KOREAN 3
FROM ZERO!

George Trombley
Reed Bullen
Jiyoon Kim
Sieun An
Myunghee Ham

Korean From Zero! Book 3
Proven Methods to Learn Korean with integrated Workbook

PREFACE

Korean From Zero! is a Korean language book series built on Korean grammar that makes sense! Each book is crafted page by page and lesson by lesson to have relevant (and sometimes fun) Korean conversation and sentence structure patterns that enhance the Korean learner's ability to speak Korean faster and understand the small nuances of Hangul and everyday Korean speech.

DEDICATION

This book is dedicated and made for those who want to truly learn Korean:

Korean culture lovers, Korean language learners, Korean drama watchers,
Korean beginners, KPOP music fans, people of Korean heritage connecting to their history,
and anyone planning travel to Korea!

This began as a project for myself (George). This is the book I wanted when I started learning Korean, but it's also for anyone like me who loves Korea and the Korean language and want to have a closer connection to Korea itself.

All of us on the *Korean From Zero!* team wish you success on your road to Korean fluency.

DISTRIBUTION

Distributed in the UK & Europe by:
Bay Foreign Language Books Ltd.
Unit 4, Kingsmead, Park Farm, Folkestone,
Kent. CT19 5EU, Great Britain
sales@baylanguagebooks.co.uk

Distributed in the USA & Canada by:
From Zero LLC.
10624 S. Eastern Ave. #A769
Henderson, NV 89052, USA
sales@fromzero.com

COPYRIGHT

Thanks for the nice comments! We love feedback!

I have already learned so much. I am excited for book 2 and 3!
Lauren C. – facebook

I'm not starting from zero but I had a ton of "now I get it moments" thanks to Korean From Zero!
Karen D. – twitter

I just finished reading Vol. 1 of this series and it was awesome! Basically under two months, I was able to get a deep understanding of the language. Some books would rely on heavy technically arranged jargon! I don't mean to say those books are awful, but they're really not handy for total beginners like me.
Andrei C. – via email

Excellent teaching. I understand so much better now. Having a native speaker present also gives me confidence that it is correct.
Permacore – youtube

I have tried other language books and software and nothing has had the affect on me that Korean From Zero has.
Josh F. – email

I tried many Korean books and found yours to be the best by far! Thanks again for such a great learning tool!
Christopher C. – email

I am from Morocco, I began to learn Korean 7 months ago and because of your book I can read, write and understand the Korean language. I really enjoyed.
Zineb B. – email

I'm so glad I've found you, you're really helping me out and I appreciate it ❤ Kamsahamnida ❤ Hwaiting!!
Bella C. – facebook

I am a Russian guy, who admires your study book. It is really perfect, I understand everything fast and easily! My Korean becomes better day by day due to you!
Mikhail S. – email

안녕하세요!! I really looove this book! It teaches really clear and I understand easily, you guys did an amazing great job!
An L. – email

feedback@fromzero.com

Korean From Zero! 3

■ Vocabulary Sentences

Introduction – Who we are

Welcome to Korean From Zero! book 3

This is the third book in the "Korean From Zero!" series. We assume that you have already completed the first and second book in the series. We will build on the concepts taught in the first two books and will also often refer to sections from those books. It is by no means required that you have the first two books in your possession.

About the authors

This book would not be possible without the collaboration of each of the authors. Each author brings a different level of Korean language understranding that help make Korean From Zero! the highly rated book series that it is. I, George, have written a synopsis of what each of the authors of the Korean From Zero! series brings to the books.

George Trombley (written by self)

I lived in Japan for 9 years and co-authored eight Japanese language text books with my Japanese wife Yukari. Since the age of 17 I have worked as a Japanese interpreter and have created over 600 instructional videos in Japanese. The similarities in the Japanese and Korean languages gave me a great advantage when I began learning Korean. Teaching language for the last 15 years and then learning Korean from scratch at age 39 gave me a unique perspective when crafting each page of Korean From Zero! Viewers of my videos are aware of my lack of love for most books that are heavy on grammar terms and overly complicated example sentences. Furthermore just because something has been taught one way for years, doesn't mean it can't be improved.

I created the Korean From Zero! series to be the book that I personally wish I had when I started learning Korean. If a grammar point brings up a question, then that question should be answered. You should NOT require a teacher to learn from this book. It's written for the independent student. In order to create the best book series I added good friend Reed Bullen to the project.

Reed Bullen

Reed learned Korean initially for his missionary work in South Korea. During his stay in Korea he lived in Daejeon and met hundreds of Koreans, volunteered for farm work, and worked with local Korean orphanages. After his mission he continued studying Korean. I first met Reed at a Korean language learning meetup in Las Vegas. We become friends and Reed spent many of those meetings patiently explaining to me the way Korean grammar worked. He had to have patience as I am relentless in my questions. One of Reeds best qualities, is that despite his knowledge of Korean, he isn't afraid to challenge what he knows. These books would absolutely not be possible with his tireless efforts.

Jiyoon Kim (Katie Kim)

Jiyoon grew up in Seoul and graduated from UNLV with a degree in hospitality management. I often communicated with Jiyoon during my intitial Korean studies. Jiyoon was able to clear up my early confusion in some of the more difficult Korean grammar concepts. She was a natural choice to join the *Korean From Zero!* team and has been instrumental in designing the sentences and debating the grammar that make up this book. Jiyoon brings a special perspective that the other authors don't share since she learned English as a second language and isn't classically trained in teaching Korean. Jiyoon is currently also studying Chinese.

Sieun An (Kelly An)

Kelly is a college student attending Sejong University, South Korea. She has introduced Korea to numerous foreigners and Korean language through her leadership in the Sejong Global Buddy organization, which is a school volunteer club for international students. She privately consulted on Korean From Zero! book 2 and is also currently co-authoring a book on Korean culture and slang.

Myunghee Ham

Myunghee is a Korean teacher at Seoul Korean Academy. She is also fluent in Japanese and has taught foriegners for over 8 years. Myunghee was added to the Korean From Zero! series after her amazing work on the 3rd revision of book 1. Myunghee has an amazing talent for breaking down a grammar point to it's base points and not over explaining. After I personally attended her classes in Korea, I knew she would be perfect for book 2.

Contributors →

Jinhyun Park (Orville Johnson)

Orville was born in Korea and his first language is Korean. He shares a unique trait among the authors as being the only half Korean in the group of authors. He was raised in Korea and moved to America before speaking any English. Orville is also currently studying Japanese. For the last 4 years he has taught Korean at the largest Korean meetup in Las Vegas. His passion for teaching Korean shows in his weekly self created lessons at the meetup where hundreds of students have learned Korean over the years. Orville has shown a special type of rare dedication to teaching Korean as he spends hours developing lessons that he voluntarily teaches at the University of Nevada Las Vegas Korean meetup.

Gayoung Choi (Kaitlin Choi)

Gayoung graduated from Sungkyul University, South Korea. When I (George) first visited Korea, Gayoung was my first native Korean friend. She helped set up my Korean cell phone and saved me when I got a horrible cold and needed medicine. We often met in coffee shops around Gangnam to do English-Korean language exchanges. Gayoung was initially just a proofreader for this book, but she quickly became a valuable asset in the book making process. Gayoung is a language lover at heart and on top of constantly improving her English, she has studied French, Italian, German and even Japanese.

Summary of Authors and Contributors

As you can see we are not a group of linguists or high level academics writing this series. We are a mix of teachers and language lovers who, more than anything, love teaching and learning languages. We hope our love of Korean will help you on your journey to Korean fluency.

Voice Actors →

Sunhee Bong

Native Korean Sunhee Bong grew up just south of Seoul in the city of Cheonan. Sunhee is a co-author of Korean From Zero! 1 and spent hundreds of hours helping create the dialogue and sentences use in the first book. Her clear voice was a natural choice for not just the book she co-authored but also for the entire series. Sunhee currently lives in Seoul and works at a medical trading company.

Hyunwoo Jang

Native Korean Hyunwoo Jang was born in Incheon, South Korea and graduated from UNLV majoring in hospitality management. While in school his academic achievements were awarded with a presidential award for academic excellence. His steady male voice gives Korean From Zero! the perfect match to Sunhee's strong female voice.

We love book reviews!

Reviews help! Not only do they help us sell more books, they also help us improve the book. Please visit any of the major book seller websites and post a review of *Korean From Zero!* We are fanatical about making the best books for students who don't have access to a Korean teacher. Your book reviews help make new books possible!

You can help with feedback!
If you love, hate, or are confused about any concept in this book please email as at feedback@fromzero.com with your feedback so we can improve future versions.

VISIT KoreanFromZero.com!

Support for your Korean Learning!
- PDF copy of *Korean From Zero!* book 1
- Mobile and Browser Audio Anytime Streaming
- FULL AUDIO sound pack for PC and WINDOWS
- Online Matching Course for book 1, 2, and 3

Thank you and enjoy your Korean journey,

The entire KFZ! team

How this book works:
Welcome to book 3!

 Getting Started

Play the sounds on mobile and in the browser!
To listen to the audio files on your mobile device or in any browser visit:
FromZero.com/korean/sounds3

Download the sound pack!
Visit **koreanfromzero.com** and download the100% Free Audio Files.

STEP 1: Download the zipped audio file to your WINDOWS or MAC computer.
The direct link to the audio is **FromZero.com/korean/audio3**

STEP 2: Unzip (uncompress) the zipped file.

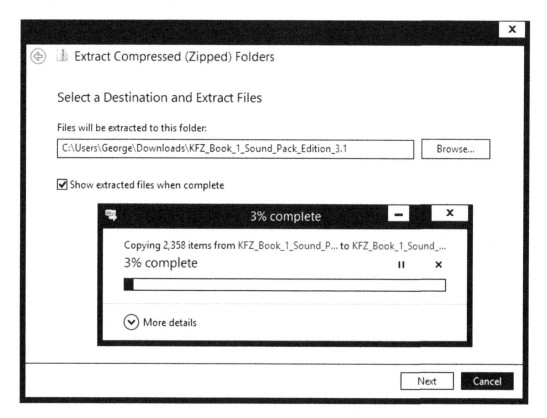

STEP 3:   Each lesson will have its own folder.

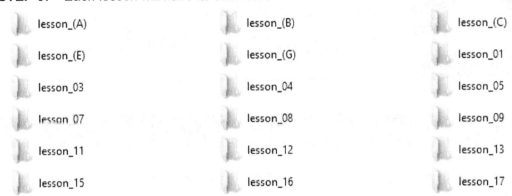

lesson_(A)   lesson_(B)   lesson_(C)

lesson_(E)   lesson_(G)   lesson_01

lesson_03   lesson_04   lesson_05

lesson_07   lesson_08   lesson_09

lesson_11   lesson_12   lesson_13

lesson_15   lesson_16   lesson_17

STEP 4:   Open any lesson to view the sections of that lesson.

Action_Verb_Usage_Examples   Additional_Vocabulary   Conversation_E-K

Descriptive_Verb_Usage_Examples   Grammar_Examples   New_Action_Verbs

New_Words   Question_and_Answer

STEP 5:   In each section folder, you will find the sounds for that section in the order that they appear in the book.

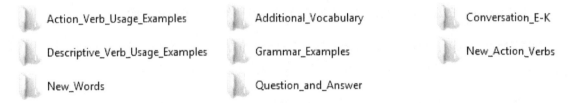

0001-What-...	1	What color do you like? 무슨 색깔을 좋아해요?
0002-What-f...	2	What foods do you dislike? 무슨 음식을 싫어해요?
0003-What-...	3	What kind of animals do you like? 어떤 동물을 좋아해요?
0004-What-t...	4	What type of things did you buy? 어떤 것을 샀어요?
0005-Which...	5	Which restaurant did you go to? 어느 식당에 갔어요?
0006-Which...	6	Which one is cheap? 어느 것이 싸요?
0007-There-...	7	There are a lot of red cars in front of my college. 제 대학교 ...
0008-I-boug...	8	I bought a black computer this Saturday. 이번주 토요일에 ...
0009-There-...	9	There are a lot of white things in hospitals. 병원에 하얀 것...
0010-Today-...	10	Today isn't so cold. 오늘은 별로 춥지 않아요.
0011-I-dont-...	11	I don't like apples that much. 나는 사과를 별로 좋아하지 않...
0012-I-dont-...	12	I don't go to America that much. 미국에는 별로 안 가요.
0013-I-dont-...	13	I don't watch basketball matches much. 농구시합을 별로 ...
0014-I-didnt...	14	I didn't get so many presents at the party. 파티에서 선물을 ...
0015-More-...	15	More water please. 물 더 주세요.
0016-I-boug...	16	I bought more fruits. 과일 더 샀어요.
0017-More-f...	17	More friends came. 친구들이 더 왔어요.

1 Korean Basics Lesson 1:
21 Advanced Phrases

Learning grammar is more important than set phrases. However some phrases don't easily make sense to beginning and intermediate students so memorization is the best option. At your level you might start grasping the phrases though!

1 Greetings 인사

1. 처음 뵙겠습니다.
   Nice to meet you. (polite)

2. 오랜만이에요.
   It's been so long.

3. 와 주셔서 감사합니다.
   Thanks for coming

4. 나중에 뵙겠습니다.
   See you later. (polite)

1 Dealing with Problems

5. 정중히 거절하겠습니다.
   I politely decline.

6. 어쩔 수 없었어요.
   It was unavoidable. / I couldn't help it.

7. 죽었다 깨어나도 못합니다.
   It's absolutely impossible.

8. 폐를 끼쳐 송구스럽습니다.
   I'm very sorry to have troubled you.

1 | Congratulatory

9. 귀하의 앞날에 무궁한 발전을 기원합니다.
   I wish you tremendous success in everything you do.

10. (득남을/ 득녀를) 축하드립니다.
    Congratulations on the arrival of your new (son / daughter)

11. 새해 복 많이 받으세요.
    Happy New Year.
    This literally means "in the new year receive many blessings".

1 | Emotional

12. 고인의 명복을 빕니다.
    RIP (rest in peace)
    This literally means "I pray for happiness from worries in the next word".

13. 당신의 충고를 가슴에 새기겠습니다.
    I will take your advice to heart.

14. 자나 깨나 당신을 생각해요.
    I think of you night and day.

15. 간 떨어질 뻔 했어요!
    You scared me!
    This literally means "I almost fell down".

1 | Talking to Friends

16. 아무것도 안하고 그냥 있어.
    I am just chilling.

17. 와! 불금이다!
    Wow! TGIF! (Thank God it's Friday)

18. 배고파 죽겠어요.
I am starving.
This literally means "I am so hungry I will die".

1 | **Injustice**

19. 새치기 하지 마세요.
Don't cut in line.

20. 바가지 씌우지 마세요.
Don't rip me off.

1 | **Interruption**

21. 실례합니다.
Excuse me.
This is used to interrupt someone so you can ask a question.

Fun in Korea:
Funny Mistakes

If you aren't making mistakes, you aren't pushing your limits in Korean. Reed and I (George) both learned Korean from scratch, and have both lived in Korea for a while. In both of our histories we have had some embarrassing, frustrating, and sometimes funny moments.

● Reed: You have a great heart?

Early on in my missionary work in Korea, while attending a church function, I got into deep discussion with one of the girl's from our church. I was impressed with her compassion and wanted to tell her that I thought she had a great heart. The word for heart is 마음. Unfortunately there is another word that I used instead of 마음. Here is what I said:

몸이 좋아요.

Some of you already know what I said. She was pretty shocked to hear a missionary say "You have a good body".

● George: Is this tea sweet?

I have never been a fan of sweet tea. But much to my dismay many of the teas sold in Korea are sweetened. The word for "sweet" is 달다. To ask if something is sweet you can say 달아요? I was determined to not drink sweet tea, so at the coffee shop I would ask if the tea was sweet. This is how I asked it:

이 차는 달라요?

The staff always said "Yes" to this question. I was in shock that every single tea in Korea was sweet. After a while I realized the problem. I was saying "Is this tea different?" by mistake. Which of course it was different. Eventually I learned the proper phrase 이 차는 달아요?

We would love to hear about your mistakes (especially the fun ones). Feel free to post them on our official Facebook page:

http://www.facebook.com/KoreanFromZero

2

Korean Basics Lesson 2:

Base Requirements

Korean From Zero! 3 assumes that you have learned important concepts taught in the first 2 books of the series.

2 | Grammar Review 문법 복습

● **2-1. The BASIC form conjugation rules for regulars**

BASIC form can be used as future tense, present tense, or a command. The BASIC form of all Korean regular verbs and adjectives can be created using the rules below:

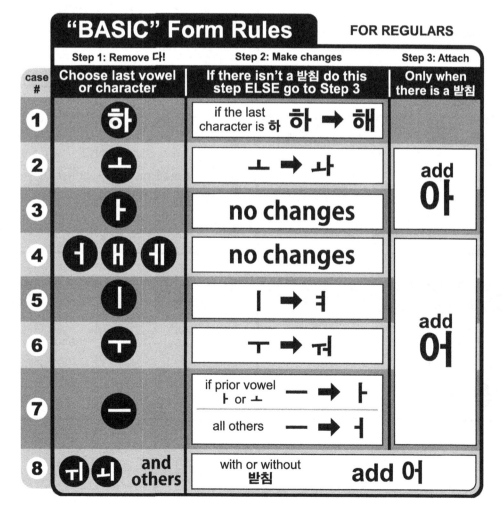

	"BASIC" Form Rules	FOR REGULARS	
case #	Step 1: Remove 다! **Choose last vowel or character**	Step 2: Make changes **If there isn't a 받침 do this step ELSE go to Step 3**	Step 3: Attach **Only when there is a 받침**
1	하	if the last character is 하 하 ➡ 해	add 아
2	ㅗ	ㅗ ➡ ㅘ	add 아
3	ㅏ	no changes	add 아
4	ㅓ ㅐ ㅔ	no changes	add 어
5	ㅣ	ㅣ ➡ ㅕ	add 어
6	ㅜ	ㅜ ➡ ㅝ	add 어
7	ㅡ	if prior vowel ㅏ or ㅗ ㅡ ➡ ㅏ all others ㅡ ➡ ㅓ	add 어
8	ㅟ ㅚ and others	with or without 받침 add 어	

Using the rules chart and some verbs you might not know, make sure you can make the BASIC form.

나누다 (to split, share)		
1	Stem	나누
	Last Vowel	ㅜ (case 6)
	받침?	NO (use step 2)
2	Change	ㅜ to ㅝ
	BASIC FORM	나눠

지키다 (to keep, to obey)		
1	Stem	지키
	Last Vowel	ㅣ (case 5)
	받침?	NO (use step 2)
2	Change	ㅣ to ㅕ
	BASIC FORM	지켜

기대하다 (to expect)		
1	Stem	기대하
	Last Char	하 (case 1)
	받침?	NO (use step 2)
2	Change	하 to 해
	BASIC	기대해

걸어오다 (to come by foot)		
1	Stem	걸어오
	Last Vowel	ㅗ (case 2)
	받침?	NO (use step 2)
2	Change	ㅗ to ㅘ
	BASIC	걸어와

끝내다 (to finish)		
1	Stem	끝내
	Last Vowel	ㅐ (case 4)
	받침?	NO (use step 2)
2	Change	none
	BASIC	끝내

잠그다 (to lock, to fasten)		
1	Stem	잠그
	Last Vowel	ㅡ (case 7)
	받침?	NO (prior char has ㅏ)
2	Change	ㅡ to ㅏ
	BASIC	잠가

사귀다 (to have relations with)		
1	Stem	사귀
	Last Vowel	ㅟ (case 8)
	받침?	NO
2	Change	add 어
	BASIC	사귀어

닦다 (to wipe, to clean)		
1	Stem	닦
	Last Vowel	ㅏ (case 3)
	받침?	YES (use step 3)
3	Change	add 아
	BASIC	닦아

● 2-2. The BASIC form conjugation rules irregulars

The BASIC form for all irregular Korean verbs and adjectives can be made using the chart rules below. There are bigger versions of all charts in this lesson in the back of the book that you can cut out for reference

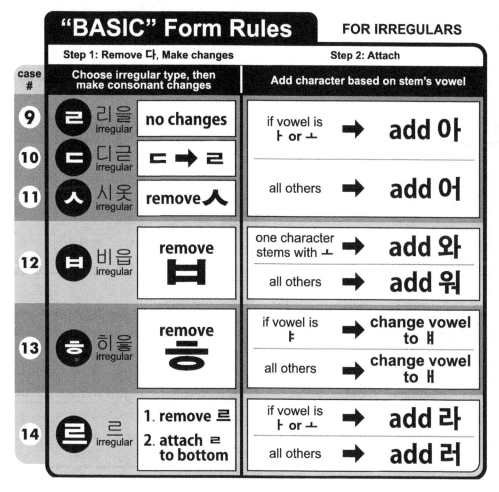

"BASIC" Form Rules FOR IRREGULARS

case #	Step 1: Remove 다, Make changes	Step 2: Attach
	Choose irregular type, then make consonant changes	Add character based on stem's vowel
9	ㄹ 리을 irregular — no changes	if vowel is ㅏ or ㅗ → add 아
10	ㄷ 디귿 irregular — ㄷ → ㄹ	
11	ㅅ 시옷 irregular — remove ㅅ	all others → add 어
12	ㅂ 비읍 irregular — remove ㅂ	one character stems with ㅗ → add 와
		all others → add 워
13	ㅎ 히읗 irregular — remove ㅎ	if vowel is ㅏ → change vowel to ㅐ
		all others → change vowel to ㅐ
14	ㄹ 르 irregular — 1. remove 르 2. attach ㄹ to bottom	if vowel is ㅏ or ㅗ → add 라
		all others → add 러

Using the rules chart and some verbs you might not know, make sure you can make the BASIC form.

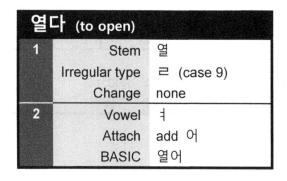

열다 (to open)

1	Stem	열
	Irregular type	ㄹ (case 9)
	Change	none
2	Vowel	ㅕ
	Attach	add 어
	BASIC	열어

깨닫다 (to realize, to grasp)

1	Stem	깨닫
	Last Vowel	ㄷ (case 10)
	Change	ㄷ to ㄹ
2	Vowel	ㅏ
	Attach	add 아
	BASIC	깨달아

짓다 (to build)

1	Stem	짓
	Irregular type	ㅅ (case 11)
	Change	remove ㅅ
2	Vowel	ㅣ
	Attach	add 어
	BASIC	지어

곱다 (to be pretty)

1	Stem	곱
	Irregular type	ㅂ (case 12)
	Change	remove ㅂ
2	Vowel	ㅗ (one char stem)
	Attach	add 와
	BASIC	고와

놀다 (to play)

1	Stem	놀
	Irregular type	ㄹ (case 9)
	Change	none
2	Vowel	ㅗ
	Attach	add 아
	BASIC	놀아

걷다 (to walk)

1	Stem	걷
	Irregular type	ㄷ (case 10)
	Change	ㄷ to ㄹ
2	Vowel	ㅓ
	Attach	add 어
	BASIC	걸어

파랗다 (blue)

1	Stem	파랗
	Irregular type	ㅎ (case 13)
	Change	remove ㅎ
2	Vowel	ㅏ
	Attach	change vowel to ㅐ
	BASIC	파래

다르다 (to be different)

1	Stem	다르
	Irregular type	르 (case 14)
	Change	remove 르 attach ㄹ
2	Vowel	ㅏ
	Attach	add 라
	BASIC	달라

하얗다 (white)

1	Stem	하얗
	Irregular type	ㅎ (case 13)
	Change	remove ㅎ
2	Vowel	ㅑ
	Attach	change vowel to ㅐ
	BASIC	하얘

머무르다 (to stay)

1	Stem	머무르
	Irregular type	르 (case 14)
	Change	remove 르 attach ㄹ
2	Vowel	ㅜ
	Attach	add 러
	BASIC	머물러

● 2-3. Verb tenses and patterns review book 1

You should know how to make and use all of the verb patterns taught in book 1 of this series. It's okay if you are missing or forgot a few, but we assume you won't be totally lost using them. Here are some of the big ones.

Verb patterns taught in book 1

1. 매일 해요.	I do it everyday.
2. 내일 해요.	I will do it tomorrow.
3. 할 거예요.	I will do it.
4. 했어요.	I did it.
5. 하지 않아요.	I won't do it. / I don't do it.
6. 하지 않았어요.	I didn't do it.
7. 하지 않을 거예요.	I won't do it.
8. 해 주세요.	Please do it.
9. 해!	Do it!
10. 해봐!	Try to do it!
11. 할까요?	Shall we do it?
12. 합시다. / 하자.	Let's do it.
13. 하고 있어요.	I am doing it.
14. 하고 있었어요.	I was doing it.
15. 하고 있지 않아요.	I am not doing it.
16. 하고 있지 않았어요.	I wasn't doing it.
17. 하고 싶어요.	I want to do it.
18. 하고 싶었어요.	I wanted to do it.
19. 하고 싶지 않아요.	I don't want to do it.
20. 하고 싶지 않았어요.	I didn't want to do it.
21. 할 수 있어요.	I can do it.
22. 할 수 없어요.	I can't do it.
23. 못 해요.	I'm not able to do it.

● 2-4. Verb tenses and patterns review book 2

A lot of important patterns were learned in book 2 of this series. It's okay if you are missing or forgot a few, but we assume you won't be totally lost using them. If you are completely confused, please refer back to book 2 to make sure your experience with book 3 doesn't make you want to cut the book into tiny pieces and set it on fire!

Grammar patterns taught in book 2

1. [A] BASIC form + 서 [B]   Because of (verb/adjective) [A], [B].

> 날씨가 추워서 파티를 취소했어요.
> We cancelled the party because the weather was cold.

2. [A] (이)라서 [B]   Because it's (noun) [A], [B].

> 오늘은 일요일이라서 학교에 안 가요.
> I don't go to school because it's Sunday.

3. BASIC + 주다   To do verb for someone.

> 친구가 점심을 사주었어요.
> My friend bought lunch for me.

4. BASIC adjective 지다   To become more adjective.

> 날씨가 점점 더워져요.
> The weather is gradually getting hotter.

5. BASIC + 하다   Other people's emotions and feelings.

> 여동생이 슬퍼해요.
> My younger sister is sad.

6. BASIC + 보이다   To look like~ (adjective).

> 저 차는 비싸 보여요.
> That car over there looks expensive.

The remaining grammar concepts don't require a pattern, so we will just show some simple sentences for demonstration.

7. 하세요	Do it.
8. 하겠어요	I will do it.
9. 하겠습니다	I will do it. (polite)
10. 하겠습니까	Will you do it? (polite)
11. 비싸네요	It sure is expensive.
12. 할 게요	I'll do it. (includes a sort of promise)
13. 먹을 음식이 사과예요.	The food I will eat is an apple.
14. 먹는 음식이 사과예요.	The food I am eating is an apple.
15. 먹은 음식이 사과였어요.	The food I ate was an apple.
16. 가기 전에 연락하세요.	Contact me before you go.
17. 간 후에 연락하세요.	Contact me after you have gone.

● 2-5. Directly modifying

This section is copied directly from book 2 to review directly modifying.
In book 1 you learned how to directly modify with adjectives. This allows you to say things like "pretty woman" etc. The simple rule is to attach ㄴ (if there is no 받침) or add 은/는 (if there is a 받침) to the adjective STEM.

Examples
1. 예쁜 여자	a pretty woman
2. 큰 고양이	a big cat
3. 작은 개	a small dog
4. 긴 머리	long hair
5. 짧은 치마	short skirt
6. 재미있는 영화	an interesting movie
7. 맛있는 음식	delicious food

In book 2 we learned how to directly modify using VERBS. The rules are slightly different from ADJECTIVES. The sentences from the prior sections demonstrate using a verb to directly modify. It can be confusing since the PAST TENSE for verbs when directly modifying is used as a neutral tense for adjectives. For example 간 도시 means "the city that I went to", which is past tense, while 큰 사과 means "big apple" but isn't past tense.

PLEASE 100% right now go review lesson 16 of book 2 to make sure you absolutely understand directly modifying with verbs, since it's one of the most important grammar structures you will use in daily speaking.

2-6. (으) form (section 7-9 book 2)

Korean grammar uses 4 common patterns:

1. BASIC FORM + something
2. STEM + something
3. 다 FORM + something
4. **으 FORM + something**

The following chart gives the formula to make the **으 FORM**.

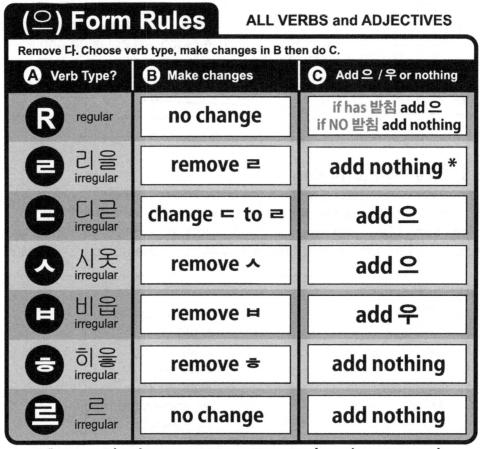

* ㄹ exception: In some grammar structures the ㄹ is not removed.

to go	가다 (regular)	→ 가~
to eat	먹다 (regular)	→ 먹으~
to do	하다 (하다)	→ 하~
to sell	팔다 (ㄹ irregular)	→ 파~
to listen	듣다 (ㄷ irregular)	→ 들으~
to build	짓다 (ㅅ irregular)	→ 지으
to be cold	춥다 (ㅂ irregular)	→ 추우~
to be red	빨갛다 (ㅎ irregular)	→ 빨가~
to not know	모르다 (르 irregular)	→ 모르~

NOTE: (으) form by itself has no meaning.

● **2-7. Review of particle 의**

In book 1 we introduce 의 as a possession marker that can be similar to the English "'s" (apostrophe s).

Examples sentences (posession)

1. 이것은 **저의** 차예요.
   This is **my** car.

2. **너의** 꿈이 뭐야?
   What is your dream?

> Remember:
> 저의 often shortens to 제 and 너의 to 네.

Examples sentences (apostrophe s)

1. 이것은 **조지의** 차예요.
   This is **George's** car.

2. **유나의** 꿈이 뭐야?
   What is **Yuna's** dream?

Another common usage of 의 is to connect 2 nouns together. The first noun modifies the second noun. It's often good to think of the 의 as "of" in this case.

Examples (noun modifier)

1. 한국**의** 정부   the government of Korea
2. 음식**의** 맛   the flavor of the food
3. 겨울**의** 날씨   winter weather
4. 치마**의** 색깔   the color of the skirt
5. 미팅**의** 시간   the time of the meeting

NOTE: Remember the 의 is often pronounced as 에. Also, remember that when speaking, 의 is often dropped when being used as a noun connector.

2 | Test Yourself Activities 연습 문제

● A2-1. BASIC conjugation practice (regular)

Use the conjugation rules in section 2-1 to convert the following regular verbs and adjectives to their BASIC form (아/어/여).

1. 켜다 (to turn on)

_____

2. 넓다 (wide)

_____

3. 배고프다 (to be hungry)

_____

4. 소개하다 (to introduce)

_____

5. 보이다 (to appear/seem)

_____

6. 쉬다 (to rest)

_____

7. 쏘다 (to shoot (gun etc.))

_____

8. 깨우다 (to wake someone up)

_____

● A2-2. BASIC conjugation practice (irregular)

Use the conjugation rules in section 2-2 to convert the following irregular verbs and adjectives to their BASIC form (아/어/여).

1. 붓다 (to pour)

_____

2. 싣다 (to load (up))

_____

3. 까맣다 (to be black)

_____

4. 빠르다 (be fast)

_____

5. 눕다 (lay down)

_____

6. 서두르다 (to hurry)

_____

7. 들다 (to lift)

_____

8. 고르다 (to choose)

_____

● A2-3. 으 form conjugation practice

Use the conjugation rules in section 2-3 to convert the following verbs and adjectives to their 으 form.

1. 날다 (to fly)
   ㄹ irregular

   _____

2. 읽다 (to read)
   regular

   _____

3. 걷다 (to walk)
   ㄷ irregular

   _____

4. 노랗다 (to be yellow)
   ㅎ irregular

   _____

5. 신다 (to put on)
   regular

   _____

6. 다르다 (to be different)
   르 irregular

   _____

7. 귀엽다 (to be cute)
   ㅂ irregular

   _____

8. 똑똑하다 (to be smart)
   하다 (regular)

   _____

2 | Self Test Answers 연습 문제 정답

● **A2-1. BASIC conjugation practice (regular)**

1. 켜
2. 넓어
3. 배고파
4. 소개해

5. 보여
6. 쉬어
7. 쏴
8. 깨워

● **A2-2. BASIC conjugation practice (irregular)**

1. 부어
2. 실어
3. 까매
4. 빨라

5. 누워
6. 서둘러
7. 들어
8. 골라

● **A2-3. 으 form conjugation practice**

1. 나
2. 읽으
3. 걸으
4. 노라

5. 신으
6. 다르
7. 귀여우
8. 똑똑하

3 Korean Basics Lesson 3:
People and Family

3 Grammar and Usage 문법과 사용법

● 3-1. Family in Korean

In English we connect our family by saying "my mother's sister" or "my father's older brother". In Korean, age, sex, marital status, and family relation determines what each family member is called.

For example, 오빠 is "older brother". However, only females can use it. Men must say 형. Older sister is 언니 for females, but 누나 for males.

If you know these differences, you know more about a person just by the words they use. We know someone is a male if they refer to someone as 누나. In English, saying "older sister" doesn't give us any extra information.

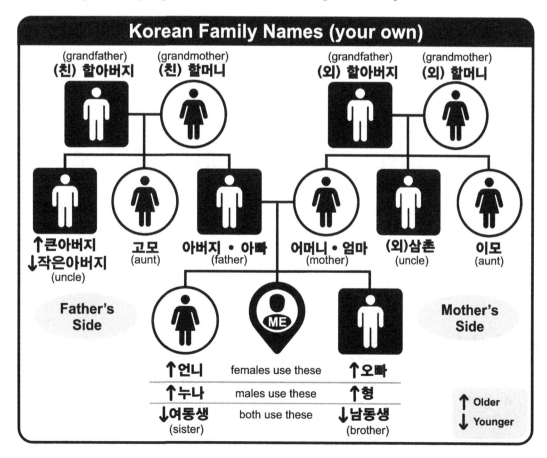

Korean Family Names (your own)

(grandfather)	(grandmother)	(grandfather)	(grandmother)
(친) 할아버지	**(친) 할머니**	**(외) 할아버지**	**(외) 할머니**

↑큰아버지 ↓작은아버지 (uncle)	고모 (aunt)	아버지 • 아빠 (father)	어머니 • 엄마 (mother)	(외)삼촌 (uncle)	이모 (aunt)

Father's Side   **Mother's Side**

↑언니	females use these	↑오빠
↑누나	males use these	↑형
↓여동생 (sister)	both use these	↓남동생 (brother)

↑ Older
↓ Younger

ME

● 3-2. Referring to your OWN family members

In Korea, people don't often refer to people older than themselves, or people in their family, with their first name like we do in the west. Instead they refer to them by their job title OR their position in the family.

Family Members: Male VS Female		
English	**Males say**	**Females say**
older brother	형	오빠
older sister	누나	언니
younger brother	동생, 남동생	
younger sister	동생, 여동생	

Family Members: Father's side VS Mother's side		
English	**Father's side**	**Mother's side**
grandfather	친할아버지	외할아버지
grandmother	친할머니	외할머니
father	아버지	
mother	아머니	

─Special Information 특별 정보─

시댁 means "husband's family" and 친정, means "wife's family". There is often conflict between married couples on Korean holidays where they have to visit both sides. Some married couples argue about setting up the visiting priority or choosing where to spend their vacation. This is especially difficult if both sides of the family don't live close to each other.

● 3-3. Referring to your SPOUSE's family members

Just like your own family, you refer to a spouse's family member by their own name. You certainly don't say "you" when talking with them. Instead you will call them by their position in the family. The following page has two charts showing which names to call them.

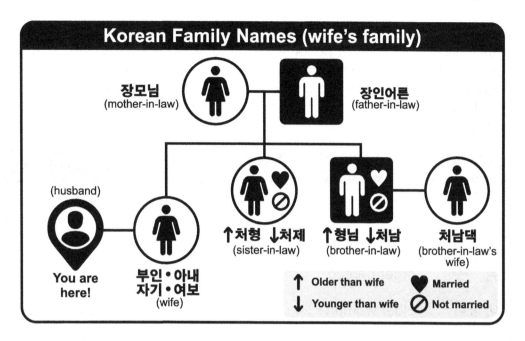

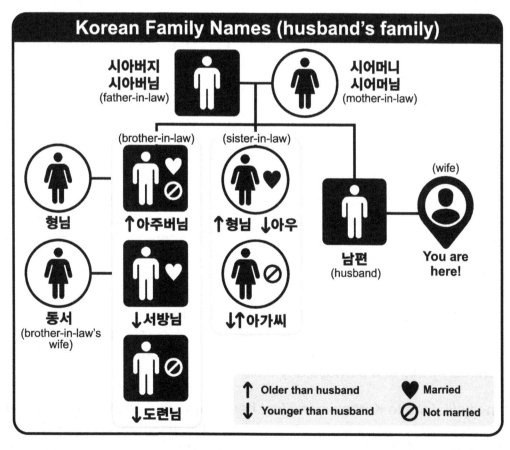

● 3-4. Referring to people outside of your family

Koreans really love calling people anything but their name. This is very opposite of western society. In America we wouldn't actually call our teacher "teacher" or someone in a higher grade as "upper classmate", but this is exactly what Koreans do. Here is a common list of words that are used instead of "you" or a person's name.

STANDARD WORD			
선배	upper classman	아저씨	older man
후배	under classman	삼촌 *	middle aged man
남	other person	총각	young single man
아줌마	older woman	오빠 (girls only)	young man
이모 *	middle aged woman	형 (men say)	young man
아가씨	young woman	언니 (girls only)	young woman
처녀	young woman, virgin	누나 (men say)	young woman

* These words are typically only used to call people in the service industry, such as a waitress.

● 3-5. Official VS being polite

One thing you should know for sure is that if you are talking to an "older woman" it's better to call her one step younger to be polite. When people call for a waitress who is by appearance an older woman they will call her 이모 instead of 아줌마 to be polite.

● 3-6. One final note on people and family

This lesson is by NO means extensive. You will learn other things as you continue to learn Korean and when you are in Korea you will hear things not covered by this and perhaps any other book.

On my first trip to Korea when I first heard someone call the waitress 이모 it was new to me. I was pretty confused actually. It certainly doesn't help that the same sounding word means "potato" in Japanese (いも). If you visit Japan, please do NOT call anyone a potato!

3 Test Yourself Activities 연습 문제

● A3-1. Multiple choice
Circle the word that best matches the set conditions.

1. What do you call your husband's mother?
   A. 엄마   B. 처형   C. 시어머니   D. 처남댁

2. Which one of the following is NOT okay to call your wife?
   A. 누나   B. 부인   C. 여보   D. 자기

3. What do you call your husband's younger married sister?
   A. 아우   B. 처남   C. 처형   D. 처님

4. What do you call your wife's mother?
   A. 이모   B. 동서   C. 장모님   D. 아우

5. What do you call aunt on your mother's side?
   A. 엄마   B. 이모   C. 삼촌   D. 아빠

6. If you are male, what do you call your older sister?
   A. 남편   B. 바보   C. 언니   D. 누나

● A3-2. Fill in the blanks
Write the names for the family members that are missing.

A. _____ B. _____ C. _____ D. _____

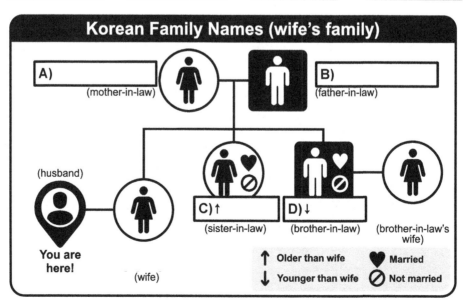

● **A3-3. Word match**
Write the letter next to the English word in the blank space next to the Korean word. You can check your answers in the Answer Key at the end of the lesson.

선배 ( )		A. young woman
아우 ( )		B. older sister
남편 ( )		C. upper classman
아가씨 ( )		D. aunt
이모 ( )		E. older man
아줌마 ( )		F. husband's younger sister
부인 ( )		G. wife
아저씨 ( )		H. husband
누나 ( )		K. older woman

3 | Self Test Answers 연습 문제 정답

● A3-1. Multiple choice (answers)

1. What do you call your husband's mother?
   A. 엄마   B. 처형   C. 시어머니   D. 처남댁

2. Which one of the following is NOT okay to call your wife?
   A. 누나   B. 부인   C. 여보   D. 자기

3. What do you call your husband's younger married sister?
   A. 아우   B. 처남   C. 처형   D. 처형

4. What do you call your wife's mother?
   A. 이모   B. 동서   C. 장모님   D. 아우

5. What do you call aunt on your mother's side?
   A. 마마   B. 이모   C. 삼촌   D. 아빠

6. If you are male, what do you call your older sister?
   A. 남편   B. 바보   C. 언니   D. 누나

● A3-2. Fill in the blanks (answers)

A. 장모님   B. 장인어른   C. 처형   D. 처남

● A3-3. Connect the words

선배 (C)	A. young woman
아우 (F)	B. older sister
남편 (H)	C. upper classman
아가씨 (A)	D. aunt
이모 (D)	E. older man
아줌마 (K)	F. husband's younger sister
부인 (G)	G. wife
아저씨 (E)	H. husband
누나 (B)	K. older woman

Korean Simplified History #1:
The Three Kingdoms

Before Korea became the North and South Korea that we are all familiar with today, it was part of a larger territory that extended well into what is now China and Russia. The period between 57 BC to 668 AD is referred to as "The Three Kindoms" period. The three kingdoms were Gogureo, Baekje, and Shilla.

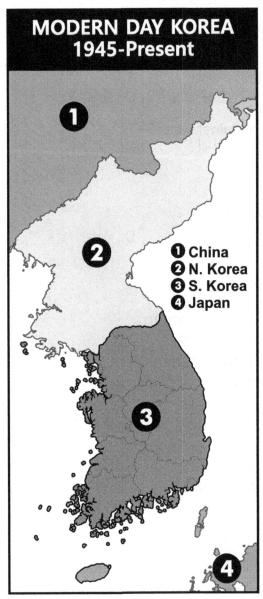

MODERN DAY KOREA
1945-Present

❶ China
❷ N. Korea
❸ S. Korea
❹ Japan

THE THREE KINGDOMS
57BC-668AD

❶ 고구려
❷ 백제
❸ 신라
❹ 가야

It's important to note the in the 삼국시대 (Three Kindom Era) 가야 disappeared when it was conquered by 신라 in 562AD.

Now that we have a basic understanding of what the three kindoms are, let's learn some "simplified" history using the Korean you mostly already know.

The following are words used in this section that haven't been taught in this series yet, or that might need to be refreshed.

 New Words and Grammar

New Words

오래	long time
전	before, ago
생기다	to be formed
왕	king
나중에	later
나라	country

Quick Grammar

~(이)라는	called, named, titled

Korean History (Korean version)

- 오래 전에는 나라가 없었어요.

- BC2333년쯤에 부여라는 나라가 생겼어요.

- 부여의 왕은 해모수와 금와에요.

- 부여에서 주몽이라는 사람이 태어났어요.

- 주몽은 나중에 고구려라는 나라를 만들어요.

- 주몽의 아들들이 백제와 신라라는 나라들을 만들어요.

★ Korean History (English version)

- A long time ago there were no countries.

- Around 2333 BC a country called Buyeo was formed.

- The kings of Buyeo were Hemosu and Keumwa.

- A person named Jumong was born in Buyeo.

- Jumong later made a country called Gogureo.

- The sons of Jumong made countries called Baekje and Shilla.

4 Korean Basics Lesson 4:
Honorific Forms

4 | New Words 새로운 단어

New Nouns etc.

높임말	honorific speech
존댓말	formal speech
반말	casual speech

4 | Grammar and Usage 문법과 사용법

● 4-1. Why learn higher level Korean?

The Korean language, in some circles, is infamous for being complicated when it comes to honorific forms and levels of formality.

With English, language usage is fairly flat regardless of who we are conversing with. Sure, we have "polite" and "slang" English, but it isn't awkward to talk to an elder in the same way that we might talk to someone our own age. We might even talk to the president of our country using the same language used amongst friends.

Korean culture on the other hand has levels of speech that change depending on factors such as the relationship of the person being spoken to, the social position of the person, and very importantly, the age of the person.

It's very possible that you will rarely use these higher levels of Korean. You might be young, you might only rarely talk to anyone older than you, or maybe all of your Korean friends speak English. However it's 100% certain that you will hear this level of Korean directed towards you. You will hear higher formal Korean somewhere as mundane as a coffee shop when the staff is talking to you. If you are like me, you will certainly be taken aback the first time you hear such Korean if you haven't studied it.

So, to avoid any huge surprises when you are in a Korean coffee shop or restaurant, this lesson introduces some of the higher levels of Korean. We promise you they are fairly easy to remember. It's almost as simple as not calling your teacher "homie" or "dude" in many cases!

● 4-2. Making any verb honorific verbs (the easy way)

This section shows you how to convert any verb into honorific form by simply changing 다 to 시다 (no 받침) or 으시다 (with 받침).

English	Normal	Honorific
to do	하다	하시다
to go	가다	가시다
to come	오다	오시다
to be tall	키가 크다	키가 크시다
to be born	태어나다	태어나시다
to teach	가르치다	가르치시다
to read	읽다	읽으시다

You will notice that even adjectives can be made into this form.
Once you make the honorofic form, you simply conjugate it and use it in a sentence. We will do this in just a bit!

● 4-3. High level particles

Higher speech levels in Korean also have some special particles.

Function	Normal	Honorific
topic marker	은/는	께서(는)
subject marker	이/가	께서(는)
to / from	에게/한테	께

NOTE: You do not always have to replace the normal particles with honorific versions. Also, you can say 께서는 or 께서 since the 는 is dropped or added depending on the speaker's preference.

Often there are alternative words that are used when speaking 높임말.

Function	Normal	Honorific
meal / cooked rice	밥	진지
name	이름	성함
age	나이	연세
birthday	생일	생신
words	말	말씀
sickness	병	병환
person	사람	분
house	집	댁
us, our, we	우리	저희
Mr., Mrs. etc	씨	님

Also instead of using BASIC form you should use ~세요 form. Just like BASIC form, ~세요 can be future, present, or a command.

해 → 하세요
와 → 오세요

The verbs conjugate using existing rules of conjugation.

Example sentences

1. 어머니께서 아침에 청소를 하셨어요.
   My mother cleaned this morning.

2. 할머니께서 매일 산에 가셔요.
   My grandmother goes to the mountain everyday.

3. 선생님께서 3시에 우리집에 오셔요.
   Teacher is coming to our house at 3 o'clock.

4. 아버지가 어머니보다 키가 크셔요.
   My father is taller than my mother.

> We are not required to use 께서 but it sounds nice.

5. 삼촌은 12 월 25 일에 태어나셨어요.
   My uncle was born on December 25.

6. 저희 할아버지께서 학원에서 수학을 가르치세요.
   Our grandfather teaches math at a private academy.

7. 할아버지는 내일 오실 거예요.
   Grandfather will be coming tomorrow.

8. 한국어를 잘 읽으시네요!
   You sure read Korean well!

> Korean will show honor to you this way. With people you've just met this politeness is common.

4-4. Special honorific verbs

Some verbs have special replacement verbs for their honorific form. This means the technique used in the prior section of just using 시다 or 으시다 won't work. Instead you have to memorize the new verb. Here are a few common verbs with special honorific forms.

English	Normal	Honorific
to eat	먹다	드시다
to drink	마시다	드시다
마시시다 is also used		
to give	주다	드리다
주시다 (when person of higher status is giving) 드리다 (when giving to person of higher status)		
to do	하다	드리다
하시다 (when person of higher status does) 드리다 (when doing for person of higher status)		
to speak	말하다	말씀하다
to hurt	아프다	편찮다
to sleep	자다	주무시다
to meet	만나다	뵙다
to be	있다	계시다

To eat and drink both convert to 드시다 when you are showing respect to the person you are speaking to. It doesn't mean that 먹다 is disrespectful.

드시다 is actually 시다 form of the verb 들다 which is ㄹ irregular. This is why it becomes 드세요 and NOT 드시세요.

> **Example sentences**
> 1. 어머니는 삼촌과 같이 저녁을 드셨어요.
>   My mother ate dinner with my uncle.
>
> 2. 선생님께서 매일 아침 커피를 드세요.
>   Teacher drinks coffee everyday.
>
> 3. 할아버지는 도서관에 계셨어요.
>   Grandfather was at the library.
>
>   > 계시다 is never 계시세요. It must be 계세요 instead.
>
> 4. 할머니는 병원에 계세요.
>   Grandmother was at the library.
>
> 5. 할머니께서 보통 매일 산에 가시지만 오늘은 집에 계셔요.
>   My grandmother normally goes to the mountain everyday, but today she is at home.

Special Information 특별 정보

It's always best to follow Korean politeness levels perfectly! However, Koreans are a lot more forgiving of mistakes for foreigners. Most Koreans will be SUPER happy you know any Korean at all. You will certainly hear:

한국어 잘 하시네요!
Wow your Korean is good!

One exception to the rule, is that if you have an Asian face, especially 교포 (2nd or 3rd generation Korean), Koreans will have higher expectations for you to speak proper Korean. For those of you with foreign looking faces, you have a bit more time to perfect your honorifics.

● 4-5. Politely doing something

Some of the grammar patterns you already know can be changed to honorific form using the new verbs. If someone that works in a restaurant place where service is provided to you, almost any time they say they will do something for you they will use BASIC + 드릴게요 to mean "I will do it for you". With friends you would use BASIC + 줄게요.

● **4-6. 높임말 is too hard! What if I don't use it properly?**

Do not stress over the 높임말 (honorific speech). I say this because if you have gotten this far in the book series, you already understand more Korean than most foreigners. Also remember that the three levels of speech 반말 (casual), 존댓말 (formal), and 높임말 are EQUALLY important.

It would be strange to speak casual speech when formal is required. But also it would be just as strange to speak honorific speech with your friends.

As you continue your journey learning Korean, watch how Koreans change their speech levels depending on the situation. Do your best to copy this and before long you won't be saying "You wanna get some grub?" when you should be saying "Would you like to eat?".

Always remember that Koreans are humans just like us. Most English native speakers wouldn't get mad or be upset with someone who is learning English if they said something rude to you by mistake.

Special Information 특별 정보

One of the most important things you can remember is to not use 높임말 when talking about yourself. It would be awkward to use 높임말 when talking about yourself.

So, for example, when you are speaking honorific style and you are saying someone is coming to your house, you should use 집 because your shouldn't honor your own house. But when you go to a person's house who deserves honor, you should use 댁. This is the same for verbs. You should use 먹다 for youself, and not 드시다.

4 | Test Yourself Activities 연습 문제

● A4-1. Verb match

Write the letter next to the honorifc verb in the space next to its matching normal verb. Check your answers in the Answer Key at the end of the lesson.

먹다 (　　)
아프다 (　　)
있다 (　　)
마시다 (　　)
주다 (　　)
자다 (　　)
말하다 (　　)
만나다 (　　)
하다 (　　)

A. 하시다
B. 편찮다
C. 뵙다
D. 말씀하다
E. 계시다
F. 드리다
G. 계시다
H. 주무시다

● A4-2. Translation

Translate the following sentences into English.

1. 저희 할아버지는 편찮으세요.

   _____

2. 시아버지께서는 1950 년에 태어나셨어요.

   _____

3. 저희 어머니께서는 한국어를 가르치세요.

   _____

4. 내일 장모님께서 우리 집에 오세요.

   _____

5. 외할아버지께서 화가 나셨어요.

   _____

6. 어머니께서 못 주무셔서 피곤해하세요.

   _____

● **A4-3. Conversion**

Convert the polite sentences into honorific Korean. Then translate the sentence below.

1. 우리 아버지가 키가 커요.

   _____

   _____

2. 아버지가 지금 밥을 먹어요.

   _____

   _____

3. 오늘 아주머님이 한국에 갈 거예요.

   _____

   _____

4. 선생님은 지금 집에 있어요.

   _____

   _____

5. 삼촌에게 선물을 줬어요.

   _____

   _____

6. 아침에 처음으로 시어머니를 만났어요.

   _____

   _____

4 | Self Test Answers 연습 문제 정답

● **A4-1. Verb match (answers)**

먹다 (   )
아프다 (   )
있다 (   )
마시다 (   )
주다 (   )
자다 (   )
말하다 (   )
만나다 (   )
하다 (   )

A. 하시다
B. 편찮다
C. 뵙다
D. 말씀하다
E. 계시다
F. 드리다
G. 계시다
H. 주무시다

● **A4-2. Translation (answers)**

1. Our grandfather is sick.

2. My husband's father was born in 1950.

3. Our mother teaches Korean.

4. Tomorrow my wife's mother is coming to our house.

5. My grandfather (father's father) was mad.

6. My mother is wasn't able to sleep so she is tired.

● **A4-3. Conversion (answers)**

1. 저희 아버지께서(는) 키가 크세요.
   Our father is tall.

2. 아버지께서(는) 지금 진지를 드세요.
   My father is eating dinner now.

3. 오늘 아주버님께서(는) 한국에 가실 거예요.
   Today my husband's older brother will go to Korea.

4. 선생님께서(는) 지금 집에 계세요.
   My teacher is at home now.

5. 삼촌께 선물을 드렸어요.
   I gave a present to my uncle.

6. 아침에 처음으로 시어머니를 (뵈었어요 / 뵀어요).
   This morning I met my husband's mother for the first time.

Korean Simplified History #2:
The Seven Brothers

 New Words and Grammar

알 egg (round objects)
도망치다 to escape
말 horse

형제 brothers
질투하다 to be jealous
~(으)면서 while doing~

 Korean History (Korean version)

- 주몽은 알에서 태어났어요
- 주몽은 7 명의 형제들이 있었어요.
- 7 명의 형제들은 주몽을 질투했어요.
- 주몽은 말을 타면서 도망쳤어요.
- 주몽은 소서노라는 사람과 결혼을 했어요.
- 주몽과 소서노는 고구려를 같이 만들었어요.

★ **Korean History (English version)**

- Jumong was born from an egg.
- Jumon had 7 brothers.
- The 7 brothers were jealous of Jumong.
- Jumong escaped while riding a horse.
- Jumong got married with a person named Soseono.
- Jumong and Soseono made Goguryeo together.

5 Lesson 5: When

5 | New Words 새로운 단어

New Nouns etc.

우산	umbrella
헬스장	gym
정신	mind, spirit
힘	power, energy
냄새	odor, smell
햇빛	sunlight
눈빛	gaze, glare of eye
휴가	vacation, day off
휴식	short break
먼저	first of all, before anything else
계획	plans

New Adjectives

어리다	to be young
강하다	to be strong (non-physical)
세다	to be strong (physical)
약하다	to be weak (physical and non)
답답하다	to be cramped, stifled, frustrated
부럽다	to be envious

New Verbs

놀라다	to be surprised
기억하다	to remember
외우다	to memorize
서다	to stand
앉다	to sit

5 | Grammar and Usage 문법과 사용법

● **5-1. ~(으)ㄹ 때 when (verbs and adjectives)**
You can place 때 after any future base (할, 갈, 먹을) to say "when I VERB".

Remember, Korean verbs are "pronoun neutral". This means you can assume that "I, he, she, we, or they" is included. Our examples use "I" to make sentences easier to write, since English ALWAYS requires a subject.

You can use practically any verb / adjective form you have learned up until now using this form. Using just 하다 look at some possibilities.

할 때
when I do

했을 때
when I did

Examples (verbs)	
1. 할 때	When I do / am doing
2. 안 할 때	When I don't do
3. 하지 않을 때	When I don't do
4. 하지 않았을 때	When I haven't done
5. 하고 싶을 때	When I want to do
6. 하고 싶지 않을 때	When I don't want to do

IMPORTANT NOTE When saying, "When my father returns home, we will eat," you MUST use 아버지가 돌아왔을 때 (past tense) since you can only eat AFTER your father has returned home. With ~아버지가 돌아올 때 it would mean, "When father is returning home, we will eat".

아버지가 집에 **돌아올** 때~
When father **returns** home~

아버지가 집에 **돌아왔을** 때~
When father **has returned** home~

Example sentences

1. 차가운 것을 먹을 때 이가 아파요.
   When I eat cold things, my teeth hurt.

2. 우리 강아지가 죽었을 때 가족들이 다 울었어요.
   When our puppy died, all of our family cried.

3. 여자친구가 내 옆에 있을 때 항상 손을 잡아요.
   When my girlfriend is next to me, we always hold hands.

4. 저는 돈이 없을 때 부모님에게 받아요.
   When I don't have money, I get some from my parents.

5. 제가 태어났을 때 부모님은 돈이 별로 없었어요.
   When I was born, my parents didn't have much money.

Example conversation

1. A: 일어날 때 제일 처음 하는 것이 뭐예요?
   B: 먼저 샤워를 해요. 샤워를 한 후에 아침을 먹어요.
   A: 먹은 후에 뭘 해요?
   B: 주말에는 게임을 하거나 비디오를 봐요.
   A: 그럼, 평일에는 뭘 해요?
   B: 월요일부터 목요일까지 아르바이트를 해요.

   A: When you wake up what is the very first thing that you do?
   B: Before anything else I shower. After I shower I eat breakfast.
   A: What do you do after you eat?
   B: On the weekend I play games or watch videos.
   A: Well then, what do you do on the weekdays?
   B: From Monday to Thursday I do a part-time job.

2. A: 제니퍼의 생일파티 때 무슨 계획이 있어요?
   B: 제니퍼랑 사진을 찍을 계획이 있어요.
   A: 저도 같이 사진을 찍고 싶어요!
   B: 그럼, 일곱 시에 강남역 11 번 출구에서 만나요.
   A: 알겠어요. (this is the same as 알겠습니다 taught in book 1)

   A: What plans do you have on Jennifer's birthday party?
   B: Today I have plans to take pictures with Jennifer.
   A: I also want to take pictures together!
   B: Well then at 7 o'clock let's meet at exit 11 at Gangnam station.
   A: Got it.

● 5-2. ~때부터 (since) ~때까지 (until)

With the addition of 부터 (since) and 까지 (from) you can say things like 죽을 때까지 (until I die) or 태어날 때부터 (since I was born).

Example sentences

1. 한국어를 잘 할 수 있을 때까지 매일 공부하세요.
   Study everyday until you can speak Korean well.

2. 아르바이트를 시작할 때부터 끝날 때까지 술을 마시지 마세요.
   Don't drink any alcohol from when your part-time job starts until it ends.

3. 우리는 저녁을 먹을 때까지 케이크를 먹지 않았어요.
   I didn't eat any cake until we ate dinner.

4. 여행에서 돌아올 때부터 계속 피곤했어요.
   Since returning from our trip I have been constantly tired.

5. 우리는 죽을 때까지 같이 살 거예요.
   We will live together until we die.

● 5-3. 어리다 (to be young)

TYPE	regular adjective	BASIC FORM	어려

Example sentences

1. 제 여동생은 너무 어려서 운전을 할 수 없어요.
   My younger sister is too young so she can't drive.

2. 우리 어머니는 정말 어려 보여요.
   My mother really looks young.

3. 리드는 어리지만 벌써 결혼을 했어요.
   Reed is young but he already got married.

4. 아이들이 어릴 때는 우리 여행을 자주 못 했어요.
   When our children were young we couldn't travel often.

5. 에밀리는 어릴 때부터 단 것을 좋아했어요.
   Emily has liked sweet things since she was young.

● 5-4. 강하다, 세다 (to be strong), 약하다 (to be weak)

강하다	TYPE	하다 adjective	BASIC FORM	강해
세다	TYPE	regular adjective	BASIC FORM	세
약하다	TYPE	하다 adjective	BASIC FORM	약해

강하다 describes strong mental capacity, strong smells, and even a strong heart and is NOT used to describe physical strength.

세다 (to be strong) is often used in combination with 힘 (power) to say "strong" when talking about muscle power.

약하다 (to be weak) is used for BOTH physical and non-physical cases.

Example sentences
1. 여름에는 햇빛이 강해서 우산을 썼어요.
   The sunlight is strong in summer so I used an umbrella.

2. 헬스장에는 힘이 센 사람이 많아요.
   There are a lot of strong people at the gym.

3. 내 동생은 힘이 약하지만 정신이 강해요.
   My sibling is weak but mentally strong.

4. 약한 사람은 무거운 것을 들 수 없어요.
   A weak person can't carry heavy things.

5. 운동을 자주 안 해서 몸이 약해졌어요.
   Because I don't often exercise my body has gotten weak.

6. 제 정신은 강하지만 몸이 약해요.
   My mind is strong by my body is weak.

● 5-5. 답답하다 (to be cramped, stuffy, stifled, frustrated)

TYPE	하다 adjective	BASIC FORM	답답해

답답하다 is a feeling or sensation that you are cramped, or feel stuffy in a small physical location. 답답하다 can also mean you are "frustrated" by a non-physical situation, such as homework, or a relationship issue.

REMEMBER, that you can NOT say 제 친구는 답답해요 to mean "my friend is frustrated". You have to say 제 친구는 답답해해요 (book 2 lesson 11).

Example sentences (physical locations)

1. 이 방은 답답해요.
   This room is cramped.

2. 숙제가 어려워서 힘들고 답답했어요
   The homework was difficult, so I was exhausted and frustrated.

3. 저는 그녀가 한국말을 못해서 답답했어요.
   I was frustrated because she couldn't speak Korean.

4. 그녀가 한국말을 못해서 답답해 했어요.
   She was frustrated because she couldn't speak Korean.

5. 동생이 전화를 받지 않아서 답답했어요.
   Because my sister didn't pick up the phone I am frustrated.

6. 비행기 안에 사람이 많아서 답답해요.
   Because there are a lot of people on the plane I feel stuffy.

● 5-6. 부럽다 (to be envious)

TYPE	ㅂ irregular adjective	BASIC FORM	부러워

If you tell any of your Korean friends something along the lines of "I am going to Hawaii", or any other place, 9 times out of 10 they will say 부럽다.

부럽다 is often mis-translated as "jealous" but "jealousy" is considered negative, whereas envy is like a compliment. 질투하다 is "to be jealous".

Example sentences

1. 키가 크고 아름다운 제니퍼가 부러웠어요.
   I was envious of tall and beautiful Jennifer.

2. 매주 여행을 가는 리드가 부러워요.
   I am really envious of Reed who goes on a trip every week.

3. 리드 씨가 한국어를 잘해서 조지가 부러워해요.
   Because Reed can speak Korean well, George is envious.

4. 리드 씨가 한국어를 잘하는 조지를 부러워해요.
   Reed is envious of George who can speak Korean well.

> CAREFULLY read #3 and #4. Very small changes COMPLETELY change the meaning.

─Special Information 특별 정보─

If sentences 3 and 4 confused you, don't worry, even the best of us have to learn the small nuances of Korean. In sentence 3, George is envious of Reed. But in sentence 4, George is just being directly modified. He is not just "George" but he is the "George who is good at Korean".
한국어를 잘하는 조지

To further add to the confusion, because Reed is jealous "OF" George, the particle must change to 를 to mark the OBJECT of 부러워하다.

Some simpler sentences might help clear things up:

1. 저는 리드가 부러워요.   I am envious of Reed.
2. 리드가 부러워해요.   Reed is envious.
3. 리드가 조지를 부러워해요.   Reed is envious of George.

● 5-7. 놀라다 (to be surprised)

TYPE	regular verb	BASIC FORM	놀라

놀라다 is so commonly used with 깜짝 that you might only occasionally hear 놀랐어요 (I was surprised) without it in front. Using 깜짝 gives more emotion to the surprise. It elevates the level of surprise. NOTE: 놀라다 never means "to surprise someone".

> 깜짝 is more the sound of being surprised and not a word you can translate.

Example sentences

1. 한국 음식이 너무 매워서 깜짝 놀랐어요.
   I was really surprised that Korean food was so spicy.

2. 놀란 선생님의 눈빛이 강해졌어요.
   The glare of the surprised teacher strengthened.

3. 뉴욕의 겨울 날씨에 놀랐어요.
   I was surprised at New York's winter weather.

> 에 marks the thing you are surprised at.

4. 경찰은 범죄자의 계획에 놀랐어요.
   The police were surprised at the criminal's plans.

5. 제 여자친구가 공포영화에 귀신이 나올 때마다 놀라요.
   Every time a ghost appears in a horror movie my girlfriend is surprised.

Special Information 특별 정보

~때마다 (every time~)
We hope you were able to figure this out on your own, but just in case, we want to point out that sentence 5 of the last set of examples teaches a new grammar structure using 때 and 마다 to say "every time + verb".

Example sentences
1. 먹을 때마다 이가 아파요.
   Every time I eat my tooth hurts.

2. 한국에 갈 때마다 날씨가 추워요.
   Every time I go to Korean the weather is cold.

3. 운동을 할 때마다 힘들어져요.
   Every time I exercise I become exhausted.

● 5-8. 기억하다 (to remember), 외우다 (to memorize)

기억하다	TYPE	하다 verb	BASIC FORM	기억해
외우다	TYPE	regular verb	BASIC FORM	외워

The item that you remember or memorize is marked with 을/를.

Example sentences
1. 수요일마다 한국어 수업에서 단어를 외워요.
   Every Wednesday I memorize vocabulary in Korean class.

2. 어제 외운 한국어를 여기에 쓰세요.
   Write the Korean here that you memorized yesterday.

3. 내가 지난 목요일에 이야기 한 것을 기억해?
   Do you remember the things I talked about last Thursday?

4. 선생님의 얼굴은 기억하지만 이름은 기억 못 해요.
   I remember teacher's face, but I can't remember (her) name.

5. 삼 일 전에 편의점에서 만난 여자의 전화번호를 아직 기억해요.
   I still remember the phone number of the girl that I met in the convenience store 3 days ago.

● **5-9. 서다 (to stand), 앉다 (to sit)**

서다	**TYPE**	regular verb	**BASIC FORM**	서
앉다	**TYPE**	regular verb	**BASIC FORM**	앉아

The location where you are standing is marked with the location marker 에.
NOTE: The ㅈ in 앉다 is silent unless followed by an ㅇ (이응).

> **Example sentences**
>
> 1. 의자에 앉았어요.
>   I sat on the chair.
>
> 2. 콘서트에서 제일 앞에 섰어요.
>   I stood in the very front at the concert.
>
> 3. 오늘 오랫동안 섰어요. 그래서 다리가 아파요.
>   I stood a long time today. So my legs hurt.
>
> 4. 여기에 앉으세요.
>   Sit here.
>
> 5. 오랫동안 앉아서 지금은 서고 싶어요.
>   When I sat for a long time, I want to stand up now.
>
> 6. 버스에 사람이 많았지만 앉을 수 있었어요.
>   There was many people on the bus but I was able to sit.

● **5-10. Using 때 just with nouns**

때 can be used directly after some nouns. The English translation of 때 can fit the needs of the sentence. 때 can translate as "during", "when", and "the time I" etc. The following are commonly used.

School	Ages	Time Periods	Events
중학교 때 when (I) was in elementary	두 살 때 when was 2	방학 때 during school break	생일 때 on birthday
고등학교 때 during high school	열 여섯 살 때 when was 16	휴가 때 during days off	파티 때 during the party
대학교 때 during college	서른 살 때 when was 30	휴식 때 during break	회의 때 during the meeting

You can also say 그때 (at that time) and 이때 (this time~). (no spaces)

Example sentences

1. 대학교 때 차가 없었어요.
   I didn't have a car in college.

2. 여름 방학 때 항상 한국에 가요.
   I always go to Korea during school summer break.

3. 열 다섯 살 때부터 스무 살 때 까지 한국에 살았어요.
   I lived in Korea from age 15 to age 20.

4. 그때는 깜짝 놀랐어요.
   At that time I was surprised.

5. 아버지의 생일 때 맛있는 것을 먹었어요.
   We ate delicious things on my Father's birthday.

6. 고등학교 때 숙제가 많아서 놀 시간이 없었어요.
   When I was in high school, because I had a lot of homework there was
   no time to play.

5 | Test Yourself Activities 연습 문제

● **A5-1. Fix the mistake**
Correct the Korean sentence, then finish the translation on the line below.

1. 공부하는 때는 조용한 곳에 있고 싶어요.

   Korean _____

   English When I study_____

2. 어릴 때까지 미국에서 살았어요.

   Korean _____

   English Since I was young_____

3. 제 친구가 저를 부러워요.

   Korean _____

   English My friend is_____

● **A5-2. Listening skills**
 Go to **http://fromzero.com/korean/kfz3/A2** OR scan the QR code. Enter the code. Write the Korean then the English.

1. 5A Korean _____

   English _____

2. 5B Korean _____

   English _____

3. 5C Korean _____

   English _____

● **A5-3. Fill in the blanks**
Fill in the missing word or particle based on the English sentence.

1. 여행에서 돌아올 _____ 계속 피곤했어요.
   Since returning from our trip I have been constantly tired.

2. 에밀리가 제니퍼를 _____요.
   Emily is envious of Jennifer.

3. 매일 헬스장에 가고 힘이 _____졌어요.
   I went to the gym everyday and got strong.

4. 기분이 _____는 많이 먹어요.
   When I feel frustrated I eat a lot.

5. 우리는 죽을 _____ 같이 살 거예요.
   We will live together until we die.

● **A5-4. Mark and Translate**
Mark the Korean sentence WITHOUT mistakes then translate it.

1. ○ 운둥을 할 떼는 물이 제일 중요해요.
   ○ 운동을 할 태는 물이 제일 중요해요.
   ○ 운동을 할 때는 물이 제일 중요해요.

   Translation:_____

2. ○ 날시가 따뜻해질 때까지 공워에 놀 수 없어요.
   ○ 날씨가 따뜻해질 때까지 공원에서 놀 수 없어요.
   ○ 날짜가 따뜻해질 때가찌 공황에서 놀 수 없어요.

   Translation:_____

3. ○ 17 살 때부터 21 살 때까지 한국 사람이랑 사귀었어요.
   ○ 17 살 때까지 21 살 때부터 한국 사람이랑 사귀었어요.
   ○ 17 살 때부터 21 살 때가찌 한국 사람이랑 사귀었어요.

   Translation:_____

5 | Self Test Answers 연습 문제 정답

● A5-1. Fix the mistake

1. 공부할 때는 조용한 곳에 있고 싶어요.
   When I study, I like to be in a quiet place.

2. 어릴 때부터 미국에서 살았어요.
   Since I was young I lived in America.

3. 제 친구가 저를 부러워해요.
   My friend is envious of me.

● A5-2. Listening skills

1. 열 다섯 살 때부터 스무 살 때 까지 살았어요.
   I lived in Korea from age 15 to age 20.

2. 제 여동생은 너무 어려서 운전을 할 수 없어요.
   My younger sister is too young so she can't drive.

3. 제가 저녁을 먹을 때 아내가 집에 돌아왔어요.
   When I was eating dinner, my wife came back home.

● A5-2. Fill in the blanks

1. 여행에서 돌아올 때부터 계속 피곤했어요.

2. 에밀리가 제니퍼를 부러워해요.

3. 매일 헬스장에 가고 힘이 세졌어요.

4. 기분이 답답할 때는많이 먹어요.

5. 우리는 죽을 때까지 같이 살거예요.

● A5-3. Best Sentence Search

1. ○ 운둥을 할 떼는 물이 제일 중요해요.
   ○ 운동을 할 태는 물이 제일 중요해요.
   ✓ 운동을 할 때는 물이 제일 중요해요.
   Translation: When you exercise water is most important.

2. ○ 날시가 따뜻해질 때까지 공워에 놀 수 없어요.
   ✓ 날씨가 따뜻해질 때까지 공원에서 놀 수 없어요.
   ○ 날짜가 따뜻해질 때가찌 공황에서 놀 수 없어요.
   Translation: Until the weather gets warm you can't play in the park.

3. ✓ 17 살 때부터 21 살 때까지 한국 사람이랑 사귀었어요.
   ○ 17 살 때까지 21 살 때부터 한국 사람이랑 사귀었어요.
   ○ 17 살 때부터 21 살 때가찌 한국 사람이랑 사귀었어요.
   Translation: From age 17 to 21 I was dating a Korean person.

5 | Vocabulary Builder 단어 구축

Presenting a new group of words that might come up in a meeting. Now get to work and learn these words.

■ Group A: Office 사무실

사무실	office
회의실	meeting room
월급	salary
출근	go to work
퇴근	get off work
회의	meeting
발표	presentation, speech
출장	business trip
퇴직	retire

■ New 하다 verbs

Some of the new words above can be made into 하다 verbs.

출근하다	to go / come to work, to get to work
퇴근하다	to get off work
회의하다	to have a meeting
발표하다	to give a speech, make a presentation
퇴직하다	to retire

If you add 가다 to 출장 then you have a verb. Don't mistake it for 하다.

출장가다	to go on a business trip

■ Vocabulary Sentences

The following sentences might contain words and concepts not yet taught. Focus on the new vocabulary more than the grammar.

1. 지금 저는 사무실에서 일을 하고 있어요.
   I am currently working in the office.

2. 저는 회의가 싫어요.
   I don't like meetings.

3. 회의실에서 잠을 자면 안 돼요.
    You aren't allowed to sleep in the meeting room.

4. 저는 지금 발표를 준비하고 있어요.
    I am preparing for a presentation right now.

5. 당신은 어디로 출장가나요?
    Where are you going to on your business trip?

6. 저는 월급 받는 날을 항상 기다려요.
    I am always waiting for the day I get my salary.

7. 출근할 때 지하철을 타지 마세요.
    Don't ride the subway when you go to work.

8. 몇 시에 퇴근해요?
    What time do you get off of work?

9. 우리 아버지는 60 살 때 퇴직을 했어요.
    My father retired when he was 60 years old.

Korean Simplified History #3:
The Two Plans

New Words and Grammar

~가지   (counter), kinds of, variety of
사이 relationship, between
계획 plan(s)
혼란스럽다 to be confusing
속이다 to fool, to trick

~번째 (counter), order, rank
게릴라 전투 guerrilla warfare
벌이다 to wage, start, begin
무찌르다 to defeat

★ Korean History (Korean version)

- 수나라와 고구려는 사이가 나빴어요.

- 을지문덕은 두 가지 계획이 있었어요.

- 첫 번째 계획은 수나라를 속이는 거였어요.

- 두 번째 계획은 게릴라 전투를 벌이는 거였어요.

- 첫 번째 계획 때문에 수나라는 혼란스러웠어요.

- 두 번째 계획 때문에 수나라는 힘들었어요.

- 을지문덕은 피곤한 수나라 군사들을 무찔렀어요.

★ Korean History (English version)

- Sunara and Goguryeo had a bad relationship.
- Eulji Mundeok had two plans.
- The first plan was to trick Sunara.
- The second plan was to wage guerilla warfare.
- Because of the first plan Sunara was confused.
- Because of the second plan it was hard for Sunara.
- Eulji Mundeok defeated the tired military of Sunara.

6
Lesson 6:
If and must do

6 | New Words 새로운 단어

New Nouns etc.

어떻게	how?, in what way?
아직도	still (not), even now
연말	the end of the year
주소	address (for houses, businesses)
삼겹살	pork belly
스타일	style
바보	fool, idiot, dummy

New Counters

~번째	1st, 2nd, 3rd etc. (order counter)

New Adverbs

열심히	hard, diligently, enthusiastically

New Adjectives

똑똑하다	to be smart
멍청하다	to be dumb
딱딱하다	to be hard
부드럽다	to be soft
위험하다	to be dangerous
안전하다	to be safe

New Verbs

입학하다	to enter school
졸업하다	to graduate
다니다	to attend, to frequent
스키를 타다	to ski

6 | Grammar and Usage 문법과 사용법

● 6-1. BASIC + 야 되다 to have to do

If you want to say a phrase like "I have to go" you can use BASIC + 야 되다 to create a "must do / have to" form. Ignore that fact that 되다 (to become) is part of the pattern. 되다 is commonly used in many grammar patterns in the same way 하다 is.

Example sentences

1. 먹어야 돼요.   (I) have to eat.
2. 가야 돼요.   (I) have to go.
3. 해야 돼요.   (I) have to do.
4. 읽어야 돼요.   (I) have to read.
5. 봐야 돼요.   (I) have to watch / look.

Example sentences

1. 내일은 일찍 일어나야 돼요.
   I have to wake up early tomorrow.

2. 저는 일을 하기 전에 조금 운동을 해야 돼요.
   Before I work I have get a bit of exercise.

3. 아내가 기다려서 빨리 돌아가야 돼요.
   Because my wife is waiting I have to return fast.

4. 어제는 지갑을 잃어버려서 친구에게 돈을 빌려야 됐어요.
   Yesterday, because I lost my wallet I had to borrow money from a friend.

5. 빨리 먹어야 될 때는 저는 보통 빵을 먹어요.
   When I have to eat fast I normally eat bread.

Special Information 특별 정보

BASIC + 야 하다 is similar ~야 되다 except that 해야 하다 is a choice and 해야 되다 is something that isn't an option. It's similar to saying "I really gotta exercise" 운동을 해야 해요 vs "I have to pay taxes" 세금을 내야 돼요.

The truth is that, despite this distinction, Koreans most often use ~돼요 over 해요. And if you use ~돼요 when you should use ~해요 you will not have any problem being understood.

● 6-2. ~ (으)면 If

To turn an adjective or verb into "if" form, we will use the (으) form taught in *book 2 section 7-9*. The pattern is (으) form + 면. Refer to the chart if needed.

NOTE: On the (으) form chart ㄹ irregular has a note that states: In some grammar structures ㄹ is NOT removed from the stem. This is the case for 면. You will say 알면 and NOT 아면 for "if you know".

Examples

1. 가면   if (you) go
2. 먹으면   if (you) eat
3. 하면   if (you) do
4. 알면   if (you) know
5. 들으면   if (you) hear / listen
6. 모르면   if (you) don't know
7. 들면   if (you) hold it

> 듣다 is ㄷ irregular. Don't assume it's a ㄹ irregular. Check the 으 form chart.

Verb Form Usage

You can use practically any verb / adjective form you have learned up until now using 면. Using just 하다 look at the possibilities.

Examples (verbs)

1. 하면   If (I) go
2. 안 하면   If (I) don't do
3. 하지 않으면   If (I) don't do
4. 하지 않았으면   If (I) hadn't done
5. 하고 있으면   If (I) am doing
6. 하고 싶으면   If (I) want to do
7. 하고 싶었으면   If (I) had wanted to do
8. 하고 싶지 않으면   If (I) don't want to do
9. 하고 싶지 않았으면   If (I) hadn't wanted to do

The following sentences are "if" sentences using both adjectives and verbs.

Example sentences

1. 나중에 노래방에 가면 연락해 주세요.
   If you go to karaoke later, please contact me.

2. 지금 머리가 아프면 아스피린을 먹으세요.
   If your head hurts now, take this aspirin.

3. 돈이 없으면 제가 빌려 줄게요.
   If you don't have money, I will loan you some.

---

4. 술을 마실 때 운전을 하면 위험해요.
   When you drink alcohol, it's dangerous if you drive.

5. 오늘 학교에 빨리 도착하면 숙제를 할 수 있어요.
   If you arrive early to school today, you can do your homework.

6. 다음 주에 눈이 많이 오면, 스키를 탈 수 있어요.
   If it snows a lot next week, we can ski.

In Korean there are times when 면 can mean "when". Often this can happen when you are making requests, commands, and recommendations.

Example sentences

1. 시간이 있으면 우리 집에 오세요.
   If / when you have time, come to our house.

2. 우리 한국에 가면, 삼겹살을 꼭 먹자.
   If / when we go to Korea, let's definitely eat pork belly.

3. 한국어를 공부하면, 이 책이 좋아요.
   If / when you study Korean, this book is good.

Example conversation

1. A: 돈이 많이 있으면 뭘 하고 싶어요?
   B: 제일 비싼 차를 사고 싶어요.
   A: 그리고 어디로 가고 싶어요?
   B: 다른 나라에 가고 싶어요.

   A: If you had a lot of money, what would you want to do?
   B: I want to buy the most expensive car.
   A: And where do you want to go?
   B: I want to go to another country.

2. A: 선생님이 되면 제일 먼저 뭘 할거예요?
   B: 24 시간 동안 계속 자고 싶어요.
   A: 선생님이 되지 않으면요?
   B: 아마... 많이 울 거예요.

   A: If you become a teacher what is the first thing you will do?
   B: I want to sleep continuously for 24 hours.
   A: And what if you don't become a teacher?
   B: Probably... I will cry a lot.

● 6-3. ~번째 counter

This counter requires the Korean number system. This is the "order" counter.

Korean	English	Never This
첫 번째	first	한 번째
두 번째	second	둘 번째
세 번째	third	셋 번째
네 번째	forth	넷 번째
다섯 번째	fifth	
여섯 번째	sixth	
일곱 번째	seventh	
여덟 번째	eighth	
아홉 번째	ninth	
열 번째	tenth	
몇 번째	which?	

The pattern for the numbers continue up to 99. If you need to go higher than 99 you use the Chinese numbers since Korean numbers end at 99.

The rank counter sometimes adds 의 before the noun it is in front of. The 의 is more common in books than everyday speaking.

Example sentences

1. 첫 번째 집은 예뻐요.
   The first house is pretty.

2. 저의 세 번째 여자친구는 프랑스 사람이었어요.
   My third girlfriend was French.

3. 저의 다섯 번째 차는 현대였어요.
   My fifth car was a Hyundai.

4. 생일에 두 번째 기타를 받았어요.
   On my birthday I received my second guitar.

● 6-4. 똑똑하다 (to be smart), 멍청하다 (to be dumb)

똑똑하다	TYPE	하다 adjective	BASIC FORM	똑똑해
멍청하다	TYPE	하다 adjective	BASIC FORM	멍청해

Example sentences

1. 동물원에 있는 돌고래는 똑똑해요.
   The dolphins in the zoo are smart.

2. 안경을 쓰면 더 똑똑해 보여요.
   You look smarter if you wear glasses

   > 쓰다 is the verb "to wear" for glasses or other things on your head like hats.

3. 똑똑한 언니가 숙제를 해 주었어요.
   My smart sister did the homework for me.

4. 제 남동생은 공부를 열심히 해서 똑똑해 졌어요.
   My younger brother got smart because he diligently studied.

5. 남편은 회사에서는 똑똑하지만 집에서는 멍청해요.
   At the company my husband is smart, but at home he is stupid.

6. 제프는 계속 멍청한 질문을 했어요.
   Jeff continually asked stupid questions.

● 6-5. 딱딱하다 (to be hard), 부드럽다 (to be soft)

딱딱하다	TYPE	하다 adjective	BASIC FORM	똑똑해
부드럽다	TYPE	ㅂ irregular adjective	BASIC FORM	부드러워

Example sentences

1. 이 빵은 딱딱해 보이지만 속은 부드러워요.
   This bread looks hard but inside it's soft.

2. 왼쪽에서 세 번째 침대가 여기서 제일 딱딱해요.
   The third bed from the left is the hardest here.

3. 세 시간 전에는 피자가 부드러웠지만 지금은 딱딱해졌어요.
   Three hours ago the pizza was soft, but now it got hard.

4. 아이스크림은 언제나 달고 부드러워!
   Ice cream is always sweet and soft!

● 6-6. 위험하다 (to be dangerous), 안전하다 (to be safe)

위험하다	**TYPE**	하다 adjective	**BASIC FORM**	위험해

안전하다	**TYPE**	하다 adjective	**BASIC FORM**	안전해

Example sentences

1. 술을 마신 후에 운전하면 정말 위험해요!
   If you drive after you drink it's really dangerous.

2. 이 호수는 물이 깊어서 위험해요.
   Because the water is deep, the lake is dangerous.

   > 깊다 means "to be deep"

3. 위험한 동물들이 있어서 이 섬에서 캠핑을 하면 위험해요.
   Because there are dangerous animals, it's dangerous
   if you camp on this island.

4. 아기에게 안전한 물건을 주어야 돼요.
   You have to give safe items to children.

5. 일본의 자동차는 안전하지만 조금 비싸요.
   Japanese cars (automobiles) are safe, but a little expensive.

● 6-7. 입학하다 (to enter school), 졸업하다 (to graduate)

입학하다	**TYPE**	하다 verb	**BASIC FORM**	입학해

졸업하다	**TYPE**	하다 verb	**BASIC FORM**	졸업해

Example sentences

1. 올해 3 월에 한국에서 제일 좋은 대학교에 입학해요.
   This March I will enter the best college in Korea.

2. 왜 아직 졸업하지 않았어요?
   Why didn't you graduate yet?

   > 대학원 means "graduate school".

3. 대학원에 입학하면 런던에 여행 갈 거예요.
   If I enter graduate school, I will take a trip to London.

4. 저는 작년 3 월에 고등학교를 졸업하고 4 월에 대학교에 입학했어요.
   Last March I graduated high school and in April I entered college.

6-8. 다니다 (to attend, to frequent)

TYPE	regular verb	BASIC FORM	다녀

In simple English 다니다 is used to describe the action of going back and forth to a place over a period of time such as school or even a hair dresser.

Example sentences

1. 매주 토요일마다 한국어 학원에 다녀요.
   I attend a Korean language academy each Saturday every week.

2. 오랫동안 다니는 피아노 학원의 수업료가 갑자기 비싸졌어요.
   The tuition for the piano academy that I have been attending for a long time all of a sudden got expensive.

3. 중학교 때부터 노래방을 다녔지만 아직도 노래를 잘 못 해요.
   I have frequented karaoke rooms since the time I was in elementary school but I still can't sing well.

4. 연말까지 꼭 요가를 다닐 거예요.
   By the end of the year I will definitely attend yoga.

5. 영어 학원은 다니고 싶지만, 수학 학원은 다니고 싶지 않아요.
   I want to attend an English academy, but I don't want to attend a math academy.

6-9. 스키를 타다 (to ski)

TYPE	regular verb	BASIC FORM	스키를 타

타다 is used to "ride" a car and other modes of transportation. In English we have made "to ski" into a verb, but Korean just says "ride skis".

Example sentences

1. 스키를 탄 후에 우리는 밥을 먹을 거예요.
   After skiing, we will eat dinner.

2. 올해 겨울에는 매주 스키를 타고 싶어요.
   This winter I want to ski every week.

3. 여기서 스키를 타면 위험해요?
   If I ski here is it dangerous?

● 6-10. How do you~?

We will learn more about 어떻게 (how?) in lesson 16. First let's learn the most basic way we can use 어떻게 to make a sentence.

Example sentences

1. 이름은 어떻게 써요?
   How do you write your name?

2. 불고기를 어떻게 만들어요?
   How do you make bulgogi?

3. 어떻게 한국어를 배웠어요?
   How did you learn Korean?

4. 어떻게 강남역에 가요?
   How do you go to Gangnam station?

5. 어떻게 그 여자를 사랑 할 수 있어요?
   How can you love that girl?

6. 답답할 때는 어떻게 해요?
   What do you do when you are frustrated?

---

1. **Conversation between a lost foreigner and a Korean person.**
   A: 실례합니다. 이 주소에 어떻게 가요?
   B: 지하철을 타야 돼요.
   A: 지하철을 어떻게 타요?
   B: 먼저 표를 사야 돼요.

   A: Excuse me. How do I go this address?
   B: You have to ride the subway.
   A: How do I ride the subway?
   B: First you have to buy a ticket.

2. **Conversation with a friend who now lives in Korea.**
   A: 어떻게 한국의 대학교에 입학했어요?
   B: 먼저 삼 년 동안 한국어를 공부하고 시험을 봤어요.
   A: 학비가 비싸요?
   B: 아니요. 별로 안 비싸요.

   A: How did you get into a Korean college?
   B: First I studied Korean 3 years and then I took a test.
   A: Is tuition expensive?
   B: No. It's not that expensive.

6 | Test Yourself Activities 연습 문제

● **A6-1. Fix the mistake**
Correct the Korean sentence, then finish the translation on the line below.

1. 저는 내일 아침 여섯 시에 일돼야 해요.

   Korean _____

   English Tomorrow at 6 in the morning_____

2. 한국어를 잘 하고 싶면 매일 공부해야 돼요.

   Korean _____

   English If you want to_____

3. 셋 번째 신호등에서 오른쪽으로 가세요.

   Korean _____

   English At the third traffic light_____

● **A6-2. Listening skills**
Go to **http://fromzero.com/korean/kfz3/A2** OR scan the QR code. Enter the code. Write the Korean then the English.

1. 6A Korean _____

      English _____

2. 6B Korean _____

      English _____

3. 6C Korean _____

      English _____

● A6-3. Fill in the blanks

Fill in the missing word or particle based on the English sentence.

1. 여동생은 유럽에서 제일 비싼 대학교에 _____요.
   My younger sister entered the most expensive school in Europe.

2. 작년 연말까지 프랑스어 학원을 _____요.
   Until the end of last year I was attending a French language academy.

3. 일찍 _____ 빨리 연락해 주세요.
   If you arrive early contact me right away.

4. 저의 _____ 남자친구는 우리 회사에서 일하는 회사원이었어요.
   My second boyfriend was a company worker working at my company.

5. 왜 계속 _____ 질문을 해??
   Why do you keep asking stupid questions?

● A6-4. Mark and Translate

Mark the Korean sentence without mistakes then translate it.

1. ○ 남편이 기다려서 빨리 돌아가다 돼요.
   ○ 남편이 기다리서 빠리 돌아가여 돼요.
   ○ 남편이 기다려서 빨리 돌아가야 돼요.

   Translation:_____

2. ○ 관심이 있으면 나와 같이 요가를 배우자.
   ○ 관심가 있으면 나와 같이 요가를 배우자.
   ○ 관심이 있으면 나와 같이 요가을 배우자.

   Translation:_____

3. ○ 귀신이 무서우면 빨리 달려아 돼요!
   ○ 귀신이 무서우면 빨리 달려야 돼요!
   ○ 달려야 돼면을 때 귀신이 무서우면!

   Translation:_____

6 | Self Test Answers 연습 문제 정답

● **A6-1. Fix the mistake**
1. 저는 내일 아침 여섯 시에 일해야 돼요.
   Tomorrow at 6 in the morning I have to work.
2. 한국어를 잘 하고 싶으면 매일 공부해야 돼요.
   If you want to speak Korean well you have to study everyday.
3. 세 번째 신호등에서 오른쪽으로 가세요.
   At the third traffic light turn right.

● **A6-2. Listening skills**
1. 저는 일을 하기전에 조금 자야 돼요.
   Before I work I have to sleep a little.
2. 돈이 없으면 제가 빌려 줄 거예요.
   If you don't have money, I will loan you some.
3. 이 빵은 딱딱해 보이지만 속은 부드러워요.
   This bread looks hard, but the inside is soft.

● **A6-3. Fill in the blanks**
1. 여동생은 유럽에서 제일 비싼 대학교에 입학했어요.
2. 작년 연말까지 프랑스어 학원을 다니고 있었어요.
3. 일찍 도착하면 빨리 연락해 주세요.
4. 저의 두 번째 남자친구는우리 회사에서 일하는 회사원이었어요.
5. 왜, 계속 멍청한 질문을 해??

● **A6-4. Best Sentence Search**
1. ○ 남편이 기다려서 빨리 돌아가다 돼요.
   ○ 남편이 기다리서 빠리 돌아가여 돼요.
   ✓ 남편이 기다려서 빨리 돌아가야 돼요.
   Translation: I have to go quickly since my husband is waiting.
2. ✓ 관심이 있으면 나와 같이 요가를 배우자.
   ○ 관심가 있으면 나와 같이 요가를 배우자.
   ○ 관심이 있으면 나와 같이 요가을 배우자.
   Translation: If you are interested learn yoga together with me.
3. ○ 귀신이 무서우면 빨리 달려아 돼요!
   ✓ 귀신이 무서우면 빨리 달려야 돼요!
   ○ 달려야 돼면을 때 귀신이 무서우면!
   Translation: If ghosts are scary, you have to run fast.

6 | Vocabulary Builder 단어 구축

Hopefully you have banked a lot of words in your memory. Let's go ahead and deposit some more words.

■ Group B: Bank 은행

현금	cash
수표	check
입금★	deposit
예금인출★	withdrawal
이체★	transfer
송금★	send money
통장	bank book
계좌	account
계좌번호	account number
수수료	fee
비밀번호	password (secret number)

★ Any item with this mark can be made into a verb by adding 하다.

■ Vocabulary Sentences
The following sentences might contain words and concepts not yet taught. Focus on the new vocabulary more than the grammar.

1. 저는 지금 현금이 많이 필요해요.
    I need a lot of cash right now.

2. 수표로 계산하고 싶어요.
    I want to pay with a check.

3. 에이티엠에서 입금을 할 수 있어요.
    You can make deposits at ATMs.

4. 예금인출을 하는 방법을 가르쳐 주세요.
    Please teach me how to withdraw.

5. 돈을 이체할 때 항상 계좌번호를 확인하세요.
    Always check the account number when you make a transfer.

6. 저희 부모님은 한국에서 매달 저에게 송금을 해요.
   My parents send money to me every month from Korea.

7. 저는 통장에 돈이 많이 있길 바라요.
   I wish there was a lot of money in my bank book.

8. 저에게 계좌번호를 가르쳐주세요.
   Tell me your account number.

9. 다른 사람들에게 비밀번호를 가르쳐주지 마세요.
   Don't teach (tell) other people your password.

10. 계좌로 돈을 이체할 때 수수료가 붙어요.
    When you transfer money to the account there
    is a fee attached.

7 Lesson 7:
Going to do

7 | New Words 새로운 단어

New Nouns etc.

실패	failure
실수	mistake
후회	regret
취업	employment, get a job
사업	business, enterprise
성공	success
이혼	divorce
약혼	engagement
생각	idea, thought
아니면	or, either

New Adjectives

시원하다	to be cool

New Verbs

생각하다	to consider, to think of
미치다	to go crazy
시험을 보다	to take a test
축하하다	to celebrate
떠나다	to leave

7 | Grammar and Usage 문법과 사용법

● **7-1. ~(으)러 가다/오다 Going and coming to do**

(으) form + 러 가다 or 오다 allows you to say phrases like "going to eat" or "coming to eat". (으) form is taught *book 2 section 7-9*.

Examples

1. 먹으러 가다	to go to eat
2. 마시러 가다	to go to drink
3. 공부하러 가다	to go to study
4. 살러 가다	to go to live
5. 타러 가다	to go to ride
6. 구경하러 오다	to come to sight-see
7. 가르치러 오다	to come to teach
8. 놀러 오다	to come to play
9. 보러 오다	to come to see

Example sentences

1. 매주 토요일에 아침 일찍 스키를 **타러 가요**.
   Every Saturday early in the morning I **go (to go) ski**.

2. 3일 후에 영국에서 친구가 **놀러 와요**.
   3 days from now my friend is **coming to hang out** from England.

3. 고등학교를 졸업하면 유럽으로 **공부하러 가고 싶어요**.
   When I graduate high school **I want to go to study** in Europe.

4. 미팅 후 손님과 점심을 **먹으러 가거나** 커피를 **마시러 갈 거예요**.
   After the meeting I will **go eat** lunch **or go drink** coffee with my customer.

> Remember that Koreans also use 우리 to mean "my".

Example conversation

1. A: 오늘 수업 후에 우리 집에 놀러 오세요.
   B: 수업 후에는 다른 미팅이 있어서 못 가요.
   A: 그럼 미팅 후 치킨과 맥주를 먹으러 갈까요?
   B: 좋아요! 이따가 연락할게요.

   A: Come to hang out at my house after class today.
   B: After class I have another meeting so I can't go.
   A: Well then, after the meeting how about we eat chicken and (drink) beer.
   B: Great! I'll contact you after a bit.

> "how about we" sounds more natural than "shall we".

2. A: 삼촌에게 고양이를 받았어.
   B: 정말? 지금 **보러 갈게**! 고양이를 빨리 안고 싶어.
   A: 아직 너무 어려서 못 안아.
   B: 알았어. 정말 안고 싶지만 사진만 찍을게.

   A: I got a cat from my uncle.
   B: Really? I'm **going** now **to see** it! I want to hold the cat right away.
   A: You can't hold it because it's still too young.
   B: It's okay. I really want to hold it, but I'll just take pictures.

3. A: 점심에 중국음식이나 태국음식을 **먹으러 가요**.
   B: 저는 전혀 태국음식을 먹지 않아요.
   A: 그럼 회사 옆쪽에 중국 식당으로 1시까지 오세요.
   B: 네. 점심밥을 먹은 후에 커피를 **마시러 가요**.

   A: For lunch let's **go to eat** Thai food or Chinese food.
   B: I never eat Thai food.
   A: Well then, come to the Chinese restaurant on the side of the company by 1 o'clock.
   B: Got it. After eating lunch we will **go drink** coffee.

● 7-2. Chinese characters in Korea

The 어, in such words as 영어 (English) and 한국어 (Korean), comes from the 한자 (Chinese character) 語 which means "language". China, Taiwan, and Japan still use 한자 in daily life. 한자 is often tedious to write with it's many strokes and takes many years to learn the 1000s of characters.

To solve this problem, Japan introduced two phonetic systems, hiragana and katakana, and reduced the number of strokes in many of the original 한자 from China. However, it's still required to learn over 1000 한자 by the time you graduate 6th grade!

China also introduced a much more "simplified" 한자, but students are still required to learn over 2500 characters by 6th grade. Taiwan is one of the few places that is still mostly using the original or "traditional" Chinese characters.

Korea solved the 한자 issue in the 16th century, when *Sejong the Great* created the 한글 phonetic system. 한글, instead of being used in conjunction with 한자, like Japanese hiragana, simply replaced it.

In modern Korea, 한자 is more a "thing you must study in school" than something required to live and survive. It still shows up occasionally, but practically speaking, you DO NOT need to learn even one 한자 to become an amazing Korean linguist.

That being said, knowing 한자 allows you to make connections in the Korean language that can enhance your understanding.

For example there are a lot of words that contain 어 in them.

言語	언어	language
語句	어구	phrase
單語	단어	word, vocabulary
用語	용어	terminology
俗語	속어	slang
語學	어학	linguistics, the study of language

If, for example, you knew that 학 is always related to school, or study, then you might be able to figure out that 어학 meant "the study of language" because of the underlying 한자. There are MANY opportunities to link words if you know 한자. Is anyone interested in "Hanja From Zero!"?   ㅋㅋㅋ

● 7-3. 어 vs 말

한국어 is also many times called 한국말. 말 means "words" or "language" and is native Korean. In other words, it didn't come from 한자 like 어 did. Other languages can also use 말 instead of 어.

English	어	말
English	영어	never
Korean	한국어	한국말
Chinese	중국어	중국말
French	프랑스어	프랑스말
Thai	태국어	태국말
Spanish	스페인어	스페인말
Japanese	일본어	일본말

Example sentences
1. 영어 잘 하시네요!   You speak English well!
2. 스페인어를 공부하고 있어요.   I am studying Spanish.
3. 태국말을 아세요?   Do you know Thai?
4. 프랑스말은 어려워요.   French is hard.
5. 일본말과 한국말은 비슷해요.   Japanese and Korean are similar.

● 7-4. 아니면 (or)

아니면 is used between two sentences with opposing choices.

> **Example sentences**
>
> 1. 화요일에 만나요? 아니면 목요일에 만나요?
>   Will we meet on Tuesday? Or will we meet on Thursday?
>
> 2. 고양이가 좋아요? 아니면 개가 좋아요?
>   Do you like cats? Or do you like dogs?
>
> 3. 한국어가 어려워요? 아니면 쉬워요?
>   Is Korean hard? Or is it easy?

● 7-5. 생각하다 (to consider, to think of)

TYPE	하다 adjective	BASIC FORM	생각해

생각하다 for this lesson means, "to consider" even though at times it can mean, "to think". The *Special Information* section has more information. The thing you are "considering / thinking of" is marked with 을/를.

> **Example sentences**
>
> 1. 결혼을 생각해요.
>   I am considering marriage.
>
> 2. 내일 해야 할 일을 생각하고 있어요.
>   I am thinking of the work I will have to do tomorrow.
>
> 3. 너를 생각해.
>   I am thinking of you.
>
> 4. 난 매일 남자친구를 생각해.
>   I think about my boyfriend everyday.
>
> 5. 어릴 때부터 부모님은 항상 우리들에 대해 생각했어요.
>   Since we were young our parents always thought about us.

Special Information 특별 정보

Thinking in Korean

In English we have one verb "to think" but unfortunately in order to say "I think X" or "I thought it was X" in Korean there are a few additional important grammar structures that must be learned first.

These grammar structures will be covered in lesson 9 of this book.

● **7-6. 시험을 보다 (to take a test)**

TYPE	regular verb	BASIC FORM	시험을 봐

보다 means to "see" or to "watch" in book 1 of this series but when combined with "test" it means "to take".

Example sentences

1. 우리 학교는 입학 하기 전 시험을 봐요.
   Before you are admitted to our school you take a test.

2. 제니퍼는 내일 운전면허증 시험을 봐서 공부를 해야 해요.
   Because Jennifer will take the driver's license test tomorrow, she has to study.

3. 대학교에서 우리는 매달마다 시험을 봤어요.
   In college we took tests each and every month.

4. 지난달에 토익 시험을 봤고, 이번 달에 대학교에 입학했어요.
   Last month I took the TOIEC test, and this month I entered college.

5. 저는 항상 시험을 보기 전 음악을 들어요.
   I always listen to music before I take a test.

6. 시험을 보는 날에는 잘 먹어야 돼요.
   On the day you take a test you must eat well.

● **7-7. Mistakes, failures, regrets, and success!**
All of the new nouns in this lesson can be made into verbs by adding 하다.
As discussed in prior lessons using 하다 you can often create new verbs.

실패하다	to fail
실수하다	to make a mistake
후회하다	to regret
취업하다	to get a job
사업하다	to do a business
성공하다	to succeed
이혼하다	to get a divorce
약혼하다	to get engaged to be married
생각하다	to consider, think of

Example sentences

1. 제 친구는 많은 사업에 실패했지만, 지금은 성공했어요.
My friend failed many businesses, but now he has succeeded.

2. 공부를 안 해서 대학원 시험에 실패했어요.
Because I didn't study I failed my graduate school test.

3. 대학을 졸업 후 취업을 해야 돼요.
After graduating college I have to get a job.

4. 취업에도 실패하고 결혼에도 실패했어요.
I failed to get a job, and I failed at marriage.

5. 그와 결혼을 후회하면, 이혼을 생각 해야 돼요.
If you regret marrying him, you have to think of divorce.

6. 여자친구랑 약혼하고 싶지만, 하기 전에 취업을 하고 싶어요.
I want to get engaged with my girlfriend, but before I do, I want to get a job.

7. 오늘 아침을 안 먹어서 후회해요.
Because I didn't eat this morning I regret it.

8. 고등학교 친구가 어제 약혼했어요.
My high school friend got engaged yesterday.

9. 성공을 하고 싶으면, 열심히 일을 해야 돼요.
If you want to succeed, you have to work hard.

10. 시험을 볼 때 실수를 하면, 화를 내지 마세요.
If you make a mistake when taking a test, don't get mad.

11. 선생님도 실수할 수 있어요.
Teachers can make mistakes too.

12. 이번 콘서트에서 많은 실수를 했지만 후회는 안 해요.
I made many mistakes at the concert, but I am not regretting it.

13. 실패는 성공의 어머니입니다.
Failure is the mother of success.

● 7-8. 시원하다 (to be cool)

TYPE	하다 adjective	BASIC FORM	시원해

시원하다 means "cool" like a cool breeze, however it's also commonly used to mean "feel good" or "relaxed".

> **Example sentences**
> 1. 오늘 아침부터 비가 와서 날씨가 시원해요.
>   It's rained since morning today, so the weather is cool.
>
> 2. 시원한 콜라 두 병만 주세요.
>   Just two cold colas please.
>
> 3. 여름에는 시원하고 편한 옷을 입으세요.
>   In summer wear cool and comfortable clothing.
>
> 4. 9 월부터 점점 시원해질 거예요.
>   It will gradually get cooler from September.

● 7-9. 미치다 (to go crazy)

TYPE	regular verb	BASIC FORM	미쳐

If you listen to KPOP or watch any KDRAMA, certainly you have heard 미치다 at least 400 times. Crazy right? The thing you are crazy for is marked with 에 or 에게 and the thing that makes you crazy is marked with 로/으로.

If you want to say someone IS crazy you have to say they have GONE crazy using past tense for 미치다.

> **Example sentences**
> 1. 우리 선생님은 진짜 미쳤어요.
>   Our teacher is really crazy.
>
> 2. 남자친구를 만날 수 없어서 미치겠어요.
>   I am going to go crazy because I can't see my boyfriend.
>
> 3. 우리 학교에서 미친 사람이 많아요!
>   There are many people that have gone crazy in our school.
>
> 4. 너 미쳤어!?
>   Have you gone crazy!?

● **7-10. 축하하다 (to celebrate)**

TYPE	regular verb	BASIC FORM	축하해

Example sentences
1. 축하합니다!!
   Congratulations!!

2. 생일 축하합니다!!
   Happy birthday!!

> 생신 is the honorific form of 생일.

3. 60 번째 생신을 축하합니다!
   Congratulations on your 60th birthday!

4. 친구와 오랫동안 싸웠지만 그 친구는 우리 결혼식을 축하하러 왔어요.
   I was fighting with my friend for a long time, but that friend came to celebrate our wedding.

● **7-11. 떠나다 (to leave, depart, go off)**

TYPE	regular verb	BASIC FORM	시험을 봐

Example sentences
1. 내가 떠날 때 울지마.
   Don't cry when I leave.

2. 삼촌은 아침에 떠났어요.
   My uncle departed in the morning.

3. 프랑스로 여행을 떠나기 전에 프랑스어를 배울 거예요.
   Before I leave on my trip to France, I will learn French.

4. 결혼식 후 결혼식장을 떠날 때 많이 울었어요.
   I cried a lot when I left the wedding hall after the wedding ceremony.

5. 엄마는 비행기가 떠날 때까지 공항에서 기다렸어요.
   My mother waited at the airport until the plane left.

7 | Test Yourself Activities 연습 문제

● **A7-1. Fix the mistake**
Correct the Korean sentence, then finish the translation on the line below.

1. 지난달에 제 친구가 한국에 남편을 찾으로 갔어요.

   Korean _____

   English To go find a husband_____

2. 한국 학생들이 어릴 때부터 영말을 배워요.

   Korean _____

   English From when they are young_____

3. 우리 학원에서는 매주 금요일에 시험을 해야 돼요.

   Korean _____

   English We have to take a test_____

● **A7-2. Listening skills**
Go to **http://fromzero.com/korean/kfz3/A2** OR scan the QR code. Enter the code. Write the Korean then the English.

1. 7A Korean _____

   English _____

2. 7B Korean _____

   English _____

3. 7C Korean _____

   English _____

● **A7-3. Fill in the blanks**
Fill in the missing word or particle based on the English sentence.

1. 우리 학교는 _____ 시험을 봐요.
   Before you are admitted to our school you take a test.

2. 스키를 _____까요?
   Shall we go skiing?

3. 우리 회사에는 _____ 사람이 거의 없어요.
   There are almost no crazy people at our company.

4. 아버지는 다른 나라로 _____요.
   My father left for another country.

5. 시험 후에 _____ 거예요?
   Are you going to come hang out after the test?

● **A7-4. Mark and Translate**
Mark the Korean sentence without mistakes then translate it.

1. ○ 성공하고 싶어면 이 책을 꼭 읽으세요.
   ○ 성공하고 싶으면 이 책을 꼭 읽으세요.
   ○ 성공하고 싶으면 이 책이 꼭 읽으세요.

   Translation:_____

2. ○ 취업하면 매일 깨끗한 옷이 입어야 돼요.
   ○ 취업하면 매일 깨끗한 옷을 입어야 돼요.
   ○ 취업하면 매일 깨끗하는 옷이 입어야 돼요.

   Translation:_____

3. ○ 미국에 오면 같이 유명한 곳에 구경하로 가자.
   ○ 미극에 오면 같이 유명한 곳에 구경하러 가자.
   ○ 미국에 오면 같이 유명한 곳에 구경하러 가자.

   Translation:_____

7 | Self Test Answers 연습 문제 정답

● A7-1. Fix the mistake
1. 지난달에 제 친구가 한국에 남편을 <mark>찾으러</mark> 갔어요.
   To go find a husband my friend went to Korea last month.

2. 한국 학생들이 어릴 때부터 <mark>영어를</mark> 배워요.
   From when they are young Korean students learn English.

3. 우리 학원에서는 매주 금요일에 시험을 <mark>봐야</mark> 돼요.
   We have to take a test every Friday at our academy.

● A7-2. Listening skills
1. 여자친구랑 약혼하고 싶지만, 하기 전에 취업을 하고 싶어요.
   I want to get engaged with my girlfriend, but before I do, I want to get a job.

2. 남자친구를 만날 수 없어서 미치겠어요.
   I am going to go crazy because I can't see my boyfriend.

3. 수업 후에는 다른 미팅이 있어서 못 가요.
   After class I have another meeting so I can't go.

● A7-3. Fill in the blanks
1. 우리 학교는 <mark>입학하기 전에</mark> 시험을 봐요.
2. 스키를 <mark>탈</mark>까요?
3. 우리 회사에는 <mark>미친</mark> 사람이 거의 없어요.
4. 아버지는 다른 나라로 <mark>떠났어요</mark>.
5. 시험 후에 <mark>놀러 올</mark> 거예요?

● A7-4. Best Sentence Search
1. ○ 성공하고 싶어면 이 책을 꼭 읽으세요.
   ✓ 성공하고 싶으면 이 책을 꼭 읽으세요.
   ○ 성공하고 싶으면 이 책이 꼭 읽으세요.
   Translation: If you want to succeed, definitely read this book.

2. ○ 취업하면 매일 깨끗한 옷이 입어야 돼요.
   ✓ 취업하면 매일 깨끗한 옷을 입어야 돼요.
   ○ 취업하면 매일 깨끗하는 옷이 입어야 돼요.
   Translation: If (when) you get a job, you have to wear clean clothes.

3. ○ 미국에 오면 같이 유명한 곳에 구경하로 가자.
   ○ 미극에 오면 같이 유명한 곳에 구경하러 가자.
   ✓ 미국에 오면 같이 유명한 곳에 구경하러 가자.
   If (when) you come to America let's go to sightsee famous places together.

7 | Vocabulary Builder 단어 구축

These flowers might not be known where you live, but they are very common in Korea.

■ Group D: Flowers etc. 꽃 등

장미	rose
튤립	tulip
유채꽃	canola flower
해바라기	sunflower
국화	chrysanthemum
백합	lily
나팔꽃	morning glory
벚꽃	cherry blossoms
민들레	dandelion
선인장	cactus
무궁화	rose of sharon

■ Group E: Trees 나무

대나무	bamboo
참나무	oak wood
소나무	pine
벚나무	cherry tree
전나무	fir

■ Vocabulary Sentences

The following sentences might contain words and concepts not yet taught. Focus on the new vocabulary more than the grammar.

1. 한국에서 노란 장미는 질투의 의미입니다.
   Yellow roses show jealousy in Korea.

2. 그는 그녀에게 아름다운 튤립 한 다발을 보냈어요.
   He sent her a beautiful bouquet of roses.

3. 요즘 제주도에는 유채꽃이 한창입니다.
   These days, the canola flowers are in full bloom on Jeju.

4. 사막에는 선인장이 여러가지 있어요.
There are many types of cactus in the desert.

5. 해바라기는 태양이 움직이는 것을 따라서 움직입니다.
Sunflowers follow the sun as it moves around.

6. 한국에서는 보통 흰 국화를 장례식장에 보내요.
In Korea, It is common to send white chrysanthemums to the funeral.

7. 백합은 순결의 상징이예요.
Lily is the symbol of purity.

8. 우리집 울타리는 나팔꽃 덩굴들로 엉켜있어요.
Our fence is tangled with morning glory vines.

9. 어제부터 벚꽃 축제가 시작되었어요.
The cherry blossom festival started from yesterday.

10. 대한민국의 꽃은 무궁화 입니다.
Korea's national flower is the rose of sharon.

11. 대나무는 가볍고 속이 비었지만 단단해요.
Bamboo is lightweight, hollow, but strong.

12. 이 식탁은 참나무로 만들어 졌어요.
This dining table was made of oak wood.

13. 소나무의 수명은 보통 500 년이 넘어요.
The life of a pine is normally longer than 500 years.

14. 봄이 되면 벚나무에 벚꽃이 만발해요.
In spring, the cherry trees are in full bloom.

15. 전나무는 크리스마스트리로 사용되는 대표적인 나무에요.
Firs are a typical type of tree used as for Christmas trees.

 **Super Review and Quiz #1:**
Lessons 5-7

SR | Question and Answer 질문과 대답

Hide the English and try to translate the Korean. Take notes on words or grammar patterns that confuse you then review them if necessary.

1. Q: 학교에 어떻게 가요?
  A: 학교에 갈 때 버스를 타요.
  A: 돈이 있을 때 택시를 타요.
  A: 걸어가요.

  Q: How do you go to school?
  A: I ride the bus when I go to school.
  A: When I have money I take a taxi.
  A: I walk.

2. Q: 작년에 유나 씨를 만났어요?
  A: 네, 한국에서 한국말을 배울 때 만났어요.
  A: 네, 처음으로 유나씨를 만났을 때 너무 예뻐서 놀랐어요.
  A: 아니요, 유나 씨는 제가 한국에 갔을 때 너무 바빴어요.

  Q: Did you meet Yuna last year?
  A: Yes, I met her when I was learning Korean in Korea.
  A: Yes, when I first met Yuna I was surprised because she was so pretty.
  A: No, Yuna was too busy when I went to Korea.

3. Q: 방학 때 뭘 했어요?
  A: 한국어 단어를 많이 외웠어요.
  A: 눈이 올 때 친구와 스키를 타러 갔어요.
  A: 영어 학원에 다녔어요.

  Q: What did you do during the school break?
  A: I memorized many Korean vocabulary.
  A: When it snowed I went skiing with a friend.
  A: I attended an English academy.

4. **Q:** 언제 차를 샀어요?
   A: 고등학교 때 샀어요.
   A: 아르바이트를 시작한 후에 샀어요.
   A: 대학교에 입학할 때 샀어요.

   Q: When did you buy a car?
   A: I bought it when I was in high school.
   A: I bought it after I started my part-time job.
   A: I bought it when I entered college.

5. **Q:** 이 약을 지금 꼭 먹어야 돼요?
   A: 네, 식사 후에 꼭 먹어야 돼요.
   A: 당연하지요. 지금 안 먹으면 아플 거예요.
   A: 아니요, 이따가 먹으세요.

   Q: Do I definitely have to take this medicine now?
   A: Yes, you definitely have to take it after a meal.
   A: Of course. If you don't take it now, you will get sick.
   A: No, take it later.

6. **Q:** 새로운 여자친구는 어때요?
   A: 여자친구가 한국말을 못해서 답답해요.
   A: 똑똑하고 예뻐서 놀랐어요.
   A: 너무 어리지만 정신은 강해요.

   Q: How is your new girlfriend.
   A: I am frustrated because she (my girlfriend) can't speak Korean.
   A: I was surprised that she is smart and pretty.
   A: She is really young but has a strong mind.

SR | Conversation 대화 K-E

Hide the English and try to translate the Korean. Take notes on words or grammar patterns that confuse you then review them if necessary.

1. **Conversation between mutual friends of Sunhee.**
   현우: 선희 씨의 결혼식에 왜 안 갔어요?
   시은: 갔어요. 그런데 제가 결혼식에 갔을 때 결혼식이 벌써 끝났어요.
   현우: 그래요? 선희 씨가 결혼식 때 많이 울었어요.
   시은: 남편도 울었어요?
   현우: 아니요, 남편은 웃었어요.

현우: Why didn't you go to Sunhee's wedding ceremony?

시은: I went. But when I went to the ceremony it was already over.

현우: Is that so? Sunhee cried a lot during the ceremony.

시은: Did her husband cry too?

현우: No, the husband laughed.

2. Polite conversation between classmates.

미영: 오늘 수업이 끝나면 같이 숙제를 할까요?

유리: 그런데 수업이 12시에 끝나요. 점심을 먹어야 돼요.

미영: 그럼 먼저 샌드위치를 먹으러 가요.

유리: 좋은 생각이에요.

미영: Shall we do homework together after class ends today?

유리: But class ends at 12 o'clock. We have to eat lunch.

미영: Well, let's go eat sandwiches first.

유리: It's a good idea.

3. Polite conversation between college classmates.

지영: 이번 시험 잘 봤어요?

대숭: 아니요. 실수를 많이 했어요.

지영: 대숭 씨는 똑똑해서 다음 번에는 잘 할거예요.

대숭: 끝날 때까지 열심히 해서 후회하지 않을 거예요.

지영: Did you do well on the test this time?

대숭: No. I made many mistakes.

지영: Because you are smart you will do well the next time.

대숭: I will do my best until the end and not have any regrets.

4. A polite conversation between friends.

효린: 쿠키를 먹으러 올래?

보라: 좋아! 한 시간 후에 갈게.

효린: 딱딱한 쿠키가 좋아? 아니면 부드러운 쿠키가 좋아?

보라: 나는 부드러운 쿠키가 좋아!

효린: Do you want to come eat cookies?

보라: Great! I'll go in an hour.

효린: You like hard cookies? Or do you like soft cookies?

보라: I like soft cookies.

SR   Quiz Yourself 퀴즈

● **1. Sentence maker**

Combine the items below using 때, then translate the complete sentence into English on the following line.

Noun + 때

Sample

Ex) 결혼식 / 한복을 입었어요.

　　Combined: <u>결혼식 때 한복을 입었어요.</u>

　　Translated: <u>During the wedding ceremony I wore a hanbok.</u>

1. 고등학교 / 프랑스말을 배웠어요.

　　Combined: _____.

　　Translated: _____.

2. 7살 / 한국에 왔어요.

　　Combined: _____.

　　Translated: _____.

3. 작년 크리스마스 / 남자 친구하고 헤어졌어요.

　　Combined: _____.

　　Translated: _____.

4. 이번 휴가 / 하와이에 갈 거예요.

　　Combined: _____.

　　Translated: _____.

5. 서른 살 / 대학원을 졸업했어요.

　　Combined: _____.

　　Translated: _____.

Verb/Adj+ (으)ㄹ 때

> **Sample**
> Ex) 선생님이 이야기합니다. 잘 들으세요.
>   Combined: <u>선생님이 이야기할 때 잘 들으세요.</u>
>   Translated: <u>When the teacher speaks listen well.</u>

6. 머리가 아파요. 이 약을 먹어요.

   Combined: _____.

   Translated: _____.

7. 밥을 먹고 싶지 않아요. 빵을 먹어요.

   Combined: _____.

   Translated: _____.

8. 한국에 도착 했어요. 눈이 오고 있었어요.

   Combined: _____.

   Translated: _____.

9. 술을 마셨어요. 운전을 하지 마세요.

   Combined: _____.

   Translated: _____.

10. 날씨가 더워요. 시원한 콜라를 마시세요.

    Combined: _____.

    Translated: _____.

● **2. Translate and answer**
Translate the question then answer it as if asked directly to yourself.

> **Sample**
> 미국인이에요? 아니면 한국인이에요?
> **Translation:** Are you American? Or are you Korean?
> **Answer:** 저는 미국인이에요.

1. 빨리 달릴 때 다리가 아파요? 아니면 팔이 아파요?

   Translation: _____.

   Answer: _____.

2. 달은 태양보다 더 밝아요? 아니면 더 어두워요?

   Translation: _____.

   Answer: _____.

3. 당신의 집에서 공항까지는 멀어요? 아니면 가까워요?

   Translation: _____.

   Answer: _____.

4. 아침에 항상 일찍 일어나요? 아니면 늦게 일어나요?

   Translation: _____.

   Answer: _____.

5. 매운 게 좋아요? 아니면 싫어요?

   Translation: _____.

   Answer: _____.

● 3. Reading comprehension

Read the following selection then answer the questions in KOREAN.

New words: 자동판매기 (vending machine), 리필 (refills)

> 저는 어릴 때 9 년 동안 일본에서 살았어요. 그리고 20 살 때 일본을 떠났어요. 그래서 미국에 대해 모르는 게 많이 있었어요. 일본에는 자동판매기가 많이 있지만 미국은 별로 없어요. 그리고 미국에 있는 식당에서는 무료로 음료를 리필 할 수 있어요. 그런데 일본에서는 리필할 때 돈을 내야 돼요.

1. 이 사람은 몇 살 때부터 일본에 살았어요?

_____

2. 미국에서는 리필은 얼마에요?

_____

3. 미국에서는 자동판매기가 많이 있어요?

_____

4. 이 사람은 몇 살 때 미국에 돌아왔어요?

_____

● 4. English to Korean Translation

Translate the following sentences into Korean.

1. I attended a Korean language academy when I was in Korea.

_____

2. My first Korean friend lives in Busan.

_____

3. Until we arrive please read this book.

_____

SR | Answer Key 해답

● 1. Sentence maker (answers)

1. 고등학교 때 프랑스말을 배웠어요.
   I learned French when I was in high school.

2. 7 살 때 한국에 왔어요.
   I came to Korea when I was 7 years old.

3. 작년 크리스마스 때 남자 친구하고 헤어졌어요.
   Last year on Christmas I broke up with my boyfriend.

4. 이번 휴가 때 하와이에 갈 거예요.
   On this vacation I'm going to Hawaii.

5. 서른 살 때 대학원을 졸업했어요.
   I graduated graduate school when I was 30 years old.

6. 머리가 아플 때 이 약을 먹어요.
   When your head hurts take this medicine.

7. 밥을 먹고 싶지 않을 때 빵을 먹어요.
   When you don't want to eat, eat bread.
   When I don't want to eat, I eat bread

8. 한국에 도착 했을 때 눈이 오고 있었어요.
   It was snowing when I arrived in Korea.

9. 술을 마셨었을 때 운전을 하지 마세요.
   When you have drunk alcohol, don't drive.

10. 날씨가 더울 때 시원한 콜라를 마시세요.
    When the weather is hot drink a refreshing cola.

● 2. Translate and answer (answers)

1. When you run fast will your legs hurt? Or will your arms hurt?
   다리가 아파요. / 팔이 아파요.

2. Is the moon brighter than the sun? Or is it darker?
   어두워요.

3. Is your house far from the airport? Or is it close?
   멀어요. / 가까워요.

4. Do you always wake up early in the moring? Or do you wake up late?
   일찍 일어나요. / 늦게 일어나요.

5. Do you like spicy things? Or do you not like them?
   좋아요. / 싫어요.

● **3. Reading comprehension (answers)**

I lived in Japan for 9 years when I was young. When I left Japan I was 20 years old. So when there were many things I didn't know about America. In Japan there are many vending machines, but in America there aren't many. And you can refill drinks at restaurants in America for free. But in Japan you have to pay money for refills.

1. Translation: From what age did this person live in Japan?
   Answer: 11 살 때부터 살았어요.

2. Translation: How much are refills in America?
   Answer: 무료예요.

3. Translation: Are there a lot of vending machines in America?
   Answer: 별로 없어요.

4. Translation: At what age did this person come back to America?
   Answer: 20 살 때 돌아왔어요.

● **4. English to Korean Translation (answers)**

1. 저는 한국에 있을 때 한국어 학원을 다녔어요.

2. 첫 번째 한국 친구는 부산에 살고 있어요 / 살아요.

3. 우리가 도착할 때까지 이 책을 읽어요 / 읽으세요 / 읽어 주세요.

Korean Simplified History #4:
The Great King

 New Words and Grammar

땅 land
대왕 great king
빼앗다 to take, to steal
사이 between, relationship

무덤 grave
싸우다 to fight
그래서 therefore
~게 되다 to become this way

 Korean History (Korean version)

- 고구려에는 광개토대왕이 있었어요.

- 고구려와 백제는 사이가 나빴어요.

- 그래서 고구려와 백제는 많이 싸우게 되었어요.

- 광개토대왕이 백제의 땅을 많이 빼앗았어요.

- 광개토대왕은 중국도 공격했어요.

- 그래서 광개토대왕의 무덤은 중국에 있어요.

 Korean History (English version)

- In Goguryeo there was King Gwanggaeto the great.

- Goguryeo and Baekje's relationship was bad.

- Therefore, Goguryeo and Baekje came to fight a lot.

- King Gwanggaeto the great took a lot of Baekje's land.

- King Gwanggaeto the great also attacked China.

- Therefore, King Gwanggaeto the great's grave is in China.

8 Lesson 8: Comparing and Choice

8 | New Words 새로운 단어

New Nouns etc.

딸기	strawberry
방학	vacation (only from school)
집안일	housework
초등학교	elementary school
중학교	middle school
고등학교	high school
출구	exit; way out
친척	relatives
호선	line # (only for subways)

New Adverbs

가장	most (similar to 제일)
훨씬	much, far, a lot, considerably, way
오래	long, a long time

New Adjectives

심심하다	to be bored
지루하다	to be boring
엄격하다	to be strict
높다	to be high
낮다	to be low

New Verbs

고르다	to choose
청소를 하다	to clean
갈아타다	to change/to transfer
눕다	to lay down

8 | Grammar and Usage 문법과 사용법

● 8-1. ~보다 ~더 Comparing items

보다 is a comparison marker that means "than". It comes after any item that you are comparing to another. There are two sentence orders you can use to make comparisons. Order #2 is very similar to English but both are common.

Making Comparisons #1

A 보다 B가 더 adjective

Compared to A, B is more [adjective]

Making Comparisons #2

B는 A 보다 더 adjective

B is more [adjective] than A

Example sentences

1. 태양보다 달이 더 작아요.
   The moon is smaller than the sun.

2. 낚시보다 골프가 더 좋아요.
   Golf is better than fishing.

3. 제니퍼는 에밀리보다 더 똑똑해요.
   Jennifer is smarter than Emily.

4. 일보다 공부가 더 쉬웠어요.
   Study is easier than work.

5. 치즈 닭갈비는 떡볶이보다 더 매워요?
   Are cheese chicken ribs spicier than spicy rice cakes?

6. 이번 주는 지난주보다 더 바빠요.
   This week is busier than last week.

7. 엄마보다 아빠가 더 엄격해요.
   My father is stricter than my mother.

You can use 훨씬 before OR in place 더 to show special emphasis on just how much better something is when comparing to others.

Example sentences

1. 태양보다 달이 <u>훨씬</u> 더 작아요.
   The moon is <u>considerably</u> smaller than the sun.

2. 낚시보다 골프가 <u>훨씬</u> 더 좋아요.
   Golf is <u>way</u> better than fishing.

3. 제니퍼는 에밀리보다 <u>훨씬</u> 더 똑똑해요.
   Jennifer is <u>much</u> smarter than Emily.

● **8-2. ~중에서/~에서 Among a group / in an area**
중에서 and 에서 define the group or area from which a selection is made. 에서 is used for locations and 중에서 is used for groups.

Locations 에서

세상에서
in the world

미국에서
in the United States

집에서
in the house

Example sentences (~에서)

1. 세상<u>에서</u> 제일 좋아하는 나라는 어디예요?
   Where (what) is your most favorite country <u>in</u> the world?

2. 미국<u>에서</u> 제일 유명한 사람은 누구예요?
   Who is the most famous person <u>in</u> the United States?

3. 제 방은 집<u>에서</u> 제일 조용한 방이에요.
   My room is the quietest room <u>in</u> the house.

Groups 중에서

사람들 중에서
out of all the people

과일 중에서
out of all the fruit

신발 중에서
out of all the shoes

Example sentences (~중에서)

1. 학생들 중에서 김유나가 성적이 제일 높아요.
   Out of all the students Yuna Kim has the highest grade.

2. 과일 중에서 제일 맛있는 과일은 뭐예요?
   Out of all the fruit which is the most delicious fruit?

3. 신발 중에서 하이힐이 제일 비싸요.
   Out of all the shoes the high heels are the most expensive.

가장 is similar to 제일. Let's replace 제일 in the following sentences.

Example sentences (~에서 and ~중에서)

1. 동물원에서 제일 좋아하는 동물은 사자 입니다.
   In the zoo the animal that I like the most is the tiger.

2. 꽃 중에서 가장 아름다운 꽃은 튤립입니다.
   The most beautiful flower out of all flowers are tulips.

3. 과일 중에서 제일 맛있는 과일은 사과입니다.
   The most delicious fruit out of all fruits are apples.

4. 제니퍼는 학교에서 수학을 가장 잘 해요.
   Jennifer is the best at math in the school.

5. 음식 중에서 한국음식이 가장 짜요.
   Out of all food Korean food is the saltiest.

Example conversation

1. A: 조지씨가 편의점에서 가장 좋아하는 것이 뭐예요?
   B: 음식 중에서는 삼각김밥을 가장 좋아하고, 삼각김밥 중에서 매운 치즈 닭갈비 맛을 제일 좋아해요.
   A: 삼각김밥은 싸지만 너무 작아요.
   B: 맞아요. 그래서 항상 2 개를 먹거나 라면을 더 먹어요.

   A: What do you like the most at the convenience store George?
   B: Out of the food I like triangle-shaped gimbap the most and out of the triangle-shaped gimbap I like the flavor of the spicy cheese chicken rib the most.
   A: The triangle-shaped gimbap is cheap but it's too small.
   B: You're right. So, normally I eat two or eat more ramen noodles.

● **8-3. BASIC 서 (action order, this then that)**
In book 2 you learned BASIC form + 서 to mean "because, since".

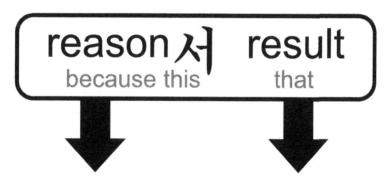

The RESULT can never be a
command or suggestion.

Example sentences

1. 돈이 없어서 여행을 할 수 없어요.
   Because I don't have money, I can't go on a trip.

2. 사람들이 많아서 이 식당은 시끄러워요.
   Because there are many people, this restaurant is loud.

3. 아침을 많이 먹어서 지금 배고프지 않아요.
   Because I ate too much breakfast, I'm not hungry now.

BASIC + 서 can also be used to show sequential or connected events.
NOTE: When the events are NOT connected then ~고 should be used.

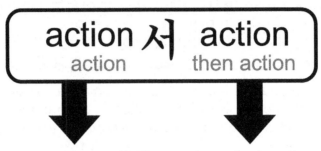

One subject ALWAYS completes both actions.
The first action ends before the final action.

1. 숙제를 해서 선생님께 드렸어요. (honorific)
   I did homework, then I gave it to my teacher.

2. 친구들이랑 만나서 같이 식당에 갔어요.
   I met with friends then I went to a restaurant with them.

3. 엄마가 고기를 사서 요리했어요.
   Mother bought meat then cooked it.

NOTE: Above notice that the same objects are on both sides of the 서.
1: homework → it   2: friends → them   3: meat → it

The first action is never past tense stem.

먹어서 ✓   먹었서 ✗

The final action always determines the tense of the first.

Example sentences
1. 아침에 여덟 시에 일어나서 운동을 할 거예요.
   I will wake up at 8 in the morning, then exercise.

2. 아침에 여덟 시에 일어나서 운동을 했어요.
   I woke up at 8 in the morning, then exercised.

3. 아침에 여덟 시에 일어나서 운동을 하고 싶어요.
   I want to wake up at 8 in the morning, then exercise.

4. 아침에 여덟 시에 일어나서 운동을 하세요.
   Wake up at 8 in the morning, then exercise.

● **8-4. Multiple action comparison ~고, ~(으)ㄴ 후, ~서**
Some grammar structures in English and Korean seem similar. Let's take a moment and review a few of the ways we now know how to use multiple actions.

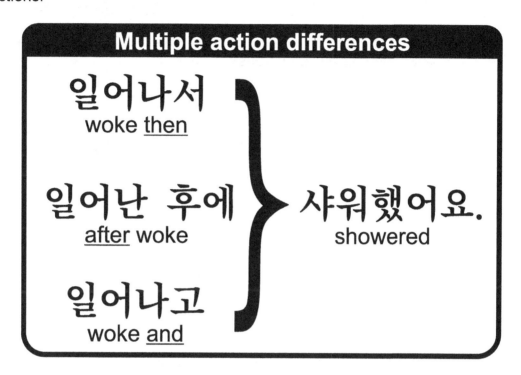

Multiple action differences

일어나서
woke <u>then</u>

일어난 후에
<u>after</u> woke

} 샤워했어요.
showered

일어나고
woke <u>and</u>

VERB BASIC + 서 – shows connected actions

VERB (으)ㄴ 후에 – puts stress on first action

VERB STEM + 고 – shows multiple unrelated actions

Example sentences
1. 컴퓨터를 끈 후에 불을 꺼 주세요.
   After turning off the computer please turn off the lights.

2. 친구랑 이야기하고 사진을 찍었어요.
   I talked with a friend and took a picture.

3. 강남역에서 갈아타서 잠실역쪽으로 갔어요.
   I transferred at Gangnam station then went towards Jamsil station.

● **8-5. 심심하다 (to be bored), 지루하다 (to be boring)**

심심하다	TYPE	하다 adjective	BASIC FORM	심심해

지루하다	TYPE	하다 adjective	BASIC FORM	지루해

심심하다 is used to describe feelings of being bored. If you want to say something is boring you will need to use 지루하다.

Example sentences

1. 어제 수업보다 오늘 수업이 훨씬 지루했어요.
   Today's class is much more boring than yesterday's class.

2. 한국에서 돌아온 후 집에만 있어서 심심해요.
   After returning from Korea I'm bored since I've only been in the house.

3. 이 영화는 한국영화 중에서 제일 지루하네요.
   Out of all the Korean movies this movie is the most boring.

4. 심심해서 노래를 불렀어요.
   I sang a song because I was bored.

5. 심심할 때는 지루한 영화를 보고 싶지 않아요.
   When I am bored I don't want to watch a boring movie.

● **8-6. 엄격하다 (to be strict)**

TYPE	하다 adjective	BASIC FORM	엄격해

Example sentences

1. 고등학교 선생님은 초등학교 선생님보다 엄격해요.
   High school teachers are stricter than elementary school teachers.

2. 우리 학교에서 수학 선생님이 가장 엄격해요.
   At our school the math teacher is the most strict.

3. 아빠보다 엄마가 더 엄격해서 아빠가 더 좋아요.
   Because my mother is stricter than my father, I like my father more.

4. 올해부터 우리 대학교의 규칙이 훨씬 더 엄격해졌어요.
   From this year the rules at our college have become considerably more strict.

● 8-7. 높다 (to be high), 낮다 (to be low)

높다	TYPE	regular adjective	BASIC FORM	높아

낮다	TYPE	regular adjective	BASIC FORM	낮아

Example sentences

1. 제 여자친구는 항상 높은 구두를 신어요.
   My girlfriend always wears high shoes.

   > The verb "to wear on feet" is 신다 (lesson 11)

2. 내일 구경할 산은 정말 높아요.
   The mountain I will see tomorrow is really tall.

3. 조지의 수학 성적은 영어성적 보다 낮아요.
   George's math grade is lower than his English grade .

4. 이 빌딩은 서울에서 가장 높아요.
   This building is the tallest in Seoul.

   > TOEIC is a common test used to test English proficiency.

5. 공부를 안 해서 토익 점수가 낮아졌어요.
   Because I didn't study my TOIEC score got lower.

● 8-8. 고르다 (to choose)

TYPE	르 irregular verb	BASIC FORM	골라

Example sentences

1. 냉장고에서 가장 맛있는 딸기를 고르세요.
   Please choose the most delicious strawberries from the refrigerator.

2. 파티에서 입을 옷을 골랐어요.
   I chose the clothing I will wear at the party.

3. 이 클럽에서 가장 예쁜 여자를 고르세요.
   Choose the prettiest girl at this club.

4. 한국 음식 중에서 먹고 싶은 것을 고르세요.
   Choose what you want to eat out of the Korean food.

● 8-9. 청소를 하다 (to clean)

TYPE	하다 verb	BASIC FORM	청소를 해

Example sentences

1. 방학 후 내 방 청소를 할 거야!
   After vacation I will clean my room!

2. 이따가 청소하고 학교에 갈 거예요.
   Later I will clean and go to school.

3. 내일은 남편과 청소를 하고 영화를 볼 거예요.
   Tomorrow I will clean with my husband and watch a movie.

4. 우리 친척이 집에 오기 전에 엄마는 오래 청소를 했어요.
   My mother cleaned a long time before our relatives came to the house.

● 8-10. 갈아타다 (to change/to transfer)

TYPE	regular verb	BASIC FORM	갈아타

Example sentences

1. 사동역에서 갈아타세요.
   Transfer at Sadong station.

2. 강남역에서 갈아타서 역삼역에서 내리세요.
   Transfer at Gangnam station then get off at Yeoksam station.

3. 2호선에서 5호선으로 갈아타면 더 빨리 도착해요.
   If you transfer from line 2 to line 5 you will arrive quicker.

4. 이태원으로 가고 싶으면 지하철을 두 번 갈아타야 돼요.
   If you want to go to Itaewon you have to transfer twice on the subway.

● **8-11. 눕다 (to lay down)**

TYPE	ㅂ irregular verb	BASIC FORM	누워

Example sentences

1. 세 시간 동안 집안일을 해서 눕고 싶어요.
   I want to lay down since I did house work for 3 hours.

2. 밥을 먹은 후 눕지 마세요.
   After eating dinner don't lay down.

3. 머리가 아파서 누웠어요.
   I layed down since my head hurt.

4. 너무 피곤해서 생각 없이 침대에 누웠어요.
   I was so tired I layed down on the bed without thinking.

8 | Test Yourself Activities 연습 문제

● A8-1. Fix the mistake

Correct the Korean sentence, then finish the translation on the line below.

1. 튤립은 성인장보다 도 예뻐요.

   Korean _____

   English Tulips_____

2. 세상중에서 가장 큰 나라는 어디예요?

   Korean _____

   English Where is the_____

3. 저는 고등학교를 졸업해고 유럽여행을 했어요.

   Korean _____

   English I graduated_____ then I _____

● A8-2. Listening skills

Go to **http://fromzero.com/korean/kfz3/A2** OR scan the QR code. Enter the code. Write the Korean then the English.

1. 8A Korean _____

   English _____

2. 8B Korean _____

   English _____

3. 8C Korean _____

   English _____

● A8-3. Fill in the blanks
Fill in the missing word or particle based on the English sentence.

1. 서울에서 제일 _____ 빌딩은 어디예요?
   Where is the tallest building in Seoul?

2. 강남역에 갈 때는 교대역에서 _____ 2호선을 타야 돼요.
   When you go to Gangnam Station you have to transfer at Gyodae station and then ride line 2.

3. 피곤_____ 소파에서 조금 누우세요.
   If you are tired lay a bit on the sofa.

4. 아버지가 집에 돌아_____ 방을 청소해!
   Clean your work before father comes home!

5. _____ 부모님이 있으면 많은 학원을 다녀야 돼요.
   If you have strict parents you must attend many private academies.

● A8-4. Mark and Translate
Mark the Korean sentence without mistakes then translate it.

1. ○ 학생중에서 가장 꼳꼳한 학생은 누구예요?
   ○ 학생중에서 가장 똑똑한 학생은 누구예요?
   ○ 학생종에서 가장 떡떡한 학생은 누구예요?

   Translation:_____

2. ○ 숙제를 다 하는 후에 친구들이랑 영화를 보러 갔어요.
   ○ 숙제를 다 할 후에 친구들이랑 영화를 보러 갔어요.
   ○ 숙제를 다 한 후에 친구들이랑 영화를 보러 갔어요.

   Translation:_____

3. ○ 오늘 날씨가 어제보다 훨씬 더 춥지 않아요?
   ○ 오늘 날씨가 어제보도 훨씬 도 춥지 않아요?
   ○ 오늘 날씨가 어제훨씬 보다 더 춥지 않아요?

   Translation:_____

8 | Self Test Answers 연습 문제 정답

● A8-1. Fix the mistake

1. 튤립은 성인장보다 더 예뻐요.
   Tulips are prettier than cactuses.

2. 세상에서 가장 큰 나라는 어디예요?
   Where is the biggest country in the world.

3. 저는 고등학교를 졸업해서 유럽여행을 했어요.
   I graduated then I travelled Europe.

● A8-2. Listening skills

1. 컴퓨터를 끈 후에 불을 꺼 주세요.
   After turning off the computer please turn off the lights.

2. 이 영화는 한국영화 중에서 제일 지루하네요.
   Out of all the Korean movies this movie is the most boring.

3. 한국 음식이 너무 매워서 깜짝 놀랐어요.
   I was really surprised that Korean food was so spicy.

● A8-3. Fill in the blanks

1. 서울에서 제일 높은 빌딩은 어디예요?

2. 강남역에 갈 때는 교대역에서 갈아타서 2호선을 타야 돼요.

3. 피곤하면 소파에서 조금 누우세요.

4. 아버지가 집에 돌아오기 전에 방을 청소해!

5. 엄격한 부모님이 있으면 많은 학원을 다녀야 돼요.

● A8-4. Best Sentence Search

1. ○ 학생중에서 가장 꼳꼳한 학생은 누구예요?
   ✓ 학생중에서 가장 똑똑한 학생은 누구예요?
   ○ 학생종에서 가장 떡떡한 학생은 누구예요?
   Translation: Who is the smartest student out of the students?

2. ○ 숙제를 다 하는 후에 친구들이랑 영화를 보러 갔어요.
   ○ 숙제를 다 할 후에 친구들이랑 영화를 보러 갔어요.
   ✓ 숙제를 다 한 후에 친구들이랑 영화를 보러 갔어요.
   Translation: I went to see a movie with friends after doing all the homework.

3. ✓ 오늘 날씨가 어제보다 훨씬 더 춥지 않아요?
   ○ 오늘 날씨가 어제보도 훨씬 도 춥지 않아요?
   ○ 오늘 날씨가 어제훨씬 보다 더 춥지 않아요?
   Translation: Isn't today's weather is much colder than yesterday?

9 Lesson 9: I think… I thought

9 | New Words 새로운 단어

New Nouns etc.

성별	gender
경기	competition
일	happening, event
부부	married couple, husband and wife
밖	outside

New Adjectives

안타깝다	to be unfortunate, regrettable

New Verbs

이기다	to win, to beat
지다	to lose

9 | Fun in Korea 즐기는 한국

Often new words added to the Korean language are mixed with misappropriated English words. Words of this type are referred to as "Konglish".

오픈카	convertible car (from "open car")
런닝머신	treadmill (from "running machine")
핸드폰	mobile phone (from "hand phone")
셀카	selfie (from "self camera")
소개팅	blind date (combined with 소개 "introduction" and the "ting" portion of "meeting")

9 | Grammar and Usage 문법과 사용법

● 9-1. Thinking in Korean is not one verb

Languages often share a 1 to 1 relationship. For example, there is one word in English for "pencil" and also just one word in Korean. What makes learning any language a challenge is when a 1 to 1 relationship doesn't exist.

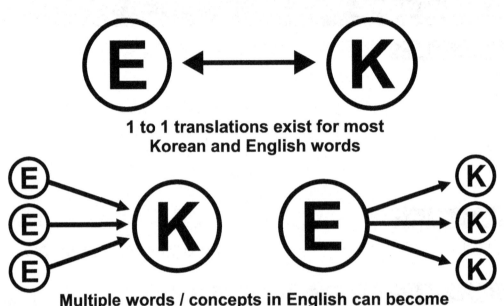

**1 to 1 translations exist for most
Korean and English words**

**Multiple words / concepts in English can become
a single concept in Korean and vice-versa.**

"To think" in English is one verb. By conjugating the verb "to think" we can say all of the following things:

1. I **think** today will be hot.	오늘 더울 것 같아요.
2. I **think** it's hot today.	오늘 더운 것 같아요.
3. I **thought** it would be hot today.	오늘 더운 줄 알았어요.
4. I am **thinking** of marriage.	결혼을 생각하고 있어요.

English simply conjugates the verb "think" to say the sentences above, but Korean requires three different grammar structures.

Because this concept can be very challenging, we considered teaching it over multiple lessons. However, in order to help the student avoid mistakes using "to think", we decided to introduce the concepts all in the same lesson.

Due to how common it is to say "I think", we recommend you spend additional time reviewing to reinforce the concept. The workbook is also a **must do**!

● 9-2. (으)ㄹ 것 같다 (I think it will~) FUTURE

(으)ㄹ 것 같다 is YOUR opinion / guess / assumption of a **future** event. This pattern can be translated to "it seems it will~" or "it's likely that~". However, in most cases "I think it will~" is a more accurate translation.

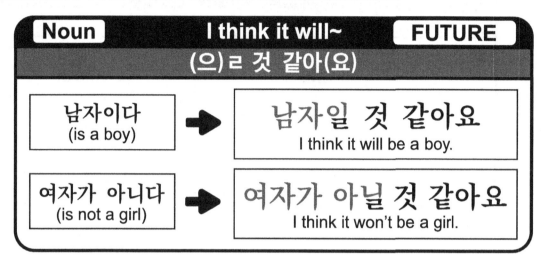

Noun | **I think it will~** | **FUTURE**
(으)ㄹ 것 같아(요)

남자이다 (is a boy) ➡ 남자일 것 같아요 I think it will be a boy.

여자가 아니다 (is not a girl) ➡ 여자가 아닐 것 같아요 I think it won't be a girl.

Example sentences
1. 파티가 다음 주일 것 같아요.   I think the party will be next week.
2. 버스가 노란색일 것 같아요.   I think the bus will be yellow.
3. 파티가 오늘이 아닐 것 같아요.   I think the party won't be today.
4. 버스가 분홍색이 아닐 것 같아요.   I think the bus won't be pink.

Example Q&A

1. A friend finds out a friend is pregnant.

Q: 성별이 뭐예요?
A: 여자**일 것 같아요**.
A: 잘 모르겠지만, 남자가 **아닐 것 같아요**.

Q: What's the gender?
A: I think it will be a girl.
A: I don't really know, but I think it's not a boy.

2. Close friends talk about future plans.

Q: 언제 결혼할 거야?
A: 내년**일 것 같아**.
A: 올해는 **아닐 것 같아**.

Q: When will you get married?
A: I think it will be next year.
A: I think it won't be this year.

Adjectives and verbs follow the exact same pattern. (으)ㄹ 것 같다 is normally only YOUR own opinion / thought a not another's.

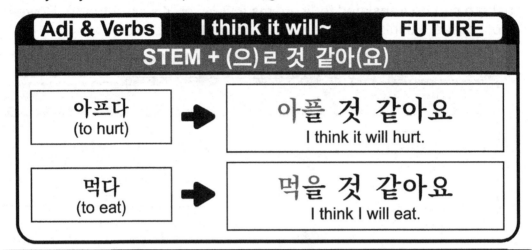

Example sentences

1. 내일 비가 올 것 같아요.
   I think it will rain tomorrow.

2. 파티에 사람들이 많을 것 같아요.
   I think there will be many people at the party.

3. 내년에 미국에 가고 싶은데 못 갈 것 같아요.
   I want to go to America next year, but I think I won't be able to go.

4. 이 책이 재미있을 것 같아요.
   I think this book will be interesting.

5. 부모님들이 공항에 8 시 반 쯤에 도착할 것 같아요.
   I think my parents will arrive at the airport around 8:30.

6. 오늘 날씨가 따뜻할 것 같아요.
   I think the weather will be warm today.

Example Q&A

1. A polite conversation between husband and wife.

Q: 언제 잠을 잘 것 같아요?
A: 오늘 피곤해서 빨리 잘 것 같아요.
A: 오늘 일이 많아서 못 잘 것 같아요.

Q: When do you think you will sleep?
A: I think I'll go to sleep early (fast) since I am tired.
A: I have so much work today, so I think I won't be able to sleep.

2. **A conversation between people watching the olympics.**
    Q: 이번 경기에서 누가 이길 것 같아요?
    A: 한국이 이길 것 같아요.
    A: 아마도 태국이 이길 것 같아요.

    Q: Who do you think will win this competition?
    A: I think Korea will win.
    A: I think maybe Thailand will win.

● 9-3. (으)ㄴ 것 같다 (I think it is~) PRESENT
(으)ㄴ 것 같다 works exactly like (으)ㄹ 것 같다 except that instead of future the thought is now present tense (see verb note).

Example sentences (future tense)
1. 식사가 한식**일** 것 같아요.   I think the meal **will be** Korean.
2. 식사가 한식**이 아닐** 것 같아요.   I think the meal **won't be** Korean.
3. 이 물건이 **비쌀** 것 같아요.   I think this item **will be** expensive.
4. 엄마가 회사에 **갈** 것 같아요.   I think my mother **will go** to work.

Example sentences (present tense)
1. 식사가 한식**인** 것 같아요.   I think the meal **is** Korean.
2. 식사가 한식**이 아닌** 것 같아요.   I think the meal **isn't** Korean.
3. 이 물건이 **비싼** 것 같아요.   I think this item **is** expensive.

VERB NOTE: (으)ㄴ 것 같다 with verbs makes the thought past tense.
*** See next section for present tense "thinking" with verbs.

4. 엄마가 회사에 **간** 것 같아요.   I think my mother **went** to work.

Example sentences (으)ㄴ 것 같다
1. 파티에 사람들이 많은 것 같아요.
   I think there are many people at the party.

2. 어제 비가 온 것 같아요.
   I think it rained yesterday.

   > Since this is a verb the thought is past tense.

3. 이 책이 재미있는 것 같아요.
   I think this book is interesting.

   > 있다 and 없다 change to 있는 and 없는 for present tense.

4. 이 반찬이 맛없는 것 같아요.
   I think these side dishes don't taste good.

● **9-4. STEM + 는 것 같다 (I think it is~) PRESENT**

STEM + 는 것 같다 is used with verbs and adjectives ending with 있다, 없다. This is used when you think the action is occurring now.

Verbs	I think it is / they are~	PRESENT

STEM + 는 것 같아(요)

공부하다 (to study)

누나가 매일 공부하는 것 같아요
I think my sister **studies** everyday.

누나가 공부하고 있는 것 같아요
I think my sister is **studying**.

놀다 (to play)

아이가 자주 밖에서 노는 것 같아요
I think the child often **plays** outside.

아이가 밖에서 놀고 있는 것 같아요
I think the child is **playing** outside.

Example sentences ~는 것 같다

1. 지금 비가 오는 것 같아요.
   I think it's raining now.

2. 파티에 사람들이 많이 있는 것 같아요.
   I think there are a lot of people at the party.

3. 제 친구가 영어 학원을 다니는 것 같아요.
   I think my friend is attending an English academy.

4. 우리 아파트 위에 사는 부부가 싸우는 것 같아요.
   I think the married couple above our apartment are fighting.

5. 최미나 씨랑 박민수가 사귀는 것 같아요.
   I think Mina Choi and Minsoo Park are dating.

6. 친구 지금 운전하고 있는 것 같아요. 그래서 전화를 안 받아요.
   I think my friend is driving now. That's why they don't answer the phone.

──Special Information 특별 정보──

When you ~고 있는 것 같다 the English verb typically should always end in "ing" (running, driving, doing etc.). ~는 것 같다 however can serve two different functions. It can be used to say both "does" and also "doing".

Example sentences

1. 누나가 지금 수영장에서 **수영하는** 것 같아요.
   I think my sister is **swimming** at the pool now.

   수영하는~ becomes "swimming" because the word 지금 (now) forces it to the "on-going present tense". The sister is DOING this now.

2. 누나가 매일 수영장에서 **수영하는** 것 같아요.
   I think my sister **swims** at the pool everyday.

   수영하는~ becomes "swims" because the word 매일 (everyday) forces it to the "present tense". The sister DOES this everyday.

3. 누나가 수영장에서 **수영하고 있는** 것 같아요.
   I think my sister is **swimming** at the pool.

   수영하고 있는~ is always just swimming right now.

● **9-5. ~ㄴ 줄 알다 (I thought it was~) PAST**

We have learned how to say "think" for future and present tenses. Past tense requires a new structure. (으)ㄴ 줄 알다 is used to say "I thought~". It's used with mistaken assumptions. For example, "I thought it was Monday" (but it's not). It can be used easily with nouns, adjectives, and verbs.

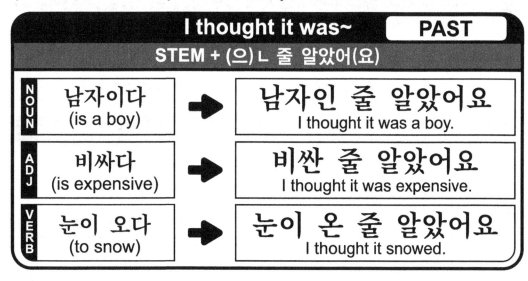

I thought it was~	PAST
STEM + (으)ㄴ 줄 알았어(요)	

NOUN 남자이다 (is a boy)	➡	남자인 줄 알았어요 I thought it was a boy.
ADJ 비싸다 (is expensive)	➡	비싼 줄 알았어요 I thought it was expensive.
VERB 눈이 오다 (to snow)	➡	눈이 온 줄 알았어요 I thought it snowed.

Example sentences

1. 오늘은 월요일 인 줄 알았어요.
   I thought today was Monday.

2. 방에 있는 램프가 더 밝은 줄 알았어요.
   I thought the lamp in the room was brighter.

3. 처음에 한국어가 쉬운 줄 알았어요.
   At first I thought Korean was easy.

4. 여동생의 생일이 어제인 줄 알았어요.
   I thought my younger sister's birthday was yesterday.

5. 선생님이 중국에 간 줄 알았어요.
   I thought the teacher went to China.

6. 김유나가 키가 더 큰 줄 알았어요.
   I thought Yuna Kim was taller.

7. 여기서 휴대폰을 판 줄 알았어요.
   I thought they sold cell phones here.

> When there is a 받침 you must add 은.

● 9-6. Summary of what we know about thinking

We learned how to "think" with *nouns*, *adjectives* and to some extent *verbs*.
We will work more with verbs later. This is what we know so far.

Tense	Nouns	
future	남자일 것 같아요.	I think it **will be** a boy.
present	남자인 것 같아요.	I think it **is** a boy.
past	남자인 줄 알았어요.	I thought it **was** a boy. (but it wasn't)

Tense	Adjectives	
future	좋을 것 같아요.	I think it **will be** good.
present	좋은 것 같아요.	I think it **is** good.
past	좋은 줄 알았어요.	I thought it **was** good. (but it wasn't)

Tense	Verbs	
future	5 시에 **도착할** 것 같아요.	I think I **will arrive** at 5.
present	항상 비행기가 5 시에 **도착하는** 것 같아요.	I think the flight **always arrives** at 5.
present on going	부모님이 **도착하고 있는** 것 같아요.	I think my parents **are arriving**.
past	5 시에 **도착한 줄** 알았어요.	I thought (they) **had arrived** at 5.

Context is VERY important in Korean. Notice how context changes the meaning in the following sentences.

1. 김선생님은 남자인 줄 알았어요.
   context: NONE   → **I thought Mr. Kim was a boy.**
   context: baby gender   → **Mr. Kim thought it was a boy.**

To avoid context misunderstandings include subjects in the sentence.

2. 김선생님은 **아기가** 남자인 줄 알았어요.
   Mr. Kim thought **the baby** was a boy.

HUGE IMPORTANT NOTE: (으)ㄹ 것 같다 and (으)ㄴ 것 같다 is rarely used for 3rd person. In other words, you can ASK people and SAY your own thoughts but you can't say someone elses thoughts.

2. 김선생님은 좋을 것 같아요.

This will almost never translate to "Mr. Kim thinks it's good." Instead it will translate to "I think Mr. Kim will be good." This is because you can't know Mr. Kim's thoughts. Later we will learn how to say "Mr. Kim thinks it's good."

In English, we often say what other people think. So it's easy to assume you can do the same in Korean. However, it's not natural to use (으)ㄹ 것 같다 and (으)ㄴ 것 같다 for other people. It's typically only used for yourself.

In lesson 12 we will learn another form of "think" that allows us to say other people's thoughts.

● 9-7. 이기다 (to win, beat, defeat), 지다 (to lose, be beaten)

이기다	TYPE	regular adjective	BASIC FORM	이겨

지다	TYPE	regular adjective	BASIC FORM	져

이기다 (to win) and 지다 (to lose) are used when talking about defeating or losing to an opponent. For money related winnings, such as gambling, then 따다 is used. The opponent or thing you defeat or win is marked with 을/를.

> **Example sentences**
>
> 1. 에밀리는 항상 가위 바위 보를 이겨요.
>   Emily always wins at scissors, rock, paper. (rock, paper, scissors)
>
> 2. 연습을 많이 해서 경기에서 이겼어요.
>   Because I practiced a lot I won at the competition.
>
> 3. 연습을 많이 했지만 경기에서 졌어요.
>   I practiced a lot but I lost at the competition.
>
> 4. 저번에는 졌지만, 이번에는 이길 거예요.
>   I lost last time, but this time I'll win.
>
> 5. 계속 연습을 했지만 이번 시합에서 졌어요.
>   I continually practiced but this time I lost at the match.
>
> 6. 이번 시험에도 친구에게 졌네요.
>   You got beat by your friend on this test also huh.

● 9-8. 안타깝다 (to be unfortunate, regrettable)

TYPE	ㅂ irregular adjective	BASIC FORM	안타까워

안타깝다 is used to say something is unfortunate.

> **Example sentences**
>
> 1. 안타깝지만, 오늘 콘서트를 취소해야 돼요.
>   It's unfortunate, but we have to cancel today's concert.
>
> 2. 오늘 안타까운 일이 생겼어요.
>   Many unfortunate events occurred today.
>
> 3. 같이 영화를 보러 못 가서 안타까워요.
>   It's unfortunate that we couldn't go watch a movie together.

못 should never come before 보러.

Example Q&A

1. **A friend relaying bad news.**

   Q: 저는 여자친구랑 헤어졌어요.
   A: 안타까워요!
   A: 슬프네요!

   Q: I broke up with my girlfriend.
   A: That's unfortunate.
   A: Oh that's sad.

9 | Test Yourself Activities 연습 문제

● A9-1. Fix the mistake
Correct the Korean sentence, then finish the translation on the line below.

1. 오늘은 화요일인 줄 같았어요.

   Korean _____

   English I thought today_____

2. 내일은 생일이지만 비가 온 것 같아요.

   Korean _____

   English Tomorrow is my birthday_____

3. 날씨가 좋으면 경기를 이길 것 같지만 나쁘면 못 이긴 것 같아요.

   Korean _____

   English If the weather is good_____

● A9-2. Listening skills
Go to **http://fromzero.com/korean/kfz3/A2** OR scan the QR code. Enter the code. Write the Korean then the English.

1. 9A   Korean _____

   English _____

2. 9B   Korean _____

   English _____

3. 9C   Korean _____

   English _____

● **A9-3. Fill in the blanks**
Fill in the missing word or particle based on the English sentence.

1. 결혼하면 부산에서 여자친구 부모님이랑 살 _____.
   If we marry I think we will live with my girlfriend's parents in Busan.

2. 현금은 신용카드보다 훨씬 더 _____ 같아요.
   I think cash is considerally (much) easier than a credit card.

3. 2025 년까지는 중국에 _____ 같아요.
   I don't think I'll be able to go to China by 2025.

4. 한국 음식중에서 김치가 제일 _____ 같아요.
   I think that out of all Korean food Kimchee is the most delicious.

5. 이 책을 다 읽을 시간이 _____ 같아요.
   I don't think I will have time to finish all of this book.

● **A9-4. Mark and Translate**
Mark the Korean sentence without mistakes then translate it.

1. ○ 저는 오늘 21 일 인 줄 알았어요.
   ○ 저는 오늘 21 일 인 줄 것 같아요.
   ○ 저는 오늘 21 일 인 줄 생각했어요.

   Translation:_____

2. ○ 영어가 가장 어려운 언아일 갓 같아요.
   ○ 영어가 가장 어려운 언어이는 것 같아요.
   ○ 영어가 가장 어려운 언어일 것 같아요.

   Translation:_____

3. ○ 남동생 생일이 지난주안 줄 알았어요.
   ○ 남동생 생일이 지난주인 일 줄 알았어요.
   ○ 남동생 생일이 지번주인 줄 알았어요.

   Translation:_____

9 | **Self Test Answers 연습 문제 정답**

● **A9-1. Fix the mistake**
1. 오늘은 화요일인 줄 알았어요
   I thought today was Tuesday.

2. 내일은 생일이지만 비가 올 것 같아요.
   Tomorrow is my birthday but I think it will rain.

3. 날씨가 좋으면 경기를 이길 것 같지만 나쁘면 못 이길 것 같아요.
   If the weather is cold I think we can win the competition

● **A9-2. Listening skills**
1. 김유나가 키가 더 큰 줄 알았어요.
   I thought Yuna Kim was taller.

2. 계속 연습을 했지만 이번 시합에서 졌어요.
   I continually practiced but this time lost at the match.

3. 안타깝지만, 오늘 콘서트를 취소해야 돼요.
   It's unfortunate, however we have to cancel today's concert.

● **A9-3. Fill in the blanks**
1. 결혼하면 부산에서 여자친구 부모님이랑 살 것 같아요.
2. 현금은 신용카드보다 훨씬 더 쉬운 것 같아요.
3. 2025 년까지는 중국에 못 갈 것 같아요.
4. 한국 음식중에서 김치가 제일 맛있는 것 같아요.
5. 이 책을 다 읽을 시간이 없을 것 같아요.

● **A9-4. Best Sentence Search**
1. ✓ 저는 오늘 21 일 인 줄 알았어요.
   ○ 저는 오늘 21 일 인 줄 것 같아요.
   ○ 저는 오늘 21 일 인 줄 생각했어요.
   Translation: I thought today was the 21st.

2. ○ 영어가 가장 어려운 언아일 갓 같아요.
   ○ 영어가 가장 어려운 언어이는 것 같아요.
   ✓ 영어가 가장 어려운 언어일 것 같아요.
   Translation: I think English is the most difficult language.

3. ○ 남동생 생일이 지난주안 줄 알았어요.
   ○ 남동생 생일이 지번주인 일 줄 알았어요.
   ✓ 남동생 생일이 지난주인 줄 알았어요.
   Translation: I thought my younger brother's birthday was last week.

10 Lesson 10: Large Numbers

10 | New Words 새로운 단어

New Nouns etc.

가격	price
값	value, worth
술집	bar
평일	weekday
전 세계	the whole world
삼성	Samsung ©
애플	Apple ©
동료	colleague, co-worker
빌 게이츠	Bill Gates
재산	property, asset, wealth

New Adverb

약	approximately, roughly
드디어	finally

New Counters

(K#) ~권	books, magazine
(K#) ~대	machinery, equipment, cars etc.

New Verbs

출근하다	to go/come to work
퇴근하다	to get off work
출퇴근하다	to commute (to work)
팔리다	to be sold
벌다	to earn (money)
쓰다	to spend (money)
감기에 걸리다	to catch a cold

10 | Grammar and Usage 문법과 사용법

● **10-1. 출근하다 (to go/come to work), 퇴근하다 (to get off work), 출퇴근하다 (to commute)**

출근하다	TYPE	하다 adjective	BASIC FORM	출근해
퇴근하다	TYPE	하다 adjective	BASIC FORM	퇴근해
출퇴근하다	TYPE	하다 adjective	BASIC FORM	출퇴근해

Example sentences

1. 몸이 아팠지만 회사에 출근했어요.
   Even though my body aches I went to work.

2. 아버지는 오늘 양복을 입고 출근했어요.
   My father put on a suit and went to work today.

3. 너무 바빠서 요즘 오전 6 시에 출근해요.
   Because I am so busy recently I have been going to work at 6 am.

4. 평일에 출근하고 주말에 쉬어요.
   On the weekdays I go to work and on the weekends I relax.

5. 오늘 딸의 생일이라서 일찍 퇴근했어요.
   Because it's my daughter's birthday I got off work early.

6. 저는 항상 동료보다 늦게 퇴근해요.
   I always get off later than my co-workers.

7. 일이 많아서 세 시간 늦게 퇴근했어요.
   Because I had so much work I got of work 3 hours late.

8. 저는 매주 금요일 지하철로 출퇴근해요.
   Every Friday I commute to work via the subway.

9. 오늘은 늦잠을 자서 택시로 출퇴근했어요.
   Today I overslept so I commuted to work via a taxi.

10. 저는 아침 8 시에 출근하고 저녁 7 시에 퇴근해요.
    I go to work at 8 in the morning and get off work at 7 in the evening.

● 10-2. New counters ~권, ~대

All of the new counters in this lesson use Korean numbers up until the 99 limit, when they switch to Chinese counters (as all Korean counters do).

Books, magazines etc. 권		Equipment, cars, planes etc. 대	
한 권	1 book	한 대	1 units
두 권	2 books	두 대	2 units
세 권	3 books	세 대	3 units
네 권	4 books	네 대	4 units
다섯 권	5 books	다섯 대	5 units
백 권	100 books	백 대	100 units
만 권	10,000 books	만 대	10,000 units
몇 권? How many books?		몇 대? How many units?	

● 10-3. 팔리다 (to be sold)

팔리다	TYPE	regular verb	BASIC FORM	팔려

The item that is sold is marked with 이/가 unless emphasizing with 은/는.

Example sentences

1. 올해 삼성의 핸드폰이 약 9 천만 대 팔렸어요.
   This year approximately 90,000,000 Samsung phones were sold.

2. 어제 대학교 때부터 탄 차가 드디어 팔렸어요.
   Yesterday the car I rode (drove) since college finally sold.

3. 이틀전에 만든 케이크는 이미 다 팔렸어요.
   The cakes we made 2 days ago are already all sold.

4. 오랫동안 우리 집은 안 팔렸어요.
   For a long time our house didn't sell.

5. 이 책은 다른 책보다 훨씬 많이 팔렸어요.
   This book has sold considerably more than other books.

● 10-4. 벌다 (to earn money), 쓰다 (to spend)

벌다	TYPE	regular verb	BASIC FORM	벌어

쓰다	TYPE	regular verb	BASIC FORM	써

Example sentences

1. 새로운 직장에서 전보다 더 돈을 벌 수 있어요.
   At my new place of work I can make more money than before.

2. 스무 살 때 매일 네 시간만 잠을 자고 돈을 많이 벌었어요.
   When I was 20, I only slept 4 hours everyday and earned a lot money.

3. 돈을 많이 벌면 새 집을 살 거예요.
   If you earn a lot of money you can buy a new house.

4. 제 아들은 가족이랑 여행 갈 때 이 천만 원을 썼어요.
   When my son went on a trip with his family he spent 20 million won.

5. 현금을 쓰고 싶지 않지만 신용카드를 잃어버렸어요.
   I don't want to want use cash, but I lost my credit card.

6. 지난 달에 돈을 너무 많이 써서 우울해요.
   I am depressed because I used too much money last month.

─── Special Information 특별 정보 ───

Ugh! How do you say "new" in Korean???
In Korean, 새~, 새로~, 새로운~ are all used to say "new". Let's see when they are used.

새 + NOUN is used when the noun is **brand new** or never used.
새 차   brand new car
새 옷   brand new clothes

새로운~ is used for "new" things that are **new to the person**.
새로운 차   new car (new OR used)
새로운 옷   new clothes (new OR used)

새로 is an "adverb" used with verbs. It essentially means "**newly**".
새로 산 차   newly bought car
새로 태어난 아기   newly born baby

● **10-5. Do you wanna…? / I wanna… (으)ㄹ래**

With friends you can use a much more friendly, casual way to ask ~고
싶어요? It's made by using future tense stem + 래.

Examples

1. 먹다 → 먹을래(요)?   Do you wanna eat?
2. 가다 → 갈래(요)?   Do you wanna go?
3. 보다 → 볼래(요)?   Do you wanna see?
4. 하다 → 할래(요)?   Do you wanna do?
5. 듣다 → 들래(요)?   Do you wanna listen?
6. 놀다 → 놀래(요)?   Do you wanna play / hang out?
7. 마시다 → 마실래(요)?   Do you wanna drink?
8. 죽다 → 죽을래(요)?   Do you wanna die?

> Don't laugh. This phrase is common amongst friends.

Example Q&A

1. **Friends meetup at 홍대 for lunch.**

   Q: 뭐 먹을래요?
   A: 피자 먹을래요!
   A: 피자 먹고 싶어요!

   Q: What do you wanna eat?
   A: I wanna eat pizza.
   A: I want to eat pizza.

2. **Friends chatting on a Saturday.**

   Q: 오늘 밤에 나랑 같이 영화 볼래?
   A: 응! 몇시에 볼래?
   A: 오늘은 계획이 있어. 내일은 어때?

   Q: Do you wanna watch a movie with tonight?
   A: Yeah! What time you wanna watch?
   A: I have plans today, How about tomorrow?

3. **Co-workers talking at after lunch.**

   Q: 오늘 퇴근한 후에 뭐 할래?
   A: 먼저 낮잠을 잘래요.
   A: 술집에 바로 갈래!

   Q: What do you want to do today after you get off work?
   A: First I want to take a nap.
   A: I want to immediately go to a bar!

   > In South Korea you can drink from age 19 (actual age).

● 10-6. ~는 동안 (while I was doing~)

STEM + 는 동안 is used to describe events that take place during the time of another event. Since it's a time, you can optionally mark it with the time marker 에.

Example sentences

1. 제가 방을 청소하는 동안 엄마는 요리를 했어요.
   While I was cleaning my room, my mother cooked.

2. 기다리는 동안 차 한 잔 마시세요.
   Drink a cup of tea while you wait.

3. 아르바이트하는 동안 한국어를 공부했어요.
   While I was working I studied Korean.

   > You can use 동안 with events in the same way 때 is used.

4. 여름 방학 동안에 파리에 가봤어요.
   During school summer break, I went to Paris.

5. 우리 가족이 유럽에 여행을 하는 동안 개가 죽었어요.
   While my family was on vacation in Europe, our dog died.

6. 공부를 하는 동안 아이폰을 보지 않을 거예요.
   I won't look at my iPhone while I am studying.

7. 친구를 기다리는 동안 커피를 마실래요?
   Do you wanna drink coffee while waiting for your friend ?

8. 출퇴근하는 동안 자주 음악을 들어요.
   While commuting to work I often listen to music.

9. 엄마가 요가를 하는 동안 아버지가 핸드폰으로 축구 시합을 봤어요.
   My father watched a soccer match on his phone while mom did yoga.

● 10-7. Numbers above 99,999

Korean currency is the 원 (won) and even just a drink from a vending machine can cost 1,000 won so Korean numbers can easily jump to above 100,000 won which is actually just around 90 US dollars or 80 Euro. So your rent might be 800,000 won and your car might cost you 16 million won!

In English we have units of a **billion**, a **million**, and a **thousand**. And each unit can have up to 999 units. In Korean, each unit can have 9,999 units.

So when you count in Korean there aren't 1 to 1 equivalents of billion and million. Instead they count like this 9,999 조 9,999 억 9,999 만.

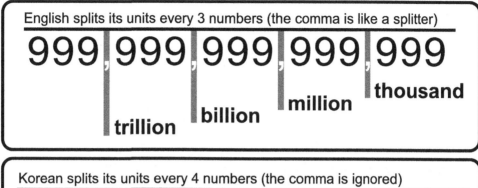

English Number	(Visual)	한국어	(Visual)
10,000	10 thousand	**만**	1 만
100,000	100 thousand	십만	10 만
1,000,000	1 million	백만	100 만
10,000,000	10 million	천만	1000 만
100,000,000	100 million	**억**	1 억
1,000,000,000	1 billion	십억	10 억
10,000,000,000	10 billion	백억	100 억
100,000,000,000	100 billion	천억	1000 억
1,000,000,000,000	1 trillion	**조**	1 조
10,000,000,000,000	10 trillion	십조	10 조
100,000,000,000,000	100 trillion	백조	100 조
1,000,000,000,000,000	1 quadrillion	천조	1000 조

Don't fret! The worst case scenario is you suck at numbers. You aren't alone!

Example sentences

1. 중국에는 약 십삼억 명이 살고 있어요.
   Roughly 1,300,000,000 (1 billion 300 million) people are living in China.

2. 우리 사장님은 딸의 결혼식 때 십억 원을 썼어요.
   For our boss's daughter's wedding ceremony he spent 1 billion won.

3. 지금까지 아이폰이 오억 대 정도 팔렸어요.
   Up until the iPhone has sold approximately 500,000,000 units.

4. 어제 천만 원을 벌었지만, 오늘 이천만 원을 썼어요.
   Yesterday I earned 10 million won, but today I spent 20 million won.

5. 빌 게이츠는 칠십칠조 달러 정도의 재산을 가지고 있어요.
   Bill Gates possesses (has) approximately 77 billion dollars of assets.

6. 어젯밤 꿈속에서 백억 원을 주워서 너무 행복했어요.
   I was so happy because in my dream yesterday night you gave me 10 billion won.

7. 서울의 아파트는 거의 십억 원 해요.
   Seoul apartments costs almost 1 billion won.

   하다 can be used to mean "to cost".

● **10-8. "As a~" 로**

We have learned other usages of (으)로. One was to mark a direction we are headed towards (왼쪽으로 to the left) and another to mark a method of how something is accomplished (손으로 by hand), and one more to mark a method of transportation (버스로 by bus). This version of (으)로 is used to say "as a~" such as "I think of you as a friend" or "I received this as a gift".

Example sentences

1. 16 살 생일에 선물로 새 차를 받았어요.
   On my 16th birthday I got a new car as a present.

2. 사장님께 월급으로 백만 원을 받았어요
   I received 1 million won from the boss as salary.

3. 저는 제 남자친구를 남편으로 생각해요.
   I am considering my boyfriend as a husband.

● 10-9. 감기에 걸리다 (to catch a cold)

걸리다	TYPE	regular verb	BASIC FORM	걸려

걸리다 is used to say you "catch" or "fall" to a sickness. The sickness is marked with 에. Later on we will learn more sicknesses, but for this lesson we will stick with just the common cold (감기) to get used to using 걸리다.

Example sentences

1. 엄마가 감기에 걸린 것 같아요.
   I think my mother caught a cold.

2. 감기에 걸려서 학교에 못 가요.
   I caught a cold so I can't go to school.

3. 감기에 걸렸지만 회사에 출근할 거예요.
   I caught a cold but I'm still going to go to work.

● 10-10. The direct quote marker 라고
Just like 은/는 makes the word before it a topic, and 을/를 makes the word before it an object, 라고 makes any thing before it into a direct quote. 라고 by itself has no meaning. It's used in combination with other verbs.

"_____" 라고 말하다 To say "_____"
"_____" 라고 물어보다 To ask "_____"
"_____" 라고 대답하다 To answer "_____"
"_____" 라고 부탁하다 To request "_____"

Now we just need a phrase to put before 라고.

---

1. 친구가 "내년에 한국에 가요" **라고** 말했어요.
   My friend said "I will go to Korea next year."

2. 친구가 "화상실이 어디에 있어요?" **라고** 물어봤어요.
   My friend asked "Where is the bathroom?"

3. 친구가 "저는 애완동물이 없어요" **라고** 대답했어요.
   My friend answered "I don't have any pets."

4. 친구가 "돈을 빌려주세요" **라고** 부탁했어요.
   My friend requested "Loan me money."

Example sentences

1. 선생님이 "숙제 해!" **라고** 말했어요.
   The teacher said "Do homework!".

2. 준호 씨가 저에게 "널 사랑해" **라고** 말했어요.
   Junho said "I love you" to me.

3. 모르는 외국인이 저를 보고 "몸이 좋아요" **라고** 말했어요.
   A foreigner I don't know looked at me and said, "You have a good body".

● **10-11. Hoping and wishing with ~(으)면 좋겠어요**
Using grammar that you already know we can learn how to say "I wish~" or "I hope". ~(으)면 좋겠다 literally means "If XXX then it will be good" but it's more natural to translate it into "I wish~" or "I hope~".

하면 좋겠다   했으면 좋겠다
I hope it will~   I hope it will~

IMPORTANT NOTE Even if the ~(으)면 is in past tense form, the meaning of this grammar is always a wish for the future.

Example sentences

1. 돈을 더 많이 벌면 좋겠어요.
   I wish I could earn money.

2. 내일 날씨가 더우면 좋겠어요.
   I hope the weather is hot tomorrow.

3. 우리 책이 잘 팔리면 좋겠어요.
   I hope our book sells well.

4. 감기에 안 걸렸으면 좋겠어요.
   I hope I don't catch a cold.

5. 30 살 전에 결혼하면 좋겠어요.
   I hope I will be married before age 30.

6. 아이폰이 더 싸면 좋겠어요.
   I wish iPhonese were cheaper.

10 ▌ Test Yourself Activities 연습 문제

● **A10-1. Fix the mistake**
Correct the Korean sentence, then finish the translation on the line below.

1. 오늘 딸의 생일이라서 일찍 출근했어요.

   Korean _____

   English I got off work early_____

2. 이번 달에 우리 책은 인터넷에서 2000 대 팔았어요.

   Korean _____

   English This month our book sold_____

3. 우리 사장님은 월급으로 하나 달에 천만 원을 벌었어요.

   Korean _____

   English In one month our boss_____

● **A10-2. Listening skills**
Go to **http://fromzero.com/korean/kfz3/A2** OR scan the QR code. Enter the code. Write the Korean then the English.

1. 10A Korean _____

   English _____

2. 10B Korean _____

   English _____

3. 10C Korean _____

   English _____

● A10-3. Fill in the blanks
Fill in the missing word or particle based on the English sentence.

1. 저는 방을 _____ 엄마가 저녁를 만들었어요.
   While I cleaned my room my mother made dinner.

2. 이 서점은 해마다 책 _____ 정도 팔려요.
   This bookstore sells approximately 1 million books each year.

3. 아버지가 _____ 직장에 못 가요.
   My father caught a cold so he can't go to his place of work.

4. _____ 카피를 한 잔 마시세요.
   Drink a cup of coffee while you wait.

5. 평일마다 서울까지 _____은 차로 출퇴근해요.
   Each weekday 500,000 people commute by car to Seoul.

● A10-4. Mark and Translate
Mark the Korean sentence without mistakes then translate it.

1. ○ 저는 술을 못 마셔서 술집에서는 커피만 마실래요.
   ○ 저는 술을 안 마셔서 술집에서는 커피만 맛일래요.
   ○ 저는 술을 못 마시서 술집에서는 커피만 마실래요.

   Translation:_____

2. ○ 엄마가 너무 바빠서 오전 5 시에 출근해요.
   ○ 엄마가 나무 바빠서 오적 5 시에 출군혜요.
   ○ 엄마가 너무 바빠서 오전 5 시에 출근해요.

   Translation:_____

3. ○ 전 세계중에서 우리 고양이가 가장 귀여울 것 같아요.
   ○ 전 세계에서 우리 고양이가 가장 귀여울 것 같아요.
   ○ 전 세계에서 우리 고양이가 가장 귀여을 것 같아요.

   Translation:_____

10 | Self Test Answers 연습 문제 정답

● **A10-1. Fix the mistake**

  1. 오늘 딸의 생일이라서 일찍 퇴근했어요.
     I got off work early because it's my daughter's birthday.

  2. 이번 달에 우리 책은 인터넷에서 2000 권 팔랐어요.
     This month our book sold 2000 books on the internet.

  3. 우리 사장님은 월급으로 한 달에 천만 원을 벌었어요.
     In one month our boss earned 10 million won as salary.

● **A10-2. Listening skills**

  1. 빌 게이츠는 칠십칠조 달러 정도의 재산을 가지고 있어요.
     Bill Gates possesses (has) approximately 77 billion dollars of assets.

  2. 우리 가족이 유럽에 여행을 하는 동안 개가 죽었어요.
     While my family was on vacation in Europe, our dog died.

  3. 나랑 같이 영화 볼래?
     Do you wanna watch a movie with me?

● **A10-3. Fill in the blanks**

  1. 저는 방을 청소하는 동안 엄마가 저녁를 만들었어요.

  2. 이 서점은 해마다 책 백만 권 정도 팔려요.

  3. 아버지가 감기에 걸려서 직장에 못 가요.

  4. 기다리는 동안 커피를 한 잔 마시세요.

  5. 평일마다 서울까지 오십만 명은 차로 출퇴근해요.

● **A10-4. Best Sentence Search**

  1. ✓ 저는 술을 못 마셔서 술집에서는 커피만 마실래요.
     ○ 저는 술을 안 마셔서 술집에서는 커피만 맛일래요.
     ○ 저는 술을 못 마시서 술집에서는 커피만 마실래요.
     Translation: Since I can't drink alcohol I only want to drink coffee at the bar.

  2. ✓ 엄마가 너무 바빠서 오전 5 시에 출근해요.
     ○ 엄마가 나무 바빠서 오적 5 시에 출군헤요.
     ○ 엄마가 너무 바빠서 오전 5 시에 출근해요.
     Translation: Because my mother is so busy she goes to work at 5 am.

  3. ○ 전 세계중에서 우리 고양이가 가장 귀여울 것 같아요.
     ✓ 전 세계에서 우리 고양이가 가장 귀여울 것 같아요.
     ○ 전 세계에서 우리 고양이가 가장 귀여을 것 같아요.
     Translation: I think our cat is the cutest in the entire world.

Korean Simplified History #5:
Korea's Romeo & Juliet

New Words and Grammar

공격 attack
죄책감 feelings of guilt
왕자 prince
~때문에 because of~
~(으)려 하다 to attempt to do~

자살 suicide
공주 princess
찢다 to tear
~라고 direct quote marker

자명고 a "self beating drum" that sounded an alarm when neighboring countries attacked. It was believed to prevent attacks on 낙랑.

Korean History (Korean version)

- 낙랑공주는 호동왕자와 결혼했어요.
- 고구려는 낙랑을 공격하려 했어요.
- 낙랑에는 자명고라는 유명한 북이 있었어요.
- 호동왕자는 낙랑공주에게 "자명고를 찢어"라고 말했어요.
- 낙랑공주 때문에 낙랑이 졌어요.
- 낙랑공주는 죄책감 때문에 자살했어요.
- 호동왕자도 자살했어요.

Korean History (English version)

- Princess Nakrang married with Prince Hodong.
- Goguryeo attempted to attack the country of Nakrang.
- In Nakrang there was a famous drum called Ja Myeong Go.
- Prince Hodong told Princess Nakrang "tear the Ja Myeong Go".
- Because of Princess Nakrang, Nakrang was defeated.
- Because of her guilty conscience, Princess Nakrang committed suicide.
- Hodong also committed suicide.

 **Super Review and Quiz #2:**
Lessons 8-10

SR | Question and Answer 질문과 대답

Hide the English and try to translate the Korean. Take notes on words or grammar patterns that confuse you then review them if necessary.

1. **Q: 방학 동안에 뭘 할 거예요?**
   A: 방학 동안에 여행을 많이 할 거예요.
   A: 집안일을 할 것 같아요.
   A: 그 동안에 공부를 해야 해요.

   Q: What are you going to do during the school break.
   A: During school break I will go on many trips.
   A: I think I will do house work.
   A: During that time I have to study.

2. **Q: 강남에서 명동까지 지하철로 갈 수 있어요?**
   A: 네, 강남역에서 2 호선을 타고 사당에서 내려서 4 호선으로 갈아타세요.
   A: 네, 하지만 시간이 많이 걸릴 것 같아요.
   A: 네. 버스를 타면 한번에 갈 수 있어요.

   Q: Can you go to Myeondong from Gangnam by subway?
   A: Yes, at Gangnam station you ride line 2, get off at Sadang, then transfer to line 4.
   A: Yes, but I think it will take a lot of time.
   A: Yes, if you take the bus you can go in one shot. (this is natural English!)

3. **Q: 내일 날씨가 좋을까요?**
   A: 비가 올 것 같아요.
   A: 눈이 올 것 같아요.
   A: 아침에는 춥고, 오후에는 따뜻할 것 같아요.

   Q: Will the weather be good tomorrow?
   A: I think it's going to rain.
   A: I think it's going to snow.
   A: I think in the morning it will be cold and in the afternoon it will be warm.

4. **Q:** 여기 있는 과일 중에서 뭐가 제일 좋아요?
   A: 딸기보다 바나나가 좋아요.
   A: 귤이 가장 좋아요.
   A: 과일을 별로 좋아하지 않아요.

   Q: Out of all the fruits here, which one is the best?
   A: Bananas are better than strawberries.
   A: Tangerines are the best. / I like tangerines the most.
   A: I don't really like fruits.

5. **Q:** 오늘 바빠요?
   A: 네, 친구랑 약속이 있어요.
   A: 아니요, 약속이 깨져서 안 바빠요.
   A: 이따가 청소를 하거나 낮잠을 잘 거예요.

   Q: Are you busy today?
   A: Yes, I have plans (an appointment) with my friend.
   A: No, I'm not busy since my plans fell through.
   A: Later I am going to clean or take a nap.

6. **Q:** 왜 아직 퇴근 안 하셨어요?
   A: 일이 많아서 늦을 것 같아요.
   A: 벌써 10 시네요. 몰랐어요.
   A: 아직 일이 안 끝나서요. 내일도 일찍 출근해야 할 것 같아요.

   Q: How come you haven't gotten off work yet?
   A: I think I'll be late since I have a lot of work.
   A: Wow it's already 10 o'clock. I didn't know.
   A: I haven't finished my work yet. I think I have go to work early
   tomorrow too.

SR | Conversation 대화 K-E

Hide the English and try to translate the Korean. Take notes on words or
grammar patterns that confuse you then review them if necessary.

1. **Polite conversation between some super friends.**
   규현: 늦어서 미안해요. 오래 기다렸어요?
   예성: 괜찮아요. 기다리는 동안 책도 읽고 음악도 들어서
   심심하지 않았어요.
   규현: 이 까페에서 먹고 싶은 것을 고르세요. 제가 살게요.
   예성: 커피가 좋을 것 같아요.

규현: Sorry for being late. Did you wait a long time?

예성: It's okay. While I waited I was read a book, and listened to music so I wasn't bored.

규현: Choose want you want to eat from this café. I will buy it for you.

예성: I think coffee is good.

2. Polite conversation between two soccer fans.

백현: 오늘 축구 경기에서 누가 이길 것 같아요?

수호: 독일이 이길 것 같아요.

백현: 저는 한국이 이기면 좋겠어요.

수호: 안타깝지만 한국이 질 것 같아요.

백현: Who do you think will win the soccer match today?

수호: I think Germany will win.

백현: I hope Korea will win.

수호: It's unfortunate but I think Korea will lose.

3. Mixed conversation between an upset wife and a guilty husband.

남편: 이번 달에 얼마를 썼어?

아내: 이백만 원 정도 썼어요.

남편: 너무 많이 쓴 것 같아. 지난 달 보다 더 많이 썼어.

아내: 미안해요. 다음 달부터 돈을 벌게요.

남편: How much did you spend this month?

아내: About 2 million won.

남편: I think you spent too much. You spent more than last month.

아내: Sorry. I'll earn more money from next month.

4. A polite conversation between friends.

미나: 왜 늦었어요? 1 시부터 기다렸어요.

초아: 약속시간이 3 시인 줄 알았어요.

미나: 초아 씨는 항상 우리 약속시간을 안 지키네요.

초아: 정말 미안해요.

미나: Why were you late? I waited from 1 o'clock.

초아: I thought our appointment time was 3 o'clock.

미나: You never keep our appointment times.

초아: I am really sorry.

SR | Quiz Yourself 퀴즈

● **1. Sentence maker**

Translate "your thought" into proper Korean.

- (으)ㄹ 것 같다 (I think it will~) FUTURE
- (으)ㄴ 것 같다 (I think it is~) PRESENT
- STEM + 는 것 같다 (I think it is~ ing) PRESENT
- ~ㄴ 줄 알다 (I thought it was~) PAST

Sample

옆집에서 생일 축하 노래가 들려요.

Your thought: I think they are having a birthday party.
한국어: <u>생일 파티를 하는 것 같아요.</u>

1. 조지 씨가 전화를 안 받아요?

   Your thought: I think he is driving.

   한국어:_____

2. 내일 몇 시에 출근할 수 있어요?

   Your thought: I think I can go to work at 8am.

   한국어:_____

3. 떡볶이 어땠어요?

   Your thought: I thought it would be spicier. (but it wasn't)

   한국어:_____

4. 사장님은 일년에 얼마를 벌어요?

   Your thought: I think he/she makes about 3 million dollars a year.

   한국어:_____

● **2. Translate and answer**
Translate the question then answer it as if asked directly to yourself.

> **Sample**
> 한국어와 일본어 중에서 뭐가 더 쉬워요?
> **Translation:** Out of Korean and Japanese which one is easier?
> **Answer:** 한국어가 더 쉬울 것 같아요.

1. 서울과 뉴욕 중에서 어느 도시가 더 추을 것 같아요?

   Translation: _____.

   Answer: _____.

2. 중국하고 러시아 중에서 어디가 더 커요?

   Translation: _____.

   Answer: _____.

3. 세상에서 제일 깨끗한 나라가 어디예요?

   Translation: _____.

   Answer: _____.

4. 엄마랑 아빠 중에서 누가 더 착해요?

   Translation: _____.

   Answer: _____.

5. 서울에서 가장 높은 빌딩은 뭐예요?

   Translation: _____.

   Answer: _____.

● 3. Particle and conjugation check

Properly conjugate all verbs and adjectives and add any required particles.
MAINTAIN THE SAME ORDER and only add particles when required.

Sample
Ex. 이것 / 이것 / 싸다
Combined: 이것보다 이것은 더 싸요.
Translation: This is cheaper than this.

1. 한국어 / 영어 / 어렵다

Combined: _____

Translation: _____

2. 초등학교 / 중학교 / 엄격하다

Combined: _____

Translation: _____

3. 피자 / 야채 / 맛있다

Combined: _____

Translation: _____

4. 여름 / 겨울 / 덥다

Combined: _____

Translation: _____

5. 할머니 / 할아버지 / 친절하다

Combined: _____

Translation: _____

● 4. Reading comprehension
Read the following selection then answer the questions in Korean.

8 달 후에 한국에 일하러 가요. 한국에 가기 전에 한국말을 배워야 돼요.
그래서 매주 화요일하고 금요일에 한국어 학원을 다니고 있어요. 한국어가
처음에는 어려웠어요. 하지만 점점 쉬워졌어요. 한국에 갈 때까지 매일
다섯 시간 정도 공부할 거예요.

1. 이 사람은 왜 한국어를 배워요?

    _____

2. 이번 달은 1 월이라면 이 사람은 몇 월에 한국에 가요?

    _____

3. 이 사람은 수요일에 몇 시간 한국어를 공부해요?

    _____

4. 이 사람은 언제 학원에 가요?

    _____

● 5. English to Korean Translation
Translate the following sentences into Korean.

1. Out of all my friends I like Jiyoon the most.

    _____

2. I always wake up at 8 am, then exercise.

    _____

3. I think my parents are too strict.

    _____

4. While my mother was cleaning the house my father was taking a nap.

    _____

SR | Answer Key 해답

● 1. Sentence maker (answers)

1. 조지 씨가 전화를 안 받아요?
   Is George not answering his phone?

   Your thought: I think he is driving.
   운전하는 것 같아요.

2. 내일 몇 시에 출근할 수 있어요?
   What time can you come to work tomorrow?

   Your thought: I think I can go to work at 8am.
   아침 열덟 시에 출근할 것 같아요.

3. 떡볶이 어땠어요?
   How was the spicy rice cake?

   Your thought: I thought it would be more spicier. (but it wasn't)
   더 매운 줄 알았어요.

4. 사장님은 일년에 얼마를 벌어요?
   How much does the president earn in one year?

   Your thought: I think he/she makes about 3 million dollars a year.
   일년에 삼백만 (달러 / 불) 을 버는 것 같아요.

● 2. Translate and answer (answers)

1. Between Seoul and New York which city do you think is colder?
   Possible answers:
   서울은 더 추운 것 같아요.
   뉴욕은 더 추운 것 같아요.

2. Which is bigger between China and Russia?
   Possible answers:
   중국은 더 커요. / 중국은 더 큰 것 같아요.

3. Where is the cleanest country in the world?
   Possible answers:
   싱가포르가 제일 깨끗해요.
   싱가포르이 제일 깨끗한 것 같아요.

4. Between your mother and father who is kinder?
   Possible answers:
   엄마가 더 착해요.
   아빠가 더 착해요.

5. What is the tallest building in Seoul?
Possible answers:
몰라요.
남산타워인 것 같아요.

● **3. Particle and conjugation check (answers)**

1. 한국어가 영어보다 더 어려워요.
Korean is more difficult than English.

2. 초등학교가 중학교보다 더 엄격해요.
Elementary school is stricter than Junior high school.

3. 피자가 야채보다 더 맛있어요.
Pizza is tastier than vegetables.

4. 여름이 겨울보다 더 더워요.
Summer is hotter than winter.

5. 할머니가 할아버지보다 더 친절해요.
Grandmother is kinder than grandfather.

● **4. Reading comprehension (answers)**

After 8 months I am going to go work in Korea. I have to learn Korean before I go to Korea. So I am attending a Korean academy every Tuesday and Friday. Korean was difficult at first. However it's gradually getting easier. I will study Korean for about 5 hours a day until I go to Korea.

1. 이 사람은 왜 한국어를 배워요?
Why is this person learning Korean?
한국에 일하러 갈 거예요 / 가요.

2. 이번 달은 1 월이라면 이 사람은 몇 월에 한국에 가요?
If this month is January, what month is this person going to Korea?
9 월에 갈 거예요 / 가요.

3. 이 사람은 수요일에 몇 시간 한국어를 공부해요?
How many hours will this person study Korean on Wednesday?
다섯 시간쯤 공부할 거예요 / 공부해요.

4. 이 사람은 언제 학원에 가요?
When does this person go to academy?
매주 화요일과 금요일에 가요.

● **5. English to Korean Translation (answers)**

1. 친구들 중에서 지윤 씨를 제일 좋아해요.

2. 저는 항상 아침 열덟 시에 일어나서 운동을 해요.

3. 제 부모님이 너무 엄격한 것 같아요.

4. (어머니 / 엄마)가 집을 청소하는 동안 (아버지 / 아빠)가 낮잠을 하고 있었어요.

11

Lesson 11:
Verbs as nouns

11 | New Words 새로운 단어

New Nouns etc.

건강	health
취미	hobby
악기	musical instrument
소설	novel (book)
유리	glass
종이	paper
팬케이크	pancakes
사용	usage
퍼즐	puzzle
고속도로	highway

New Counters

(K#) ~장	flat objects, paper
(K#) ~조각	pieces, slices

New Adjectives

간단하다	to be easy, to be simple

New Verbs

치다	to play a stringed instrument
불다	to play a wind instrument
연주하다	to play an instrument (any)
금지하다	to be forbidden, to be prohibited
허가하다	to permit, to grant
사용하다	to use
인쇄하다	to print

11 | Grammar and Usage 문법과 사용법

● 11-1. New counters ~장, ~조각

The new counters in this lesson use Korean numbers up until the 99 limit, when they switch to Chinese counters (as all Korean counters do).

Pieces of paper, thin items 장	
한 장	1 piece
두 장	2 pieces
세 장	3 pieces
네 장	4 pieces
다섯 장	5 pieces
백 장	100 pieces
만 장	10,000 pieces
몇 장? How many pieces?	

Slices, pieces (split items) 조각	
한 조각	1 piece
두 조각	2 pieces
세 조각	3 pieces
네 조각	4 pieces
다섯 조각	5 pieces
백 조각	100 pieces
만 조각	10,000 pieces
몇 조각? How many pieces?	

장 counter can be used with items that are flat and thin such as the following:

paper, tickets, stamps	leaves	credit cards
CD, DVD, Discs	various clothing	photographs
flags	tissues, napkins	playing cards

flat, thin objects ~장

조각 counter is used with pieces and slices of a bigger originally intact items:

broken glass	cake slices	pizza slices
chess pieces	chocolate squares	chunks cheese
slices of bread	cuts of meat	cuts of gimbap
puzzle / game pieces	slices of fruit	pieces of chicken

pieces, slices ~조각

Example sentences

1. 어젯밤 저녁을 안 먹어서 팬케이크를 열 장 먹을 것 같아요.
   Last night I didn't eat dinner so I think I can eat 10 pancakes!

2. 종이 100 장만 주세요.
   Just give me 100 pieces of paper.

3. 미국 사람들은 보통 지갑 속에 신용카드가 3 장 있어요.
   Americans normally have 3 credit cards in their wallet.

4. 오늘 친구와 카페에서 케이크 두 조각을 먹고 커피를 마셨어요.
   Today I ate two pieces of cake and drank coffee with a friend at a café.

5. 피자 세 조각과 콜라 한 병 주세요.
   Three slices of pizza and one bottle of cola please.

6. 아까 치킨 다섯 조각을 먹었지만 아직 배고파요.
   Just now I ate 5 pieces of chicken but I am still hungry.

Special Information 특별 정보

If you order an entire pizza use (K#) ~판 counter. Also, when saying a page number you can use (C#) ~페이지 or (C#) ~장.

● 11-2. 치다 (to play stringed instruments), 불다 (to play wind instruments)

치다	TYPE	regular verb	BASIC FORM	쳐
불다	TYPE	ㄹ irregular verb	BASIC FORM	불어

치다 and 불다 both translate to just "play" in English, but in Korean you have to consider the type of instrument being played. 치다 is used for string instruments or instruments that you hit such as:

기타 guitar	피아노 piano	드럼 drums
우쿨렐레 ukulele	탬버린 tambourine	실로폰 xylophone

stringed and instruments you strike ~치다

불다 is used for any wind instruments such as below:

플루트 flute	트럼펫 trumpet	리코더 recorder
색소폰 saxophone	하모니카 harmonica	튜바 tuba

wind instruments you blow ~불다

The instrument that you play is marked with object marker 을/를.

Example sentences

1. 저는 어릴 때부터 튜바를 불었어요.
   I have played the tuba since I was young.

2. 우리 아버지가 10 년 동안 "기타를 치고 싶어요" 라고 말했어요.
   My father for 10 years said, "I want to play guitar".

3. 저는 우리 학교 학생들 중에서 제일 트럼펫을 잘 불어요.
   I play the trumpet best out of all the students in our school.

4. 드럼을 칠 수 있지만 시끄러워서 밤에 못 쳐요.
   I can play the drums but since they are loud I can't play at night.

5. 오 년 전에는 하모니카를 많이 불었지만 요즘은 별로 안 불어요.
   5 years ago I played harmonica a lot, but these days I don't play much.

6. 제 여자 친구가 취미로 피아노를 쳐요.
   My girlfriend plays piano as a hobby.

> Use 연주하다 (to perform) when you don't know the type of instrument.

Example Q&A

1. **People talking at a music store.**
   Q: 무슨 악기를 연주할 수 있어요?
   A: 어릴 때는 기타를 칠 수 있었지만 다 잊어버렸어요.
   A: 하모니카를 불을 수 있어요.
   A: 저는 악기를 (아무것도) 못 연주해요.

   Q: What musical instrument can you play (perform)?
   A: When I was young I could play the guitar but I forgot it all.
   A: I can play the harmonica.
   A: I can't play (any) instruments.

2. **Friends chatting on a Saturday.**
   Q: 드럼을 칠 수 있어요?
   A: 아니요. 하지만 노래방에서 탬버린을 자주 쳐요.
   A: 네, 5 년 동안 배워서 잘 칠 수 있어요.
   A: 치고 싶지만 못 쳐요.

   Q: Can you play the drums?
   A: No. But I often play the tambourine at karaoke.
   A: Yes, I have been learning for 5 years, so I can play well.
   A: I want to play but I am unable to.

● 11-3. ~는 것,~는 게 (~ing form of a verbs)
To make a verb into a noun you use the **STEM + 는것** pattern.

Examples (verbs)

1. 사는 것   buying
2. 하는 것   doing
3. 읽는 것   reading
4. 있는 것   having
5. 자는 것   sleeping

Examples (verb phrases)

1. 새 차를 사는 것   buying a new car
2. 소설을 읽는 것   reading a novel
3. 혼자서 수영하는 것   swimming alone
4. 버스를 타는 것   riding the bus
5. 음악을 듣는 것   listening to music

Once you have a nominalized verb (a verb turned into a noun) you can use it in a sentence with various particles (markers) as if it was a normal noun.

subject   수영하는 것이 재미있어요.   Swimming is interesting.
topic   수영하는 것은 취미예요.   Swimming is my hobby.
object   수영하는 것을 좋아해요.   I like swimming.
comparator   수영하는 것보다 안전해요.   It's safer than swimming.

Example sentences

1. 늦게 먹는 것이 건강에 나빠요.
   Eating late is bad for your health.

   > 에 means "for" here.

2. 새 차를 사는 것은 힘들어요.
   Buying a new car is exhausting.

3. 제 취미는 소설을 읽는 것이에요.
   My hobby is reading novels

4. 혼자서 수영하는 것은 위험해요.
   Swimming alone is dangerous.

   > 수업 시간 means "during class".

5. 수업 시간에 음악을 듣는 것이 금지해요.
   Listening to music during class is prohibited.

6. 버스를 타는 것은 택시를 타는 것보다 더 싸요.
   Riding the bus is cheaper than taking a taxi.

7. 기타를 치는 것을 좋아해요.
   I like playing guitar.

8. 매일 야채를 먹는 것은 어려워요.
   Eating vegetables everyday is difficult.

9. 독일어를 배우는 것은 어려울 것 같아요.
   I think learning German is difficult.

─── Special Information 특별 정보 ───

Often 것이 is contracted to 게 and 것을 to 걸. Review lesson 15 of book 2 for common Korean contractions.

Example sentences
1. 아침 일찍 일어나는 게 힘들어요.
   Waking up early in the morning is rough.

2. 친구들이랑 노는 걸 좋아해요.
   I like hanging out with friends.

3. 고속도로에서 운전하는 게 어려워요.
   It's difficult to drive on the highway.

● **11-4. 금지하다 (to be prohibited), 허가하다 (to permit, grant)**

금지하다	TYPE	하다 verb	BASIC FORM	금지해
허가하다	TYPE	하다 verb	BASIC FORM	허가해

Example sentences
1. 다음 주부터 길에서 음식을 파는 것을 허가합니다.
   Starting next week selling food on the street will be permitted.

2. 여기서 휴대폰 사용을 금지했어요.
   Cell phones usage has been prohibited here.

3. 박물관에서 사진을 찍는 것을 금지해요.
   Taking pictures in the museum is prohibited.

허락하다 (to allow) is a much lighter form of 허가하다.

4. 우리 선생님이 교실에서 먹는 것을 **허락**해요.
   Our teacher **allows** eating in the classroom.

● **11-5. 인쇄하다 (to print)**

인쇄하다	TYPE	하다 verb	BASIC FORM	인쇄해

Example sentences
1. 보고서를 100 부 인쇄해야 돼요.
   I have to print 100 copies of a report.

   > 부 means "portion". Here it is the "copies" counter.

2. 이것을 인쇄하기 전에 노란색 잉크를 샀어요.
   Before I printed this I bought yellow ink.

● **11-6. 사용하다 (to use)**

사용하다	TYPE	하다 verb	BASIC FORM	사용해

Example sentences
1. 요즘 아이폰을 사용해서 사진을 많이 찍어요.
   These days I use an iPhone so I take many pictures.

2. 30 분 동안 핸드폰을 사용하지 마세요.
   Don't use your cell phone for a period of 30 minutes.

   > 이용하다 is better but Koreans often use 사용하다.

3. 계단을 오르는 게 힘들어서 항상 엘리베이터를 사용해요.
   Because going up stairs is exhausting I always use the elevator.

4. 월요일부터 수요일까지 이 헬스장을 무료로 사용할 수 있어요.
   From Monday to Wednesday you can use this gym for free.

● **11-7. 간단하다 (to be easy, to be simple)**

간단하다	TYPE	하다 adjective	BASIC FORM	간단해

Example sentences
1. 이번 숙제는 정말 간단했어요.
   The homework this time was really easy.

2. 한국어는 간단하지 않아요.
   Korean is not easy.

3. 저는 항상 점심으로 간단한 음식을 먹어요.
   I always eat simple food for lunch.

11 | Test Yourself Activities 연습 문제

● **A11-1. Fix the mistake**
Correct the Korean sentence, then finish the translation on the line below.

1. 이 퍼즐은 만 장이 있어서 오래 걸릴 것 같아요.

   Korean _____

   English Since this puzzle has 1,000 pieces_____

2. 미국 학생들은 거의 다 리코더를 놀 수 있어요.

   Korean _____

   English Almost all American students_____

3. 친구가 어두운 방에 혼자 있은 걸 무서워해요.

   Korean _____

   English My friend is scared being_____

● **A11-2. Listening skills**
Go to **http://fromzero.com/korean/kfz3/A2** OR scan the QR code. Enter the code. Write the Korean then the English.

1. 11A Korean _____

   English _____

2. 11B Korean _____

   English _____

3. 11C Korean _____

   English _____

● **A11-3. Fill in the blanks**
Fill in the missing word or particle based on the English sentence.

1. 친구랑 _____이 혼자보다 더 재미있어요.
   Swimming with a friend is more fun than alone.

2. 영화관에서는 휴대폰 사용을 _____.
   Cell phone usage is prohibited in the movie theatre.

3. 교실 안에 핸드폰을 _____ 마세요.
   Don't use your cell phone in the classroom.

4. 돈을 _____ 힘들어요.
   It's tough to earn money. / Earning money is tough.

5. 저는 기타를 _____ 사람들이 부러워요.
   I am envious of people who can play the guitar.

● **A11-4. Mark and Translate**
Mark the Korean sentence without mistakes then translate it.

1. ○ 내 취미은 소설을 읽는 거야.
   ○ 내 취미는 소설을 읽는 거야.
   ○ 내 취미는 소설을 읽은 거야.

   Translation:_____

2. ○ 매일 야채를 먹는 것을 겅간에 좋아요.
   ○ 매일 야채가 먹는 것이 겅간에 좋을 것 같아요.
   ○ 매일 야채를 먹는 게 겅간에 좋아요.

   Translation:_____

3. ○ 제 할아버지는 피아노를 잘 불 수 있어요.
   ○ 제 할아버지는 피아노를 잘 불 수 없어요.
   ○ 제 할아버지는 피아노를 잘 칠 수 있어요.

   Translation:_____

11 | Self Test Answers 연습 문제 정답

● A11-1. Fix the mistake

1. 이 퍼즐은 천 조각이 있어서 오래 걸릴 것 같아요.
   Since this puzzle has 1000 pieces, I think it will take a long time.

2. 미국 학생들은 거의 다 리코더를 불 수 있어요.
   Almost all America students can play the recorder.

3. 친구가 어두운 방에 혼자 있는 게 무서워해요.
   My friend is scared being in a dark room alone.

● A11-2. Listening skills

1. 드럼을 칠 수 있어요?
   Can you play the drums?

2. 버스를 타는 것은 택시를 타는 것보다 더 싸요.
   Riding the bus is cheaper than taking a taxi.

3. 우리 선생님이 교실에서 먹는 것을 허가해요.
   Our teacher allows eating in the classroom.

● A11-3. Fill in the blanks

1. 친구랑 수영하는 것이 혼자보다 더 재미있어요.
2. 영화관에서는 휴대폰 사용을 금지해요.
3. 교실 안에 핸드폰을 사용하지 마세요.
4. 돈을 버는 게 힘들어요.
5. 저는 기타를 칠 수 있는 사람들이 부러워요.

● A11-4. Best Sentence Search

1. ○ 내 취미은 소설을 읽는 거야.
   ✓ 내 취미는 소설을 읽는 거야.
   ○ 내 취미는 소설을 읽은 거야.
   Translation: My hobby is reading novels.

2. ○ 매일 야채를 먹는 것을 겅간에 좋아요.
   ○ 매일 야채가 먹는 것이 겅간에 좋을 것 같아요.
   ✓ 매일 야채를 먹는 게 겅간에 좋아요.
   Translation: Eating vegetables everyday is good for your health.

3. ○ 제 할아버지는 피아노를 잘 불 수 있어요.
   ○ 제 할아버지는 피아노를 잘 불 수 없어요.
   ✓ 제 할아버지는 피아노를 잘 칠 수 있어요.
   Translation: My grandfather is can play the piano well.

11 | Vocabulary Builder 단어 구축

In Lesson 12 we will learn a "TON" of verbs related to clothing and accessory related verbs!

■ Group F: Clothing 옷

모자	hat
바지	pants
장갑	gloves
속옷	underwear
원피스	one piece dress
코트	coat
드레스	dress
셔츠	shirt
넥타이	necktie

■ Group G: Accessories etc. 액세서리

머리 띠	headband
팔찌	bracelet
목도리	scarf
귀걸이	earrings
안경	glasses
벨트	belt
마스크	mask
반지	ring

■ Vocabulary Sentences

The following sentences will use grammar / verbs / adjectives that may or may not have been covered in this or book 2. Focus on the new vocabulary.

1. 그 모자 어디에서 샀어요?
   Where did you buy that hat?

2. 골프를 칠때 장갑을 사용하면 좋아요.
   It's good to use gloves when playing golf

3. 대학생들이 머리띠를 자주 사용해요.
    College students use headbands often.

4. 겨울에는 목도리를 사용하세요.
    Use scarfs during the winter.

5. 제 귀걸이는 서울에서 샀어요.
    I bought the earrings in Seoul.

6. 안경을 바꿀때가 됐어요.
    It is time for me to change my glasses

7. 중요한 날에는 예쁜 속옷을 입어야 돼요.
    We need to wear pretty underwear on an important day

8. 제 벨트가 고장났어요.
    My belt broke.

9. 그녀가 입은 원피스가 예뻐요.
    The one piece dress that she is wearing is beautiful

Korean Simplified History #6:
The Sixty Days Battle

 New Words and Grammar

조카 nephew, niece
용감하다 to be brave
이기다 to win
죽이다 to kill

군인 soldier
없애다 to eliminate
보내다 to send
~(으)려고 하다 to attempt / try to do

★ Korean History (Korean version)

- 고구려에는 연개소문라는 사람이 있었어요.

- 연개소문은 정말 용감하고 무서운 사람이었어요.

- 연개소문은 고구려의 왕을 죽이고 조카를 왕으로 만들었어요.

- 신라와 당나라 (China)는 고구려를 싫어했어요.

- 신라와 당나라는 같이 고구려를 없애려고 했어요.

- 당나라는 113 만 명의 군인들을 보냈어요.

- 연개소문은 60 일 동안 싸우고 이겼어요.

★ Korean History (English version)

- In Goguryeo there was person named Yeon Gaesomun.

- Yeon Gaesomun was a really brave and scary person.

- Yeon Gaesomun killed the king of Goguryeo and made his nephew King.

- Shilla and Dangnara didn't like Goguryeo.

- Together Shilla and Dangnara tried to eliminate Goguryeo.

- Dangnara sent 1,130,000 soldiers.

- Yeon Gaesomun fought for 60 days and won.

12 Lesson 12: **The Wearing Verbs**

12 New Words 새로운 단어

NOTE: Make sure you review the vocabulary builder words in lesson 11 since a lot of the words introduced are used in this lesson.

New Nouns etc.

향수	perfume, cologne
결혼반지	wedding rings
렌즈	contact lens
신발 끈	shoelaces
구두	dress shows
시계	clock, watch
생일날	birthday

New Verbs

입다	to wear clothes
쓰다	to wear on head
매다	to tie, to wear ties etc.
착용하다	to fasten
끼다	to put on gloves, glasses etc.
신다	to wear on feet
차다	to put on a watch
하다	to put on accessories
뿌리다	to put on perfume etc.
벗다	to take off clothes etc
빼다	to take off rings, gloves etc.
풀다	to take off ties, hair ribbons

12 | Grammar and Usage 문법과 사용법

● **12-1. Why so many verbs to say "wear"?**
Here is some solid advice that will save you a lot of stress.

> ***Avoid asking why when learning a language.***

Asking why can slow you down. Imagine if a Korean asked you why English pronounces, "nite", "night", and "knight" the same way but spells them differently. The answer is related to the history of English but it's not important to the overall progress of the student.

That being said… Korean has multiple ways to say "wear" and "take off" depending on the clothing type. You simply have to learn the differences.

The wearing and removing verbs		
wear, put on	**applies to**	**take off, remove**
쓰다	hats, beanies, glasses*, masks *, wigs	벗다
매다	ties, neckties, bow tie, belts, shoelaces, scarf	풀다
끼다	contact lenses, rings	빼다
끼다	glasses*, gloves, watches, bracelets*, masks *	벗다
하다	accessories, bracelets*, earrings, hair bows	벗다
하다	makeup	지우다
차다	watches, bracelets*	벗다
신다	socks, shoes, boots, nylons	벗다
입다	shirts, pants, underwear, jackets, suits, robes	벗다
뿌리다	perfume, aftershave, cologne	(not used)
All of the verbs above mark the item being worn or removed with 을/를.		

* this item can use two verbs

● 12-2. 입다 (to wear clothes)

TYPE	regular verb	BASIC FORM	입어

Example sentences

1. 날씨가 추워서 코트를 입었어요.
   I wore a coat because the weather is cold.

2. 어제 이 원피스을 입었지만 오늘도 입을 거예요.
   I wore this one piece yesterday, but I'm going to wear it again today.

3. 친구에게서 빌린 드레스를 이번 생일날 입을 거예요.
   I'm going to wear a dress that I borrowed from a friend this birthday.

● 12-3. 끼다 (to put on gloves, glasses etc.)

TYPE	regular verb	BASIC FORM	껴

Example sentences

1. 스키를 타기 전에 모자를 쓰고 장갑을 끼세요.
   Before you ski put on a hat and gloves.

2. 저는 눈이 안 좋아서 렌즈를 껴요.
   I wear lenses since my eyes aren't good.

3. 오늘 남자친구에게 선물로 받은 반지를 꼈어요.
   Today I wore the pants that I got from my boyfriend as a present.

● 12-4. 신다 (to wear on feet)

TYPE	regular verb	BASIC FORM	신어

Example sentences

1. 저 신발 한 번 신어 봐요.
   Try on those shoes over there once.

2. 저는 다른 신발 보다 운동화를 더 자주 신어요.
   I wear tennis shoes more often than other shoes.

3. 내일은 검은색 양말을 신고 흰색 구두를 신을 거예요.
   Tomorrow I will wear black socks and white dress shoes.

● 12-5. 쓰다 (to wear on head)

TYPE	regular verb	BASIC FORM	써

Example sentences

1. 저는 눈이 나빠서 안경을 써요.
   I wear glasses because my eyes are bad.

2. 교실에서 모자를 쓰지 마세요.
   Don't wear a hat in the classroom.

3. 감기가 걸려서 마스크를 쓰고 학교에 갔어요.
   I went to school wearing a mask since I caught a cold.

● 12-6. 매다 (to tie, to wear ties etc.), 착용하다 (to fasten)

매다	TYPE	regular verb	BASIC FORM	매
착용하다	TYPE	하다 verb	BASIC FORM	착용해

착용하다 (to fasten, to tie) overlaps with 매다 enough that it can be confusing. 착용하다 is a generic verb that mean "to wear". Perhaps it most common usage is with seat belts but it pops up for many types of clothing from masks to even bras. Sometimes 매다 must be used, and other times 착용하다. Some clothing can use both. Here is a quick helper list.

매다 vs 착용하다			
item being worn		매다	착용하다
넥타이	neck tie	✔	✔
안전벨트	seat belt	✔	✔
헬멧	helmet	✘	✔
마스크	mask (surgical)	✘	✔
신발 끈	shoelaces	✔	✘
옷고름	coat strings	✔	✘
Things that you snap or buckle tend to be 착용하다. Things you can only tie tend to be 매다.			

Example sentences

1. 파티가 있을 때 저는 항상 하얀색 셔츠를 입고 빨간색 넥타이를 매요.
   When there is a party I always wear a white shirt and a red necktie.

2. 달리기 전에 꼭 신발 끈을 매세요.
   Before running make sure to tie your shoelaces.

3. 바지가 너무 커서 벨트를 착용할 거예요.
   I'm going to put on a belt because my pants are so big.

12-7. 차다 (to put on a watch)

TYPE	regular verb	BASIC FORM	차

Example sentences

1. 엄마는 아빠에게 선물로 받은 시계를 찼어요.
   My mother is wearing the watch that my father gave to her as a present.

   Remember Korean uses past tense to say "wearing".

2. 저는 매일 아침 시계를 차고 회사에 가요.
   Everyday I put on my watch and go to work.

   회사에 가요 sounds better as "go to work" in English.

3. 지금 찬 시계는 요즘 유행하는 시계예요.
   The watch I'm wearing now is (a) fashionable (watch) these days.

12-8. 하다 (to put on accessories)

TYPE	하다 verb	BASIC FORM	해

Example sentences

1. 귀걸이도 하고 목걸이도 할 거예요.
   I'm going to wear a necklace and also earrings.

2. 그녀는 오늘 머리띠를 해서 더 예뻐요.
   She is prettier because today she is wearing a headband.

3. 감기에 걸려서 목도리를 했어요.
   Because I have a cold I put on a scarf.

● 12-9. 뿌리다 (to put perfume, to spray etc.)

TYPE	regular verb	BASIC FORM	뿌려

Example sentences

1. 향수를 너무 많이 뿌리지 마세요.
   Don't put on too much perfume / cologne.

2. 지금 뿌린 향수 이름이 뭐예요?
   What's the name of the perfume / cologne you just sprayed now?

3. 제 남자친구는 항상 향수를 세번 뿌려요.
   My boyfriend always sprays cologne three times.

● 12-10. 벗다 (to take off clothes etc.)

TYPE	regular verb	BASIC FORM	벗어

Example sentences

1. 제 방에서는 신발을 벗어 주세요.
   Please take off your shoes in my room.

2. 갑자기 더워져서 코트를 벗고 싶어요.
   Because it got hot suddenly I want to take off my coat.

3. 지금 쓴 모자를 벗고 다른 모자를 쓸게요.
   I'll take off the hat I am wearing now (that I put on) and put on
   a different one.

● 12-11. 빼다 (to take off rings, gloves etc., to remove)

TYPE	regular verb	BASIC FORM	빼

Example sentences

1. 날씨가 너무 추워서 장갑을 빼고 싶지 않아요.
   Because it's so cold I don't want to take off my gloves.

2. 십년 동안 낀 반지를 오늘 뺐어요.
   Today I took off the ring I wore for 10 years.

● **12-12. 풀다 (to untie, to let down)**

TYPE	ㄹ irregular verb	BASIC FORM	풀어

Example sentences

1. 저녁을 너무 많이 먹어서 벨트를 풀었어요.
   Since I ate too much dinner I took off my belt.

2. 그녀는 항상 퇴근 후 머리를 풀어요.
   After getting off work she always let's down her hair.

3. 여자친구가 머리를 풀면 더 예뻐 보여요.
   When my girlfriend unties her hair she looks prettier.

● **12-13. 지우다 (to remove makeup, to erase)**

TYPE	regular verb	BASIC FORM	지워

Example sentences

1. 잠을 자기 전에 화장을 꼭 지워야 해요.
   Before sleeping I definitely have to remove my makeup.

2. 그녀는 화장을 지우면 다른 사람 같아요.
   If she takes off her make up she looks like another person.

3. 너무 피곤해서 화장을 못 지웠어요.
   I was so tired that I couldn't remove my makeup.

12 | Test Yourself Activities 연습 문제

● A12-1. Fix the mistake
Correct the Korean sentence, then finish the translation on the line below.

1. 저는 눈이 나쁘지만 안경을 안 입어요.

   Korean _____

   English I am nearsighted however_____

2. 결혼식에 갈 때 넥타이를 껴야 돼요.

   Korean _____

   English You have to put on a necktie_____

3. 저는 아버지가 저에게 준 시계를 처음으로 뿌렸어요.

   Korean _____

   English I put on the watch my_____

● A12-2. Listening skills
Go to **http://fromzero.com/korean/kfz3/A2** OR scan the QR code. Enter the code. Write the Korean then the English.

1. 12A Korean _____

   English _____

2. 12B Korean _____

   English _____

3. 12C Korean _____

   English _____

● **A12-3. Fill in the blanks**
Fill in the missing word or particle based on the English sentence.

1. 머리띠를 하고 _____ 식당에 일해서 해야 돼요.
   I don't want to wear a headband but since I work at a restaurant I have to.

2. 신발 끈을 안 _____ 위험해요.
   It's dangerous if you don't tie your shoelaces.

3. 교회에 있을 때 모자를 _____.
   When you are in a church take off your hat.

4. 어떤 향수를 _____요?
   What kind of perfume are you wearing?

5. 저는 아침마다 화장을 해요. 근데 밤에는 다 _____.
   Each morning I put on makeup. But at night I remove it all.

● **A12-4. Mark and Translate**
Mark the Korean sentence without mistakes then translate it.

1. ○ 제 배를 아파서 앉을 때 벨트를 풀어야 돼요.
   ○ 제 배가 아파서 앉을 때 벨트를 풀려야 돼요.
   ○ 제 배가 아파서 앉을 때 벨트를 풀어야 돼요.

   Translation:_____

2. ○ 내 여자친구가 화장실을 지우면 다른 사람 같아 보여.
   ○ 내 여자친구가 화장을 지으면 다른 사람 같아 보여.
   ○ 내 여자친구가 화장을 지우면 다른 사람 같아 보여.

   Translation:_____

3. ○ 스포츠를 할 때 운동화를 안 신으면 다리가 아플 줄 같아요.
   ○ 스포츠를 할 때 온둥화를 안 신으면 다리가 아플 것 같아요.
   ○ 스포츠를 할 때 운동화를 안 신으면 다리가 아플 것 같아요.

   Translation:_____

12 | Self Test Answers 연습 문제 정답

● A12-1. Fix the mistake

1. 저는 눈이 나쁘지만 안경을 안 써요.
   I have bad eyes but I don't wear glasses.

2. 결혼식에 갈 때 넥타이를 매야 돼요.
   You have to put on a necktie when you go to a wedding ceremony.

3. 저는 아버지가 저에게 준 시계를 처음으로 찼어요.
   I put on the watch my father gave me for the first time.

● A12-2. Listening skills

1. 어제 뿌린 향수 이름이 뭐예요?
   What is the name of the perfume / cologne you wore yesterday?

2. 여름에는 코트를 입으면 더울 것 같아요.
   If you wear a coat in summer I think you will be hot.

3. 안경을 끼고 싶지 않아서 저는 보통 렌즈를 껴요.
   Because I don't want to wear glasses, I normally put in contact lens.

● A12-3. Fill in the blanks

1. 머리띠를 하고 싶지 않지만 식당에 일해서 해야 돼요.
2. 신발 끈을 안 매면 위험해요.
3. 교회에 있을 때 모자를 벗으세요.
4. 어떤 향수를 뿌렸어요?
5. 저는 아침마다 화장을 해요. 근데 밤에는 다 지워요.

● A12-4. Best Sentence Search

1. ○ 제 배를 아파서 앉을 때 벨트를 풀어야 돼요.
   ○ 제 배가 아파서 앉을 때 벨트를 풀려야 돼요.
   ✓ 제 배가 아파서 앉을 때 벨트를 풀어야 돼요.
   Translation: Since my stomach is hurts, when I sit I have to remove my belt.

2. ○ 내 여자친구가 화장실을 지우면 다른 사람 같아 보여.
   ○ 내 여자친구가 화장을 지으면 다른 사람 같아 보여.
   ✓ 내 여자친구가 화장을 지우면 다른 사람 같아 보여.
   If (when) my girlfriend removes her makeup, she looks like a different person.

3. ○ 스포츠를 할 때 운동화를 안 신으면 다리가 아플 줄 같아요.
   ○ 스포츠를 할 때 온둥화를 안 신으면 다리가 아플 것 같아요.
   ✓ 스포츠를 할 때 운동화를 안 신으면 다리가 아플 것 같아요.
   When you play sports if you don't wear sneakers I think your legs will hurt.

12 | Vocabulary Builder 단어 구축

Sickness happens throughout life. It's good to know how to say each sickness JUST IN CASE! And of course if you do get sick you might want to get medicine at the pharmacy.

■ Group G: Sickness 병

감기	cold
열	fever
병	sickness
두통	headache
몸살	body aches
당뇨병	diabetes
암	cancer
치매	Alzheimer's
폐렴	pneumonia
빈혈	anemia
심장병	heart disease

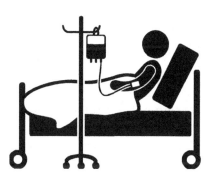

■ Group H: Symptoms 증상

증상	symptons
기침	cough
콧물	running nose (mucus)
전염병	infection
영양실조	malnutrition
타박상	bruise
불면증	insomnia
설사	diarrhea
메스꺼움	nausea

■ Vocabulary Sentences

The following sentences will use grammar / verbs / adjectives that may or may not have been covered in this or book 2. Focus on the new vocabulary.

1. 감기에 걸리면 열이 나고 기침과 콧물과 두통이 와요.
   If you get a cold you get a fever, cough, runny nose, and headache.

2. 어제 할머니가 치매에 걸렸다는 소식을 들어서 슬펐어요.
   Since I heard the news that my grandmother got Alzheimer's I'm sad.

3. 케이크를 많이 먹으면 당뇨병에 걸릴 수 있어요.
   If you eat lots of cake than you can get diabetes.

4. 의사가 환자를 치료하다가 전염병에 감염 되었어요.
   The doctor treated the patient and they got an infection.

5. 감기가 악화되면 폐렴이 돼요.
   If a cold gets worse it can become pneumonia.

6. 일반적으로 여자는 남자보다 빈혈의 위험이 더 커요.
   Normally girls have a greater risk of anemia than men.

7. 저희 할아버지는 심장병으로 작년에 돌아가셨어요.
   My grandfather passed away last year from heart disease.

8. 담배를 많이 피면 암에 걸릴 확률이 높아져요.
   If you smoke a lot, your chance of getting cancer increases.

9. 갑자기 설사를 해서 집으로 돌아왔어요.
   I suddenly got diarrhea so I came back home.

10. 아프리카에서는 매년 많은 어린이들이 영양실조로 죽어요.
    In Africa every year many children die from malnutrition.

11. 요즘 저는 불면증이 너무 심해서 약을 먹고 자요.
    Lately my insomnia has been severe so I take medicine and sleep.

12. 어제 계단에서 넘어져서 타박상을 입었어요.
    Yesterday I fell down the stairs and I got bruised.

13 | Lesson 13:
Indirect Speech

13 | New Words 새로운 단어

New Nouns etc.

지급일	pay day
근처	nearby, in the area
공기	air
뉴스	news (tv news cast)
점원	salesperson, store clerk
요리사	cook, chef
성형수술	plastic surgery
부탁	request
환자	patient
앨범	album (photo, record, cd)
서비스	service *** (see Special Information below)

New Verbs

부탁하다	to request, to ask
이사하다	to move (to a new place)
합격하다	to pass (a test)
생기다	to happen, to occur, to make, to form

Special Information 특별 정보

In America if we say "service" it is something we pay for. For example when a company says "We offer many services" it usual means paid services. However, in Korean 서비스 is a perk that companies give to attract customers or make current customers happy. In KPOP it's common to hear the word 팬 서비스. This usually involves the star doing something special for the fans that is perhaps out of character.
It's really just a fancy way of saying "free".

13 | Grammar and Usage 문법과 사용법

● 13-1. Overview of indirect speech

When indirectly quoting someone, even yourself, "indirect speech" is used. *Indirect speech* is any speech that communicates what someone has said.

> *He said it was a cute dog.*

> *She said it was too expensive.*

> *Jeff said he was returning to America.*

The sentences above are not *direct quotes* that can use 라고 like section 10-10, but instead are *indirectly quoting* what the person said.

When using indirect speech in Korean, it must be properly "packaged" based on the content of the speech. Nouns, adjectives, and verbs each have unique ways to package. The packaging changes additionally based on tense.

● 13-2. Indirect speech (NOUNS) ~(이)라고

When packaging 이다 (is, am, are) for indirect speech, when there is a 받침 it changes to 이라고 and when there isn't one it's changed to 라고.

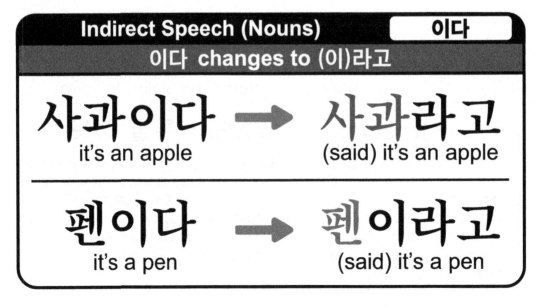

Indirect Speech (Nouns) | **이다**

이다 changes to (이)라고

사과이다 → 사과라고
it's an apple | (said) it's an apple

펜이다 → 펜이라고
it's a pen | (said) it's a pen

1. 그가 무료**라고** 했어요.
   He said it's free.

2. 몇 시**라고** 했어요?
   What time did they say it is?

3. 제가 미국사람**이라고** 했어요.
   I said I'm American.

4. 그 여자가 열여덟살**이라고** 했어요.
   That girl said she was 18 years old.

5. 선생님은 시험이 내일**이라고** 했어요?
   Did the teacher say the test is tomorrow?

With indirect speech, the verb 하다 instead of 말하다 to mean "to say". 말하다 can also be used but isn't as common.

아니다 (is not, am not, are not) changes to 아니라고. Don't forget that 아니다 always requires an 이/가 particle after the noun.

Indirect Speech (Nouns)   이니다
아니다 changes to 아니라고

사과가 아니다

사과가 아니**라고**
(said) it's not an apple

펜이 아니다

펜이 아니**라고**
(said) it's not a pen

Example sentences (with 아니다)

1. 그가 무료가 **아니라고** 했어요.
   He said it's not free.

2. 저는 중국사람이 **아니라고** 했어요.
   I said I'm not Chinese.

3. 이 핸드폰은 아이폰이 **아니라고** 했어요.
   They said the phone wasn't an iPhone.

4. 그여자가 여자친구가 **아니라고** 했어요?
   Did he say that girl wasn't his girlfriend?

5. 의사 선생님께 물어봤어요. 그런데 감기가 **아니라고** 했어요.
   I asked the doctor. However he/she said it wasn't a cold.

If the speaker isn't mentioned in the sentence you can assume who the speaker is based on the context of the conversation.

의사 means "doctor" but often people refer to doctors as the more polite 의사 선생님.

Example Q&A (with 이다 and 아니다)

1. **Parents talking about a drawing their son drew.**
   Q: 이 동물이 뭐예요?
   A: 여우**라고** 했어요.
   A: 기린**이라고** 했어요.

   Q: What is this animal?
   A: He said it was a fox.
   A: He said it was a giraffe.

2. **Co-workers in an office.**
   Q: 이 보고서는 금요일까지 필요해요?
   A: 사장님이 월요일**이라고** 했어요.
   A: 김민지 씨에게 물어봤어요. 금요일이 **아니라고** 했어요.

   Q: Is this report needed by Friday?
   A: The boss said it was Monday.
   A: I asked Minji Kim. She said it wasn't Friday.

3. **Nurses discussing a recent female patient.**
   Q: 환자는 어디가 아파요?
   A: 어깨랑 무릎**이라고** 했어요.
   A: 손목이랑 팔꿈치**라고** 했어요.

   Q: Where does the patient hurt?
   A: She said her shoulder and knee.
   A: She said her wrist and elbow.

● 13-3. Indirect speech (ADJECTIVE PRESENT) ~다고

Adjectives can be made into present tense direct speech by adding 다고 to the stem. It doesn't matter if there is a 받침 or not.

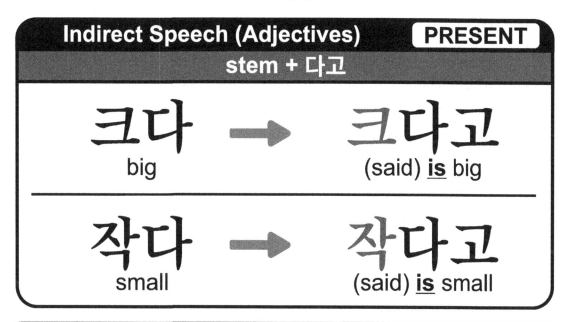

Indirect Speech (Adjectives) **PRESENT**

stem + 다고

크다 → 크다고
big | (said) **is** big

작다 → 작다고
small | (said) **is** small

Example sentences (adjectives PRESENT)

1. 리드 씨가 콘서트 티켓이 너무 비싸**다고** 했어요.
   Reed said the concert tickets are too expensive.

2. 제 친구가 영화가 재미있**다고** 했어요.
   My friend said the movie is interesting.

   > 싶다 (want to) form is always treated like an adjective.

3. 아버지가 새 차를 사고 싶**다고** 했어요.
   My father said he wants to buy a new car.

4. 박민수 씨가 지급일까지 돈이 없**다고** 했어요.
   Minsu Park said he won't have money until pay day.

5. 엄마가 날씨가 춥**다고** 했어요.
   Mother said the weather is cold.

   > 해요 can be used to say "they say" instead of 했어요 "they said".

6. 모두가 맥도날드의 커피가 맛있**다고** 해요.
   Everyone says McDonald's coffee tastes good.

7. 경찰이 근처에 위험한 범죄자가 있**다고** 했어요.
   The police said there is a dangerous criminal in the area.

Example Q&A

1. **Schoolmates talking about a family trip.**

   Q: 아버지는 왜 여행을 취소했어요?
   A: 비행기 표가 너무 비싸**다고** 했어요.
   A: 호텔이 바다에서 너무 멀**다고** 했어요.

   Q: Why did your father cancel the trip?
   A: He said airplane tickets are too expensive.
   A: He said the hotel is too far away from the ocean.

2. **선배 talking to 후배.**

   Q: 아바타를 보자!
   A: 좋아요! 친구가 아바타가 재미있**다고** 했어요.
   A: 좋아요. 그런데 친구가 아바타가 재미없**다고** 했어요.

   Q: Let's watch Avatar!
   A: Okay! My friend said Avatar was interesting.
   A: Okay. However my friend said Avatar was uninteresting.

● 13-4. Indirect speech (ADJECTIVE PAST) ~다고

Past tense indirect speech for adjectives is made by adding ~다고 after the past tense stem.

Indirect Speech (Adjectives)	PAST
past tense stem + 다고	

느리다 → 느렸다고
slow   (said) it **was** slow

밝다 → 밝았다고
bright   (said) it **was** bright

1. 비싸다 → 비쌌다고	4. 재미있다 → 재미있었다고
2. 많다 → 많았다고	5. 화가나다 → 화가났다고
3. 외롭다 → 외로웠다고	6. 조용하다 → 조용했다고

Example sentences (adjectives PAST)

1. 아빠가 어젯밤 인터넷 연결이 너무 느**렸다고** 했어요.
   Dad said the internet connection was too slow last night.

2. 우리 엄마가 아침에 피곤**했다고** 했어요.
   My mother said she was tired in the morning.

3. 그는 제 친구 중에서 제 가방이 제일 무거**웠다고** 했어요.
   He said that out of all my friends my bag was the heaviest.

4. 아버지가 옛날에 공기가 더 깨끗**했다고** 했어요.
   My father said the air was cleaner a long time ago.

5. 삼촌이 여행 가기 전에 짐이 더 가벼**웠다고** 했어요.
   My uncle said the luggage was lighter before going on the trip.

6. 여동생이 남자들 앞에서 부끄러**웠다고** 했어요.
   My younger sister said she was embarrassed in front of boys.

7. 지금은 키가 크지만 열두 살 때는 키가 작**았다고** 했어요.
   He is tall now but he said he was short when he was 12 years old.

Example Q&A

1. **Friends discussing a concert.**
   Q: 여자친구랑 같이 콘서트에 가요?
   A: 아니요. 여자친구가 지난 번에 재미없었다고 했어요.
   A: 네. 여자친구가 지난번에 재미있었다고 했어요.

   Q: Are you going to the concert with your girlfriend?
   A: No. My girlfriend said that last time was uninteresting.
   A: Yes. My girlfriend said the last time was interesting.

2. **Friends planning a trip.**
   Q: 이 호텔은 어때요?
   A: 김민지 씨가 갔을 때는 정말 더러웠다고 했어요.
   A: 김민지 씨는 이 호텔이 아주 깨끗했다고 했어요.

   Q: How is this hotel?
   A: Minji Kim said it was really dirty when she went.
   A: Minji Kim said the hotel was very clean.

● 13-5. Indirect speech with other verbs

Now that you see how indirect speech works with 하다 to say that someone "said" something, here are some other verbs often used with indirect speech.

듣다   to hear
생각하다   to think

Example sentences

1. 저는 이것이 비싸다고 **했어요**.
   I **said** this was expensive.

2. 저는 이것이 비싸다고 **들었어요**.
   I **heard** this is expensive.

   > 듣다 and 하다 often use *past tense* in direct speech but 생각하다 is most often *present tense*.

3. 프랑스가 아름답다고 **들었어요**.
   I **heard** France is beautiful.

4. 저는 이것이 비싸다고 **생각해요**.
   I **think** this is expensive.

5. 제 친구들은 제가 시끄럽다고 **생각해요**.
   My friends **think** I am loud.

Example Q&A

1. Friends talking about a new album from PSY.

Q: 새로운 앨범이 어때요?
A: 저는 아직 못 들어 봤어요. 친구는 좋다고 **생각해요**.
A: 저는 아직 못 들어 봤어요. 친구에게서 좋다고 **들었어요**.
A: 저는 아직 못 들어 봤어요. 친구는 좋다고 **했어요**.

Q: How is the new album?
A: I haven't heard it yet. My friend thinks it's good.
A: I haven't heard it yet. I heard from a friend that it's good.
A: I haven't heard it yet. My friend said it's good.

2. Friends discussing a missing friend.

Q: 민수 씨의 여자친구는 친절해요?
A: 저는 아직 못 만났지만 친절하다고 **들었어요**.
A: 한 번 만났지만 친절한 것 **같아요**.
A: 누나가 만났을 때는 불친절했다고 **했어요**.

Q: Is Minsu's girlfriend kind?
A: I haven't met her yet, but I heard she is kind.
A: I met her once, but I think she is kind.
A: When my sister met her, she said she wasn't kind.

● **13-6. Indirect speech (ADJECTIVE FUTURE) ~겠다고**

There are two common ways to make *future* tense indirect speech for adjectives. They are STEM + 겠다고 and STEM + (을) 거라고.

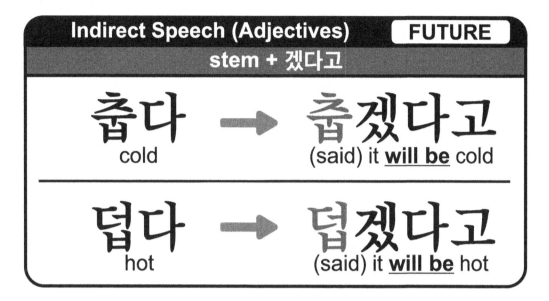

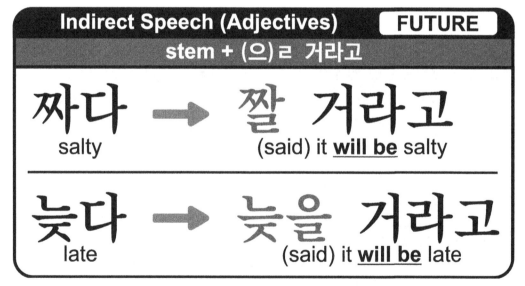

Now that we know how to create future indirect, let's take a step back and understand when to use one over the other.

~겠다 and ~을 것이다 both make assumptions of the future. However the assumptions are NOT the same.

~겠다 is used to say "it seems like it will~" or "it appears that it will~" based on experience or observation.

~을 것이다 is used to say "it will~" or "apparently it will~" based on facts rather than direct observation.

In the end BOTH versions mean something will happen in the future, the main difference being how the information was obtained.

Example sentences

1. 매일 연습을 하지 않으면 시험이 어렵**겠다고** 했어요.
   He/she said the test would be hard if you don't practice everyday.

2. 요리사가 전자레인지를 쓰면 음식이 맛없을 **거라고** 했어요.
   The cook said the food won't taste good if you use a microwave.

3. 코치가 계속 운동하면 근육이 아프**겠다고** 했어요.
   Coach said your muscles will hurt if you continue to exercise.

In the next few examples we use BASIC + 지다 (taught in book 2) to show that the item will become "more" than it is now.

4. 점원이 다음달에 핸드폰이 더 싸지**겠다고** 했어요.
   The store clerk said cell phones will get cheaper next month.

5. 수술 한 후에는 할머니가 더 편할 **거라고** 들었어요.
   I heard that my grandma will be more comfortable after surgery.

6. 아내랑 이혼하면 우울해지**겠다고** 생각해요.
   I think if you divorce with your wife you will become depressed.

7. 선생님이 한국어를 계속 공부하면 더 쉬워지**겠다고** 했어요.
   My teacher said that if I continue to study Korean it will get easier.

Example conversation

1. Two good friends trying on clothing.

   A: 이 셔츠 어때?
   B: 조금 작은 것 같아.
   A: 뭐?
   B: 너에게 너무 작겠다고 했어.

   A: How is this shirt?
   B: It think it's a bit small.
   A: What?
   B: I said it's too small for you.

Example Q&A

1. **Friends talking about another friend.**

   Q: 민지 씨는 어디에 있어요?
   A: 오늘 늦잠을 자서 늦을 거라고 했어요.
   A: 도서관에서 공부할 거라고 했어요.

   Q: Where is Minji?
   A: She said she would be late since she overslept.
   A: She said she will be studying at the library.

2. **Teachers waiting back at school.**

   Q: 학생들이 다 왔어요?
   A: 3시 전에 올 거라고 했어요.
   A: 지금 출발할 거라고 했어요.

   Q: Have all the students come?
   A: They said they would come before 3 o'clock.
   A: They said they will depart now.

● **13-7. Difference between ~다고 생각하다 and ~(으)ㄴ 것 같아요**

~다고 생각하다 can be used for 1st, 2nd, and 3rd person. However (으)ㄴ 것
같다 should not be used for 3rd person.

~다고 생각해요.

1st **좋다고 생각해요.**
I think it's good.

2nd **좋다고 생각해요?**
Do you think it's good?

3rd **친구가 좋다고 생각해요.**
Friend thinks it's good.

친구가 좋다고 생각해요?
Does friend think it's good?

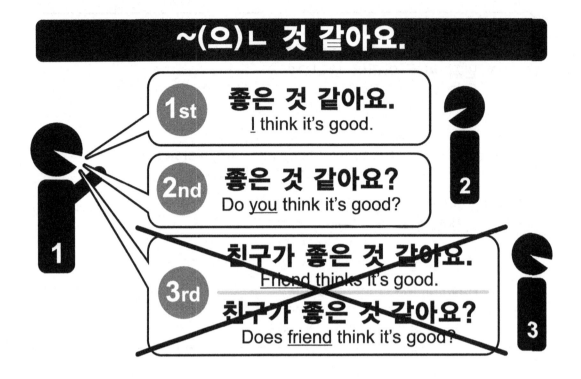

~(으)ㄴ 것 같아요.

1st 좋은 것 같아요.
I think it's good.

2nd 좋은 것 같아요?
Do you think it's good?

3rd 친구가 좋은 것 같아요.
Friend thinks it's good.

친구가 좋은 것 같아요?
Does friend think it's good?

● **13-8. 부탁하다 (to request, ask someone to do)**

TYPE	하다 verb	BASIC FORM	부탁해

부탁하다 is a very cultural word in Korean. It doesn't only mean "request".
부탁해요, or the more humble 부탁드립니다, is often used in a conversation
to have the meaning of "I leave it in your hands" or "I appreciate anything you
can do for me".

Example sentences
1. 많이 기다렸어요! 서비스로 샴페인 한 병 부탁해요.
   We waited a long time. I request one bottle of champagne for free.

2. 배가 너무 고파서 요리사에게 음식을 오 인분 부탁했어요.
   Because I was so hungry I ordered 5 servings of food.

3. 내가 어제 부탁한 보고서를 내일까지 주세요.
   Give the report I requested yesterday by tomorrow.

Example conversation between a restaurant and a customer.

1. A: 저녁을 몇 시로 예약해 드릴까요?
   B: 오후 일곱 시 부탁합니다.
   A: 몇 명 오세요?
   B: 일곱 명 예약 부탁합니다.

   > Time normally uses 에 but since this is a "time slot" it is used like a location so 로 is used

   A: What time shall I make the reservation this evening?
   B: I request 7 pm.
   A: How many people will be coming?
   B: I request a reservation for 7 people.

2. A: 오늘 수업 끝난 후에는 바빠요?
   B: 아니요. 오늘은 약속이 없어요.
   A: 그럼 제 숙제를 부탁할게요.
   B: 정중히 거절하겠습니다.

   A: Are you busy after class ends today?
   B: No. Today I have no appointments.
   A: Well then I leave my homework to you..
   B: I politely decline.

● 13-9. 생기다 (to happen, to occur, to make, to form)

TYPE	regular verb	BASIC FORM	생겨

생기다 can be used to say that an event has "happened" and also to say "made a friend" or even "made money". The thing that happens or is made is marked with 이/가.

생기다 is passive so you shouldn't use as a command to say "go make friends". Instead you should use 만들다. Depending on the sentence, 생기다 can translate to "get" or "got" to make the English sound more natural.

돈이 생기다	to make money
친구가 생기다	to make/get a girlfriend
아기가 생기다	to form a baby (to get pregnant)
시간이 생기다	to get time (time opened up)
문제가 생기다	to have a problem happen

These were originally created with 생기다 but now are words by themselves.

잘생기다	to be handsome, pretty (formed well)
못생기다	to be unattractive, ugly (not formed well)

Example sentences

1. 아르바이트를 시작한 후 돈이 많이 생겼어요.
   After starting my part-time job I made a lot of money.

2. 시험에 합격한 후 여자친구가 생겼어요.
   After I passed the test I got a girlfriend.

3. 갑자기 약속이 생겨서 바빠졌어요.
   I got busy because I suddenly got an appointment.

> Here "got an appointment" sounds better than "appointment happened".

4. 아기가 생겨서 자주 병원에 가요.
   We often go to the hospital since we made a baby.

Example conversation

1. A: 아침 먹으러 갈래요?
   B: 9시에 약속이 있지만 시간이 생기면 전화할게요.
   A: 갈 수 있으면 8시 전에 연락해 주세요.
   B: 알았어요.

   A: Do want to go eat breakfast?
   B: I have an appointment at 9 o'clock if I get some time I will call you.
   A: If you can go contact me before 8 o'clock.
   B: Got it.

2. A: 갑자기 미팅이 생겨서 오늘 데이트를 취소했어요.
   B: 중요한 미팅이에요?
   A: 네. 사장님도 나오실 거예요.
   B: 그래요? 그럼 늦지 마세요.

   A: I got a meeting all of a sudden so I cancelled my date today.
   B: Is it an important meeting?
   A: Yes. Even the president will appear.
   B: Really? So then, don't be late.

● 13-10. 이사하다 (to move (to a new place))

TYPE	하다 verb	BASIC FORM	부탁해

The place you are moving into can be marked with (으)로 or 에.

Example sentences
1. 우리 가족은 방이 다섯 개가 있는 집으로 이사했어요.
   Our family moved to a house that has 5 rooms.

2. 최근 이사한 집은 학교에서 멀어요.
   The house I recently moved to is far from school.

3. 저는 작년에 일곱 번 이사했어요.
   Last year I moved 7 times.

4. 집이 너무 작아서 더 큰 집으로 이사할 거예요.
   Because our house is so small we are moving into a bigger house.

Polite conversation between neighbors.
1. A: 언제 이사하세요?
   B: 다음 주 월요일 두시 쯤에 이사해요.
   A: 어디로 이사하세요?
   B: 회사 근처로 이사할 거예요.

   A: When are you moving?
   B: I am moving next Tuesday around 2 o'clock.
   A: Where are you moving to?
   B: I will move to a place nearby work (the company).

● 13-11. 합격하다 (to pass (a test etc))

TYPE	하다 verb	BASIC FORM	합격해

The thing that you pass is marked with 에.

Example sentences
1. 학생들 중에서 한 명만 합격했어요.
   Out of all the students only one student passed.

2. 저는 이번 시험에 합격한 줄 알았어요.
   I thought I passed this test.

3. 시험에 합격한 후에 로스앤젤레스에 갈 거예요.
   After passing the test I am going to Los Angeles.

13 | Test Yourself Activities 연습 문제

● A13-1. Fix the mistake
Correct the Korean sentence, then finish the translation on the line below.

1. 그는 제 옷이 제일 귀엽이라고 했어요.

   Korean _____

   English He said my clothes_____

2. 아버지가 내년에 새 차를 사고 싶어다고 했어요.

   Korean _____

   English My father said he wants_____

3. 저는 영화가 재미있다고 생각하지만 친구가 재미없다고 했어요.

   Korean _____

   English I thought the movie was interesting but_____

● A13-2. Listening skills
Go to **http://fromzero.com/korean/kfz3/A2** OR scan the QR code. Enter the code. Write the Korean then the English.

1. 13A **Korean** _____

   English _____

2. 13B **Korean** _____

   English _____

3. 13C **Korean** _____

   English _____

● **A13-3. Fill in the blanks**
Fill in the missing word or particle based on the English sentence.

1. 선생님은 시험이 내일_____ 했어요?
   Did the teacher say the test is tomorrow?

2. 그 남자가 남자친구가 _____ 했어요.
   He said that boy wasn't her boyfriend.

3. 친구에게 싸이 콘서트 티켓이 너무 비싸다고 _____.
   I heard from a friend that Psy concert tickets are too expensive.

4. 생일 파티는 무슨 _____ 했어요?
   What day of the week did they say the party is?

5. 그녀가 21 살이라고 했지만 친구에게 18 살이라고 _____.
   She said she was 21 years old but I heard she is 18 from a friend.

● **A13-4. Mark and Translate**
Mark the Korean sentence without mistakes then translate it.

1. ○ 감기이라고 생각했지만 의서 선생님이 열이라고 했어요.
   ○ 감기라고 생각했지만 의사 선생님이 열이라고 했어요.
   ○ 감기라고 생각했지만 의자 선생님이 열이다고 했어요.

   Translation:_____

2. ○ 선생님이 이번 주 금요일에 수업이 없아고 했어요.
   ○ 선생님이 이번 주 금요일에 수업이 없다라고 했어요.
   ○ 선생님이 이번 주 금요일에 수업이 없다고 했어요.

   Translation:_____

3. ○ 점원은 편의점이 호텔에서 너무 멀다고 했어요.
   ○ 점원은 변의점이 호텔에서 너무 머다고 했어요.
   ○ 점원은 편위점이 호텔에서 너무 뭐다고 했어요.

   Translation:_____

13 | Self Test Answers 연습 문제 정답

● A13-1. Fix the mistake

1. 그는 제 옷이 제일 귀엽다고 했어요.
   He said my clothes were the cutest.

2. 아버지가 내년에 새 차를 사고 싶다고 했어요.
   My father said he wants to buy a new car next year.

3. 저는 영화가 재미있다고 생각했지만 친구가 재미없다고 했어요.
   I thought the movie was interesting but my friend said it wasn't interesting.

● A13-2. Listening skills

1. 그는 제 친구중에서 제 가방이 제일 무거웠다고 했어요.
   He said that out of all my friends my bag was the heaviest.

2. 박민수 씨가 영화가 재미있다고 했어요?
   Did Minsoo Park say the movie was interesting?

3. 도서관에 있는 컴퓨터가 느리다고 들었어요.
   I heard the computers at the library are slow.

● A13-3. Fill in the blanks

1. 선생님은 시험이 내일이라고 했어요?

2. 그 남자가 남자친구가 아니라고 했어요.

3. 친구에게 싸이 콘서트 티켓이 너무 비싸다고 들었어요.

4. 생일 파티는 무슨 요일이라고 했어요?

5. 그녀가 21 살이라고 했지만 친구에게 18 살이라고 들었어요.

● A13-4. Best Sentence Search

1. ○ 감기이라고 생각했지만 의서 선생님이 열이라고 했어요.
   ✓ 감기라고 생각했지만 의사 선생님이 열이라고 했어요.
   ○ 감기라고 생각했지만 의자 선생님이 열이다고 했어요.
   Translation: I thought it was a cold but the doctor said it was a fever.

2. ○ 선생님이 이번 주 금요일에 수업이 없아고 했어요.
   ○ 선생님이 이번 주 금요일에 수업이 없다라고 했어요.
   ✓ 선생님이 이번 주 금요일에 수업이 없다고 했어요.
   Translation: The teacher said we don't have class this Friday.

3. ✓ 점원은 편의점이 호텔에서 너무 멀다고 했어요.
   ○ 점원은 변의점이 호텔에서 너무 머다고 했어요.
   ○ 점원은 편위점이 호텔에서 너무 뭐다고 했어요.
   The store clerk said the convenience store was very far from the hotel.

SR! Super Review and Quiz #3: Lessons 11-13

SR | Question and Answer 질문과 대답

Hide the English and try to translate the Korean. Take notes on words or grammar patterns that confuse you then review them if necessary.

1. **Q: 지금 교실에 누가 있어요?**
   A: 제 동생이 있어요. 동생은 혼자서 공부하는 것을 좋아해요.
   A: 민수가 선생님과 같이 있어요.
   A: 조지가 있는 것 같아요.

   Q: Who is in the classroom now?
   A: My sibling is there. I think my sibling likes studying alone.
   A: Minsoo is there with the teacher.
   A: I think George is there.

2. **Q: 왜 마스크를 꼈어요?**
   A: 아침부터 아파서 마스크를 꼈어요.
   A: 저는 감기가 걸리면 항상 마스크를 껴요.
   A: 여자친구가 마스크를 끼면 멋있어 보인다고 했어요.

   Q: Why did you put on a mask?
   A: I put a mask on because I have been sick from this morning.
   A: I always where I mask when (if) I catch a cold.
   A: My girlfriend said that I look cool if I wear a mask.

3. **Q: 새로 산 컴퓨터는 어때요?**
   A: 좋아요. 남자친구도 좋다고 생각해요.
   A: 빨라요. 하지만 너무 비싸다고 생각해요.
   A: 별로예요... 좀 느린 것 같아요.

   Q: How is the new computer that you bought?
   A: It's good. My boyfriend also thinks it's good.
   A: It's fast. But I think it's too expensive.
   A: No so good... I think it's a bit slow.

4. **Q: 내일 무엇을 입을 거예요?**
   A: 양복을 입고 넥타이를 맬 거예요.
   A: 출근을 안 해서 편한 옷을 입을 거예요.
   A: 새로 산 옷을 입고 부츠를 신을 거예요.

Q: **What are you going to wear tomorrow?**
A: I will wear a suit and put on a tie.
A: Because I am not going to work, I will put on comfortable clothes.
A: I will wear the new clothing I bought, and wear boots.

SR | Conversation 대화 K-E

Hide the English and try to translate the Korean. Take notes on words or grammar patterns that confuse you then review them if necessary.

1. **Polite conversation at the Pizza Hut in Myeongdong.**

   A: 피자 한 조각만 주세요.

   B: 두 조각을 사면 서비스로 한 조각을 드려요.

   A: 그래요? 한판을 사면 무슨 서비스가 있어요?

   B: 한판을 더 드려요. 한판 드릴까요?

   A: 당연하죠!

   A: Just one slice of pizza please.

   B: If you buy 2 slices I will give you 1 slice for free (as service).

   A: Is that so? If I buy one pizza what do I get (what service is there)?

   B: I will you give one more pizza. Shall I get you one (pizza)?

   A: Of course!

2. **Polite conversation between girlfriends.**

   A: 오늘 중요한 약속이 있어요?

   B: 결혼 기념일 (anniversary) 이에요.
      그래서 향수를 뿌리고 귀걸이를 했어요.

   A: 그 귀걸이는 어디에서 샀어요?

   B: 남편이 백화점에서 샀다고 했어요.

   A: Do you have any important appointments today?

   B: It's my wedding anniversary.
      So I will put on perfume and earrings.

   A: Where did you buy those earrings?

   B: My husband said he bought them at the department store.

3. **Polite conversations with a student studying to be a lawyer.**

   A: 시험에 합격한 후 시간이 생기면 무엇을 할 거예요?

   B: 먼저 새 집으로 이사할 거예요.

   A: 우리 아버지가 다음 달부터 새 집은 비싸질 거라고 했어요.

   B: 그래요? 다시 생각해볼게요.

   A: After you pass the test if you have time what will you do?

   B: First I want to move to a new house.

   A: My father said new houses will get expensive from next month.

   B: Is that so? I'll consider it again.

4. **Polite conversation between a girl and her jerk boyfriend.**

   토니: 지윤 씨는 화장을 하면 더 예쁜 것 같아요.

   지윤: 그래요? 우리 엄마는 화장을 지우면 더 예쁘다고 했어요.

   토니: 아닌것 같아요. 집에서만 화장을 지우세요.

   지윤: 알겠어요. 토니 씨를 만날 때는 꼭 화장을 할게요.

   Tony: I think you are prettier when (if) you put on make-up.

   Jiyoon: Is that so? My mother said I'm prettier when I remove my make-up.

   Tony: I don't think so. Please only remove your make-up at home.

   Jiyoon: Got it. Only when I meet you, I will definitely put on make-up.

5. **Polite conversation between friends.**

   A: 미나 씨는 무슨 악기를 연주 할 수 있어요?

   B: 하모니카와 플루트를 불 수 있어요.

   A: 저는 하모니카보다 플루트를 더 좋아해요.

   B: 하모니카를 연주하는 것은 간단해요.

   A: 다음에 같이 연주해요.

   A: Which instrument can you play Mina?

   B: I can play the harmonica and the flute.

   A: I like the harmonica more than the flute.

   B: Playing the harmonica is easy.

   A: Let's play together next time.

SR | Quiz Yourself 퀴즈

● **1. Clothing – Verb match**
Fill in the verbs that can be used for each of the items in the chart.

Item	to put on	to take off
장갑	_____	_____
손목시계	_____, _____, 하다	_____
구두, 신발	_____	_____
목도리	_____, 하다	벗다, _____
모자	_____	_____

Item	to put on	to take off
바지	_____	_____
반지	_____, 하다	_____
원피스	_____	_____
벨트	_____, 착용하다	벗다, _____
셔츠	_____	_____
넥타이	_____, 하다	벗다, _____

● **2. Picture perfect**
Circle the letter that matches the picture.

A. 하얀 드레스를 입었어요.
B. 하얀색 드레스를 꼈어요.
C. 흰색 드레스를 해요.
D. All of the above.
E. None of the above.

A. 넥타이를 꼈어요.
B. 헬맷을 찼어요.
C. 넥타이를 썼어요.
D. 헬맷을 썼어요.
E. None of the above.

A. 벨트를 했어요.
B. 벨트를 맸어요.
C. 벨트를 착용했어요.
D. All of the above.
E. None of the above.

A. 안경을 찼어요.
B. 안경을 썼어요.
C. 안경을 꼈어요.
D. B and C are correct.
E. A and B are correct.

● **3. Reading comprehension**
Read the following selection then answer the questions.

저희 가족은 악기를 연주하는 것이 취미예요. 아버지는 드럼을 치고, 어머니는 피아노를 잘 치세요. 제 여동생은 아직 어려서 악기를 연주할 수 없지만 템버린을 좋아해요. 저는 치는 것보다 부는 것이 좋아요. 그래서 트럼펫을 배우고 있어요. 가족과 같이 연주하는 게 제 꿈입니다.

1. 이 가족의 취미는 음악을 듣는 것이에요? 아니면 뭐예요?

_____

2. 어머니는 무슨 악기를 연주해요?

_____

3. 여동생은 무슨 악기를 연주해요?

_____

4. 이 사람은 무슨 꿈을 가지고 있어요?

_____

● **4. Instruments – Verb match**
Circle which verb means "to play" for each instrument below.

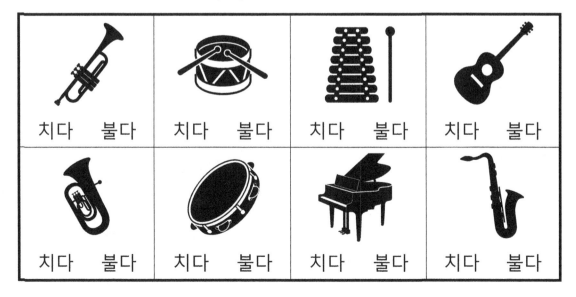

치다　불다	치다　불다	치다　불다	치다　불다
치다　불다	치다　불다	치다　불다	치다　불다

● **5. English to Korean Translation**

Translate the following sentences into Korean.

1. My father said that this present isn't expensive.

   _____

2. When I was 5 years old my cousin said he was a ghost. I was scared!

   _____

3. I heard that Paris is beautiful in the summer.

   _____

4. My aunt said that after their trip their luggage got very heavy.

   _____

SR | Answer Key 해답

● 1. Clothing – Verb match (answers)

Item	to put on	to take off
바지	입다	벗다
반지	끼다, 하다	빼다
원피스	입다	벗다
벨트	매다, 착용하다	벗다, 풀다
셔츠	입다	벗다
넥타이	매다, 하다	벗다, 풀다
장갑	끼다	벗다
손목시계	끼다, 차다, 하다	벗다
구두, 신발	신다	벗다
목도리	매다, 하다	벗다, 풀다
모자	쓰다	벗다

● 2. Picture perfect (answers)
1. A   2. D   3. D   4. D

● 3. Reading comprehension (answers)
Playing instruments is a hobby for my family. My father plays the drums, and my mother can play the piano well. My younger sister is still young so she can't play an instrument but she likes the tambourine. I like striking more than blowing. So I am learning the trumpet. Performing with my family is my dream.

1. Translation: Is this family's hobby listening to music? If not, what is it?
   Answer: 악기를 연주하는 (게, 것이) 취미예요.

2. Translation: What instrument does the mother play?
   Answer: 피아노를 쳐요 / 치세요.

3. Translation: What instrument does the younger sister play?
   Possible answers:
   ① 아직 어려서 악기를 연주 안 해요. ② 아직 어려서 악기를 연주 할 수 없어요. ③ 아직 어려서 악기를 연주 못 해요.

4. Translation: What dream does this person have?
   Answer: 가족이랑 같이 연주 하는 것이에요.

● 4. Instruments – Verb match (answers)

불다	치다	치다	치다
불다	치다	치다	불다

● 5. English to Korean Translation (answers)

1. My father said that this present isn't expensive.
    제 아버지 (아빠)가 이 선물은 비싸지 않다고 했어요.
    제 아버지 (아빠)가 이 선물은 안 비싸다고 했어요.

2. When I was 5 years old my cousin said he was a ghost. I was scared!
    제가 다섯 살 때 사촌은 귀신이라고 (말)했어요. 무서웠어요.

3. I heard that Paris is beautiful in the summer.
    파리가 여름에 아름답다고 들었어요.

4. My aunt said that after their trip their luggage got very heavy.
    제 이모/고모가 여행 후에 짐이 무거워졌다고 했어요.

14 Lesson 14: Easy to do, Hard to do

14 | New Words 새로운 단어

New Nouns etc.

그림	drawing, painting
웃음	laughter
막내	youngest (child)
급우	classmate
얘기	talk, story (same as 이야기)
여기저기	here and there
재료	ingredients
가능성	possibility, likelyhood
이기적	selflish
자연	nature
교통사고	traffic accident

New Adverbs

제대로	properly

New Adjectives

즐겁다	to be joyful
신선하다	to be fresh

New Verbs

기대하다	to expect
느끼다	to feel
숨을 쉬다	to breathe
그리다	to draw, to paint
씻다	to wash

14 | Grammar and Usage 문법과 사용법

● 14-1. ~기 쉽다/어렵다/좋다/싫다/ Hard / easy to do

We learned how to make a verb into a noun in a prior lesson and now we will learn another very common way. Regardless of if there is a 받침 or not you simply add 기 to the stem of the verb.

먹기 (eating)   하기 (doing)   읽기 (reading)   가기 (going)

Once you have made the 기 form you can add some common adjectives. You can have 가 or 는 for added emphasis after 기 but it's often omitted.

Example sentences

1. 하기 쉽다   easy to eat
2. 하기 어렵다   hard to eat
3. 하기 좋다   good to eat
4. 하기 싫다   don't like to do / don't want to do
5. 하기 힘들다   tough to do / exhausting to do

하기 싫다 is stronger than 하고 싶지않다 and has a bit more emotion.

In book 2 lesson 11 we learned how to express other people's emotion. The same rules apply here. You must use BASIC + 하다 form for other people's emotion.

> 싫어해요 is used instead of just 싫어요 since it isn't 1st person perspective.

Example sentences

1. 우리 막내가 학교에 가기 싫어해요.
   Our youngest doesn't like going to school.

2. 수영장에서는 수영하기 쉽지만 바다에서는 수영하기 어려워요
   It's easy to swim in a pool, but it's hard to swim in the ocean.

3. 한국 음식중에서 김치가 제일 먹기 싫어요.
   Out of all Korean foods, kimchi is the one I don't want to eat the most.

4. 불고기는 맛있지만 만들기는 어려워요.
   Bulgogi is delicious but making it is difficult.

5. 뉴욕에서는 운전하기 힘들어요.
   It's tough to drive in New York.

6. 중국어는 쓰기 쉽지 않아요.
   Chinese isn't easy to write.

● 14-2. ~(으)면서 While doing something

In a prior lesson we learned ~는 동안 to say "during the time of on action". The difference between ~는 동안 and ~(으)면서 is that for ~(으)면서 the person doing the simultaneous actions MUST be the same person.

Example sentences

1. 밥을 먹으면서 말하지 마세요.
   Don't talk while eating.

2. 운전하면서 문자를 보내면 위험해요.
   It's dangerous to send texts while driving.

3. 커피를 마시면서 소설을 읽었어요.
   I read a novel while drinking coffee.

> 물다 means "to bite".

4. 우리 개가 공을 물고 여기저기 달리고 있어요.
   My dog is running here are there while biting a ball.

5. 우리 엄마는 요리하면서 항상 친구랑 전화로 얘기해요.
   My mother always talks with her friends on the phone while she cooks.

● 14-3. 즐겁다 (to be joyful, enjoyable)

TYPE	ㅂ irregular adjective	BASIC FORM	즐거워

Example sentences

1. 친구와 일을 할 때는 항상 즐거워요.
   When I work with my friend it's always enjoyable.

2. 새로운 것을 배우는 것은 즐거워요.
   It's enjoyable to learn new things.

3. 여행은 힘들지만 즐거울 거예요.
   Travel is exhausting but it will be enjoyable.

Example Q&A

1. **Q: 이번 여행에서 뭐가 제일 즐거웠어요?**
   A: 맛있는 한국음식을 먹는 게 제일 즐거웠어요.
   A: 새 친구를 많이 사귀어서 즐거웠어요.

   Q: What was most enjoyable on this trip?
   A: Eating delicious Korean food was the most enjoyable.
   A: It was enjoyable because I made many new friends.

● 14-4. 신선하다 (to be fresh)

TYPE	하다 adjective	BASIC FORM	신선해

Example sentences

1. 신선한 야채를 먹는 것은 건강에 좋아요.
   Eating fresh vegetables is good for your health.

2. 여기에 있는 과일은 신선해요?
   Are the fruits here fresh?

3. 우리 식당은 신선한 재료만 사용해서 요리합니다.
   Our restaurant only cooks using fresh ingredients.

● 14-5. 숨을 쉬다 (to breathe)

TYPE	regular verb	BASIC FORM	숨을 쉬어

Example sentences

1. 머리가 아프면 밖에 가서 신선한 공기로 숨을 쉬세요.
   If you head hurts go outside and breathe with fresh air.

2. 물 속에서는 숨을 쉴 수가 없어요.
   You can't breathe in water.

3. 그녀가 너무 아름다워서 숨을 쉴 수 없었어요.
   She is so beautiful I couldn't breathe.

4. 대도시의 공기가 더러워서 숨을 쉬기가 어려워요.
   Big city air is so dirty it's hard to breathe.

Example conversation

1. A: 회사 일이 너무 많아서 숨을 쉴 수 없어요.
   B: 그럼 보고서는 비서에게 부탁하세요.
   A: 비서는 휴가 갔어요.
   B: 그럼 돌아온 후에 일을 시작하세요.

   A: I have so much company work I can't breathe.
   B: Well then, have your secretary do the reports. (request to them)
   A: My secretary went on vacation.
   B: Well then, after she comes back start the work.

● 14-6. 가능하다 (to be possible)

TYPE	하다 regular	BASIC FORM	가능해

Example sentences

1. 매일 공부를 하면 다음 주 시험에 합격이 가능할 거예요.
   If I study every day, next week it's possible I will pass the test.

2. 방학 때 아르바이트가 가능할 것 같아요.
   I think a part-time job is possible when I have school break.

3. 가능하면 월요일에 영화를 보러 가요.
   If possible I will go see a movie on Monday.

● 14-7. 그리다 (to draw, to paint)

TYPE	regular verb	BASIC FORM	그려

The item that you are drawing or painting is marked with the object marker 을/를. A picture / painting / drawing is called a 그림, so it's very common that 그림을 그리다 are used together.

Example sentences

1. 오늘 학교에서 강아지를 그렸어요.
   Today I drew a puppy at school.

2. 내가 그린 그림은 어제 팔렸어요.
   Yesterday the painting I painted sold.

> Context will change the meaning of 그리다 to "paint" or "draw".

3. 저는 선생님보다 그림을 더 잘 그려요.
   I can draw pictures better than the teacher.

Example Q&A

1. Q: 내일은 무엇을 그릴 거예요?
   A: 여자친구의 얼굴을 그리고 싶어요.
   A: 일출을 그릴 것 같아요.
   A: 내일은 바빠서 그림을 안 그릴 거예요.

   Q: What are you going to draw tomorrow?

   A: I want to draw my girlfriend's face.
   A: I think am going to draw the sunrise.
   A: I won't draw anything tomorrow since I am busy.

● 14-8. 기대하다 (to expect, to look forward to)

TYPE	하다 verb	BASIC FORM	기대해

Example sentences

1. 생일날에 아버지에게 돈을 기대해요.
   I expect money from my father on my birthday.

> The 의 is needed here to use "with Jennifer" as a modifier of the *date*.

2. 이번 주말 제니퍼 씨와의 데이트를 기대해요.
   This weekend I am looking forward to a date with Jennifer.

Example conversation

1. A: 이번 생일에 선물로 무슨 것을 받고 싶어요?
   B: 부모님께서 생일에 좋은 것을 줄 거라고 기대해요.
   A: 기대하는 선물은 뭐예요?
   B: 현금을 받으면 좋을 것 같아요.

   A: For this birthday what type of thing do you want to get as a gift?
   B: I am expect that my parents will give me something good.
   A: What is the gift you are expecting?
   B: I think if I get cash it will be good.

● 14-9. Attribute words 성 and the power of 한자

In book 2 lesson 9 we learned how 한자 (Chinese characters) affects the Korean language. Knowing the 한자 of a word can give you the capability to understand a word without ever searching a dictionary.

Many words (not all) with the suffix 성 come from the 한자 for 性 which means "nature of" or "characteristic". When it is combined with familiar words you can sometimes easily guess the meaning of the word.

In this lesson we learned 가능하다 (to be possible). When you hear 가능성 you know that the base meaning has something to do with "possible". In this case 가능성 (可能性) means "possibility". Here are some common words that use (性) 성:

필요성	必要性	necessity
중요성	重要性	importance
다양성	多樣性	diversity
위험성	危險性	riskiness, jeopardy

Example sentences
1. 교통사고 후 안전벨트의 필요성을 알았어요.
   After the traffic accident I knew the necessity of seatbelts.

2. 오늘 수업 시간에 자연의 중요성을 배웠어요.
   In today's class learned of the importance of nature.

3. 우리는 대학교에서 문화의 다양성을 공부할 거예요.
   We will study cultural diversity in college.

4. 시작하기 전에 이 일의 위험성을 생각해야 돼요.
   Before start, you must consider the dangerousness of this work.

● 14-10. 씻다 (to wash)

TYPE	ㅅ regular	BASIC FORM	씻어

Example sentences
1. 밥을 먹기 전에 손을 씻으세요.
   Before eating dinner wash your hands.

2. 식탁 위에 있는 사과를 씻어 주세요.
   Please wash the apple(s) on the table.

3. 커피를 마신 후 컵을 씻어 주세요.
   After you drink coffee please wash the cup.

● 14-11. 느끼다 (to feel, to sense)

TYPE	regular verb	BASIC FORM	느껴

느끼다 is used to say how you sense or feel about something. It is not used to say you "touched" something. The thing you feel is marked with 을/를.

Example sentences
1. 한국에 있었을 때 한국어 공부의 필요성을 느꼈어요.
   When I was in Korea I felt the necessity of Korean study.

2. 민수 씨와 있을 때 사랑을 느껴요.
   When I am with Minsoo I feel love.

3. 감기가 걸려서 맛을 느끼지 못해요.
   Because I have cold, I can't sense taste.

● **14-12. Expanding indirect speech (~고 + verb)**
We learned indirect speech last lesson. We can use this concept with many other verbs such as 기대하다 (to expect) and 느끼다 (to feel).

Example sentences
1. 이 영화가 재미있을 거라고 기대했어요.
   I expected this movie to be good.

2. 어제 외운 한국어를 다 기억할 거라고 기대하지 마세요.
   Don't expect that I will remember all the Korean I memorized yesterday.

3. 에밀리와 같이 여행하는 동안 그녀가 이기적이라고 느꼈어요.
   While travelling with Emily I felt she was selfish.

4. 민수보다 리드가 멋있다고 느껴요.
   I feel that Reed is cooler than Minsoo.

5. 항상 우리 학교가 춥다고 느껴요.
   I always feel that our school is cold.

Special Information 특별 정보

The verb doesn't always have to be said when using indirect speech. Often it can be assumed based on context. For example you might hear "뭐라고?" to mean "What did you say?".

Here are some similar examples with context to show how indirect speech can omit the verb when speaking:

Talking about a planned outdoor event
1. 내일 날씨가 추울거라고요.
   (They said / I heard) the weather will be cold tomorrow…

Talking about a boy you like
2. 여자친구가 있다고…
   (They said / I heard) they have a girlfriend…

> 요 is dropped with friends and casual situations.

Talking about a concert you want to see
3. 티켓이 이미 없다고…
   (They said / I heard) the tickets are already gone…

14 | Test Yourself Activities 연습 문제

● **A14-1. Fix the mistake**
Correct the Korean sentence, then finish the translation on the line below.

1. 화가 난 후에는 화해하기 어려다고 것 같아요.

   Korean _____

   English I think it's hard to make up_____

2. 한국어를 할 수 있으면 한국인 (한국 사람) 친구가 더 간단해요.

   Korean _____

   English It's easier to make Korean friends_____

3. 는이 만이 올 때는 운전하기 어려워요.

   Korean _____

   English It's hard to drive_____

● **A14-2. Listening skills**
Go to **http://fromzero.com/korean/kfz3/A2** OR scan the QR code. Enter the code. Write the Korean then the English.

1. 14A **Korean** _____

   English _____

2. 14B **Korean** _____

   English _____

3. 14C **Korean** _____

   English _____

● A14-3. Fill in the blanks
Fill in the missing word or particle based on the English sentence.

1. 지갑을 _____ 경찰에게 전화했어요.
   While looking for my wallet I called to the police.

2. 어제 본 영화의 제목이 _____ 어려워요.
   It's hard to say the title of the movie I watched yesterday.

3. 매일 아르바이트를 하고 있지만, 학비가 비싸서 _____요.
   I am working a part-time job everyday, but because tuition is expensive it's hard to pay.

4. 우리 선생님를 좋아해요. 그런데 그의 긴 얘기를 _____요.
   I like our teacher. But it's tough to listen to his long stories.

5. 저는 많은 사람들 앞에서 노래를 하기 _____요.
   I don't want to sing in front of a lot of people.

● A14-4. Mark and Translate
Mark the Korean sentence without mistakes then translate it.

1. ○ 시골의 공기가 너무 선선해서 숨을 쉬기 좋아요.
   ○ 시골의 공기가 너무 신선해서 숨을 쉬기 좋아요.
   ○ 시골의 공기가 너무 진전해서 숨을 쉬기 좋아요.

   Translation:_____

2. ○ 화장실에 간 후에는 손을 제대로 씻으세요.
   ○ 화장실에 갈 후에는 손을 제대로 씻으세요.
   ○ 화장실에 간 후에는 손을 제대로 씻으새요.

   Translation:_____

3. ○ 점원은 녹색 바나나가 제일 신선하다고 했아요.
   ○ 점원은 녹색 바나나가 제일 신선하가고 했어요.
   ○ 점원은 녹색 나바바가 제일 신선하다고 말했어요.

   Translation:_____

14 | Self Test Answers 연습 문제 정답

● A14-1. Fix the mistake (answers)

1. 화가 난 후에는 화해하기 어려운 것 같아요.
   I think it's hard to make up after you have been mad.

2. 한국어를 할 수 있으면 한국인 (한국 사람) 친구가 더 만들기 쉬워요.
   It's easier to make Korean friends if you can speak Korean well.

3. 눈이 많이 올 때는 운전하기 어려워요.
   It's hard to drive when it snows a lot.

● A14-2. Listening skills (answers)

1. 수영장에서는 수영하는 게 쉽지만 바다에서는 수영하기 어려워요.
   It's easy to swim in a pool, but it's hard to swim in the ocean.

2. 우리 엄마가 요리하면서 항상 친구랑 전화로 얘기해요.
   My mother always talks with her friends on the phone while she cooks.

3. 새로운 것을 배우는 것은 즐거워요.
   It's enjoyable to learn new things.

● A14-3. Fill in the blanks (answers)

1. 지갑을 찾으면서 경찰에게 전화했어요.
2. 어제 본 영화의 제목이 말하기 어려워요.
3. 매일 아르바이트를 하고 있지만, 학비가 비싸서 내기 어려워요.
4. 우리 선생님을 좋아해요. 그런데 그의 긴 얘기를 듣기 힘들어요.
5. 저는 많은 사람들 앞에서 노래를 하기 싫어요.

● A14-4. Best Sentence Search (answers)

1. ○ 시골의 공기가 너무 선선해서 숨을 쉬기 좋아요.
   ✓ 시골의 공기가 너무 신선해서 숨을 쉬기 좋아요.
   ○ 시골의 공기가 너무 진전해서 숨을 쉬기 좋아요.
   Translation: Because the country air is fresh I like to breathe it.

2. ✓ 화장실에 간 후에는 손을 제대로 씻으세요.
   ○ 화장실에 갈 후에는 손을 제대로 씻으세요.
   ○ 화장실에 간 후에는 손을 제대로 씻으새요.
   Translation: Please properly wash your hands after you go to the bathroom.

3. ✓ 점원은 녹색 바나나가 제일 신선하다고 했어요.
   ○ 점원은 녹색 바나나가 제일 신선하가고 했어요.
   ○ 점원은 녹색 나바바가 제일 신선하다고 말했어요.
   Translation: The store clerk said that the green bananas are the freshest.

14 Vocabulary Builder 단어 구축

We use many of the items listed in the following list everday.

■ Group I: Electronics 전자 제품

믹서기	blender
카메라	camera
선풍기	electric fan
전자 사전	electronic dictionary
충전기	charger
건전지	battery
토스터	toaster
녹음기	recorder
전기 칫솔	electric toothbrush
청소기	vacuum cleaner

■ Vocabulary Sentences

The following sentences will use grammar / verbs / adjectives that may or may not have been covered in this or book 1. Focus on the new vocabulary.

1. 저는 카메라로 사진을 찍는 것을 좋아해요.
   I like taking pictures with a camera.

2. 감기에 걸리지 않으려면 자기 전에 꼭 선풍기를 끄세요.
   Before you go to sleep turn off the fan so you don't get a cold.

3. 한국어를 공부할 때 저는 항상 전자 사전을 써요.
   When I study Korean I always use an electronic dictionary.

4. 건전지를 살 때 충전기도 함께 사세요.
   When you buy batteries, buy a charger together .

5. 오늘 수업시간에 녹음기로 수업을 녹음했어요.
   Today during class time I recorded class with a recorder.

6. 제 치과의사는 전동 칫솔을 사용하라고 했어요.
   My dentist told me to use an electric toothbrush.

7. 어머니께서는 하루에 한 번 청소기로 방을 청소해요.
Mother cleans the room once everyday with a vacuum.

8. 지금 남편의 셔츠를 다리미로 다리는 중이예요.
I am in the middle of ironing my husband's shirt with an iron right now.

9. 압력 밥솥으로 지은 밤은 맛있어요.
Rice that was cooked with a pressure cooker is delicious.

10. 아침마다 토스터에 빵을 구워 먹어요.
Every morning I toast bread in the toaster and eat it.

11. 빨래는 세탁기와 건조기로 해요.
Laundry is done with a washer and dryer.

12. 시원한 물은 냉장고에 있어요.
There is cool water in the refrigerator.

13. 날씨가 너무 건조해서 가습기가 필요해요.
The weather is so dry that I need a humidifier.

14. 정수기의 필터는 매 달 갈아주는 것이 좋아요.
It's good to change out the water purifier filter every month.

15. 건강을 위해서 아침마다 믹서기로 야채를 갈아 마셔요.
It's good for your health to grind vegetables in a blender and drink them everyday.

Fun With Korean:
Korean Onomatopoeia

Onomatopoeia is a word that represents the sound. Sometimes it can even represent the "sound" of something that doesn't make sound. They are used as adverbs to change the feeling of the particular action they come before.

When using Korean onomatopoeia they are often combined with the verb 거리다 which means that something is "repeating", for example a sound. There unfortunately isn't a very clear way to simply translate 거리다 so just remember that it's used with onomatopoeia.

★ Onomatopoeia 의성어

깔깔, 키득키득, 킥킥	laughing
콜록콜록	coughing
두근두근, 콩닥콩닥	heart beating
꿀꺽꿀꺽, 꼴깍꼴깍	swallowing
반짝반짝	shiny, glitter, twinkle
바삭바삭	crunching
사각사각	cutting sound
소곤소곤	whispers
욱신욱신	throbbing
부랴부랴, 허겁지겁	quickly

Example sentences
1. 부랴부랴 지하철을 내렸어요.   I quickly got off the subway.
2. 소곤소곤 말했어요.   I talked in a whisper.
3. 엄마가 깔깔 웃었어요.   Mother heartedly laughed.
4. 별이 반짝반짝 빛났어요.   The stars twinkled brightly.
5. 가슴이 콩닥콩닥 뛰어요.   My chest thumped.
6. 몸이 욱신욱신 거려요.   My body throbbed.
7. 이 샐러드는 사작사작해요.   This salad is fresh cut.
8. 물을 꿀꺽꿀꺽 마셨어요.   I gulped the water.
9. 늦어서 허겁지겁 준비했어요.   I was late so I quickly prepared.

15 Lesson 15: Anything and Anyone

15 | New Words 새로운 단어

New Nouns etc.

월말	end of month
연말	end of year
기숙사	dormitory
살	fat

New Counters

(K#) ~초	seconds
(K#) ~킬로그램	kilograms
(K#) ~킬로미터	kilometers

New Adjectives

괜찮다	to be okay, to be fine
이상하다	to be strange, weird

New Verbs

살이 찌다	to gain weight
살이 빠지다	to lose weight (become less fat)
살을 빼다	to lose weight (make effort to lose)

15 | Grammar and Usage 문법과 사용법

● 15-1. 괜찮다 (to be okay, to be fine)

TYPE	regular adjective	BASIC FORM	괜찮아

How did we not teach this already?! It's so common! Anyways… the thing you are okay with is marked with 이/가.

Example sentences

1. 제가 만든 커피는 어때요? 괜찮아요?
   How is the coffee I made? Is it okay?

2. 제니퍼는 매운 음식은 괜찮아요?
   Is spicy food okay?

3. 이 사업에 실패했지만 괜찮을 것 같아요.
   I failed at this business but I think I will be okay.

● 15-2. 이상하다 (to be strange, to be weird)

TYPE	하다 adjective	BASIC FORM	이상해

Example sentences

1. 어제 이상한 꿈을 꿨어요.
   I had a weird dream yesterday.

   새벽 means "dawn" but is anytime after midnight until dawn. In English we often just say "morning.

2. 새벽에 강남역 앞에 이상한 남자가 있었어요!
   In the early morning there was a strange man in front of Gangnam station.

3. 지난 주에 산 딸기의 맛이 이상해요.
   The taste of the strawberries I bought last week are strange.

● 15-3. Anyone, anywhere, anything
The following words are used for ambiguous places or people. The words ending in 도 must be used with a verb in a negative form, or a verb like 없다 which is negative. Vice-versa the 나 ending words are used with positive conjugations or 있다.

any (negatives + 없다)		none (positives or 있다)	
nothing / not any / anything	아무것도	anything	아무거나
no one / nobody / anyone	아무도	any body / anyone	아무나
no place / anywhere	아무 데도	any place / anywhere	아무 데나

Example sentences

1. 이 식당은 맛있는 게 **아무것도** 없어요.
   This restaurant doesn't have **any** delicious things.

2. 오늘 **아무것도** 안 했어요.
   Today I didn't do **anything**.

3. 우리 개는 **아무거나** 먹을 수 있어요.
   Our dog can eat **anything**.

4. 아버지는 **아무거나** 괜찮다고 했어요.
   My father said **anything** is okay.

5. 시험이 너무 어려워서 **아무도** 합격 못 했어요.
   Because the test was so difficult **nobody** was able to pass it.

6. 네 학교에 있는 한국어 수업은 **아무나** 다닐 수 있어?
   Can **anyone** attend the Korean class at your school? (casual)

7. 친구랑 우리 파티에 오세요. **아무나** 괜찮아요.
   Come to our party with a friend. **Anyone** is fine.

8. 화장실에 **아무도** 없어요.
   There isn't **anyone** in the bathroom.

9. 저는 오늘 밤 **아무 데도** 안 가요.
   Tonight I am not going **anywhere**.

10. **아무 데도** 가고 싶지 않아요.
    I don't want to go **anywhere**.

11. 지윤 씨가 **아무 데나** 가서 먹을 수 있다고 했어요.
    Jiyoon said she can go eat **anywhere**.

12. **아무 데나** 앉으세요.
    Sit **anywhere**.

● **15-4. Avoid a common mistake!**

나 words are most common with positives or 있다.
도 words are most common with negatives or 없다.

This rule leads to the paradox that 아무것도 and 아무거나 can BOTH mean "anything". The problem is NOT Korean but is really English.

> 1. **아무것도** 할 수 없어요. (literally: There is anything I can't do.)
>   I can't do **anything**.
>
> 2. **아무거나** 할 수 있어요.
>   I can do **anything**.

English does NOT allow double negatives. Here is a quick phrase that will help you avoid blowing up the world with a double negative paradox.

> **나 am positive. (I am positive)**

By process of elimination you know 도 is for negative. The most important thing you can do is keep your English translation matching the intent of the Korean sentence. All the sentences below essentially mean the same thing.

> 1. 화장실에 **아무도** 없어요. (literally: There isn't nobody in the bathroom)
>   No one is in the bathroom.
>   There isn't anyone in the bathroom.
>   The bathroom has no one in it.

● **15-5. New counters ~초, ~킬로그램, ~킬로미터**

All these new counters use Korean numbers in front of them. Korea uses the metric system so they will not use 마일 (miles) or 인치 (inches).

> **Example sentences**
> 1. 저는 드디어 45 킬로그램이 됐어요!
>   I am finally 45 kilograms.
>
> KTX is short for Korean Train eXpress. It's South Korea's high speed rail system.
>
> 2. 서울에서 부산까지 KTX 로 약 390 킬로미터예요.
>   It's approximately 390 kilometers by KTX from Seoul to Busan.
>
> 3. 전자레인지에 90 초 돌리세요.
>   Spin it in the microwave for 90 seconds.
>
> Koreans will say 돌리다 "to spin" in the microwave, much like we say "nuke it".

● **15-6. Indirect speech (VERB FUTURE) ~겠다고**

Future tense indirect speech for verbs uses the exact same patterns as
adjectives. One way to make future is STEM + 겠다고.

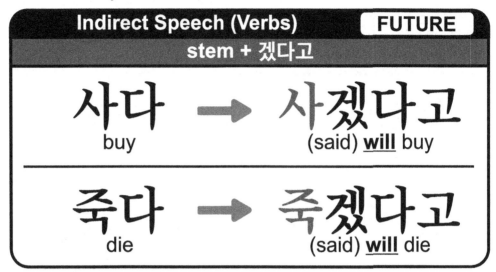

Indirect Speech (Verbs)   **FUTURE**

stem + 겠다고

사다 → 사겠다고
buy   (said) <u>will</u> buy

죽다 → 죽겠다고
die   (said) <u>will</u> die

Example Q&A (verbs PRESENT)

1. **Q: 친구가 뭐라고 했어요?**
   A: 내일 새 차를 사겠다고 했어요.
   A: 다음 주에 미국에 가겠다고 했어요.

   Q: What did your friend say?
   A: (He) said he will buy a new car tomorrow.
   A: (He) said he will go to America next week.

2. **Q: 김가영 씨가 언제 이사하겠다고 했어요?**
   A: 연말에 이사하겠다고 했어요.
   A: 월말에 이사하고 싶지만 못 하겠다고 했어요.

   Q: When did Gayeong Kim say she was going to move?
   A: She said she will move at the end of the month.
   A: She said she wants to move at the end of the month but she won't
   be able to.

3. **Q: 그가 몇 시에 오겠다고 했어요?**
   A: 오전 다섯 시에 도착하겠다고 했어요.
   A: 오후 열 시에 출발하겠다고 했어요.

   Q: What time did he say he was coming?
   A: He said he will arrive at 5 am.
   A: He said he is departing at 10 pm.

● **15-7. Indirect speech (VERB FUTURE) ~(으)ㄹ 거라고**

The other way to make a indirect future for verbs is by adding (으)ㄹ 거라고 to the stem. Both future tenses for verbs are exactly the same as adjectives.

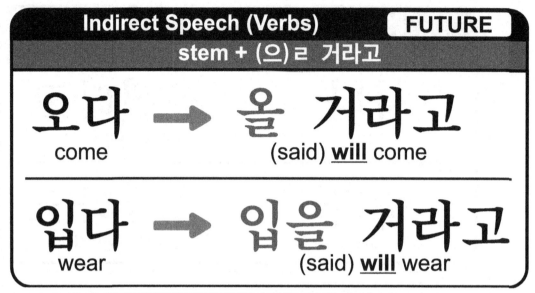

Indirect Speech (Verbs)   **FUTURE**

stem + (으)ㄹ 거라고

오다 → 올 거라고
come   (said) **will** come

입다 → 입을 거라고
wear   (said) **will** wear

Example Q&A (verbs PRESENT)

1. **친구가 뭐라고 했어요?**

   비가 오면 못 올 **거라고** 했어요.
   지하철을 타서 강남역에서 내릴 **거라고** 했어요.

   What did your friend say?

   (He) said if it rains he wouldn't be able to come.
   (He) said he will take the subway and then get off at Gangam station.

2. **누가 이 보고서를 만들 거예요?**

   제프 씨가 만들 **거라고** 했습니다.
   사장님이 다른 회사에게 부탁할 **거라고** 했어요.

   Who is going to make this report?

   Jeff said he was going to make it.
   The president said we would request to another company.

3. **여동생은 할로윈에 뭘 입을 거예요?**

   파란색 드레스를 입고 하이힐을 신을 **거라고** 했어요.
   빨간색 바지를 입고 무서운 마스크를 쓸 **거라고** 했어요.

   What is your sister going to wear on Halloween?

   She said she is going to wear a blue dress and put on high heels.
   She said she is going to wear red pants and put on a scary mask.

● **15-8. Indirect speech (VERB PRESENT) ~ㄴ/는 다고**

Present tense indirect speech for verbs is perhaps the most difficult one to master since it introduces a rule that isn't familiar to us yet. If the stem of the verb doesn't have a 받침 then you just attach a ㄴ to the bottom of it BEFORE adding 다고. If the verb stem has a 받침 then you add 는다고.

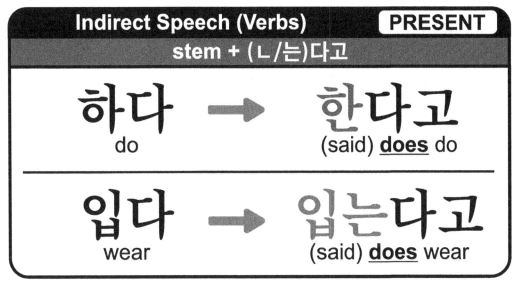

Example sentences (verbs PRESENT)

1. 친구가 매일 소설을 두 권 읽**는다고** 했어요.
   My friend said he reads 2 novels everyday.

2. 그는 저를 좋아한**다고** 했어요.
   He said he likes me.

3. 박선생님이 서울대학교에서 과학을 가르친**다고** 했어요.
   He said Mr. Park teaches science at Seoul university.

4. 그는 아기가 태어날 때부터 거의 매일 사진을 찍**는다고** 했어요.
   Since the baby was born he said he takes pictures everyday.

5. 우리 댄스 선생님은 매일 6시간 춤을 춘**다고** 했어요.
   Our dance teacher says (she) dances everyday for 6 hours.

6. 여자친구가 지금 식당에서 저를 기다린**다고** 했어요.
   My girlfriend said she is waiting for me now at the restaurant.

7. 여동생이 부끄러워서 수영할 때 비키니 위에 셔츠를 입**는다고** 했어요.
   My younger sister said that because she is embarrassed she wears a shirt over her bikini.

Example Q&A (verbs PRESENT)

1. Q: 리드 씨는 왜 한국어 잘해요?
A: 매일 한국어 학원에 다닌다고 했어요.
A: 아내가 한국 사람이라서 잘 하는 것 같아요.

Q: Why does Reed speak Korean well?
A: He said he attends a Korean language academy everyday.
A: I think he is good because his wife is Korean.

2. Q: 남자 친구가 생일에 준 목도리를 좋아한다고 했어요?
A: 날씨가 추울 때마다 맨다고 했어요.
A: 목도리의 스타일은 좋아하는데 색깔은 싫어한다고 했어요.

Q: Did your boyfriend say that he likes the scarf you gave him on his birthday?
A: He said he wears it every time the weather is cold.
A: He said he likes the style of the scarf but that he doesn't like the color.

3. Q: 숙제로 읽어야 하는 책을 언제 다 읽을 수 있어요?
A: 김 선생님이 다음 주 월요일까지 읽어야 한다고 했어요.
A: 매일 읽고 있지만 요즘 눈이 피곤해서 오랫동안 못 읽어요.

Q: When can you read the entire book that we need to read for homework?
A: Mr. Kim said we have to read it by next Monday.
A: I am reading it everyday, but these days my eyes are tired so I am unable to read for a long time.

4. Q: 집이 진짜 조용하네요. 아이들은 뭐해요?
A: 방에서 숙제를 하고 있는 것 같아요.
A: 할머니는 아이들이 지금 자고 있다고 했어요.

Q: The house sure is quiet. What are the children doing?
A: I think they are doing homework in their room.
A: Grandma said the kids are sleeping now.

5. Q: 언제쯤 미팅을 시작 하나요?
A: 한 시간 후에 시작 할 것 같아요.
A: 비서가 오 분 전에 시작했다고 했어요.

> 하나요? is a friendly sounding version of 해요? More on this later!

Q: Around when will the meeting start?
A: I think we will start in one hour (after one hour).
A: The secretary said it started 5 minutes ago.

Indirect Speech (Verbs)   **PAST**

past tense stem + 다고

가다 ➡ 갔다고

go   (said) **did** go

읽다 ➡ 읽었다고

read   (said) **did** read

Example sentences (verbs PAST)

1. 제 친구가 그 영화는 중국에서 만들었**다고** 했어요.
   My friend said that this move was made in China.

2. 아이폰이 작년보다 올해에 더 많이 팔렸**다고** 들었어요.
   I heard that the iPhone sold more this year that last year.

3. 아버지가 이미 저녁을 드셨**다고** 했어요.
   My father said he already ate.

   > Remember that 드시다 is honorific form for 먹다.

4. 그녀는 열여덟 살 때 기숙사에 살았다고 말했어요.
   She said that when she was 18 years old she lived in a dormitory.

5. 남편이 지난 달에 돈을 많이 썼다고 했어요.
   My husband said last month he spent a lot of money.

6. 이모가 감기에 걸렸다고 했어요.
   My aunt said she caught a cold.

7. 사촌이 시험에 합격했다고 했어요.
   My cousin said they passed the test.

8. 제니퍼 씨가 오늘 요가를 했다고 했어요.
   Jennifer said she did yoga today.

● **15-9. Warning about ~고 싶다**

Verbs in ~고 싶다 (want to~) form act like adjectives. This is true for all verbs using ~고 싶다.

Here are examples of how it would be wrong to treat ~고 싶다 as a verb.

Using the verb style when *direct modifying* is WRONG.

1. 읽고 싶는 책이 많아요. ← WRONG (verb style)
   (bad korean)

2. 읽고 싶은 책이 많아요. ← CORRECT (adjective style)
   There are a lot of books I want to read.

Using the verb style for *indirect speech* is wrong.
1. 조지가 먹고 싶는다고 했어요. ← WRONG (verb style)
   (bad korean)

2. 조지가 먹고 싶다고 했어요. ← CORRECT (adjective style)
   George said he wants to eat.

● **15-10. 살이 빠지다 (to lose weight) 살이 찌다 (to gain weight)**

살이 빠지다	TYPE	regular verb	BASIC FORM	살이 빠져
살이 찌다	TYPE	regular verb	BASIC FORM	살이 쪄

When saying the amount of weight you gained or lost the weight should come after 살이.

Example sentences

1. 저는 이번 여름에 살이 10 킬로그램 찐 것 같아요.
   I think I gained 10 kilograms this summer.

   > 킬로 is short for 킬로그램 and 킬로미터.

2. 고모는 병원에 있을 때 5 킬로 정도 살이 쪘어요.
   When my aunt was in the hospital she lost about 5 kilograms.

3. 살이 너무 빨리 빠지면 건강에 안 좋을 것 같아요.
   I don't think it's good for your health if you lose weight too fast.

4. 세 달 동안 아침마다 운동을 해서 살이 많이 빠졌어요.
   I exercised every morning for 3 months so I lost a lot of weight.

──Special Information 특별 정보──

If you accidentaly switch 살이 빠지다 with 살을 빼다 it won't be the end of the world, and of course Koreans would undertand you. But each have very specific usage.

살이 빠지다 is used when describing what happened with your body without any relation to your efforts. For example, if you lost weight because of a sickness 살이 빠지다 is correct.

살을 빼다 is used for weight loss that is a result of your efforts and when used it shows the effort you put towards the goal. For example if you exercised and changed your diet then 살을 빼다 works best.

In the case of personal effort to lose weight, you can still use 살이 빠지다 because it is the result of your efforts. However the feeling of the sentence changes and different information is relayed.

1. 운동해서 살이 빠졌어요. (my fat went away)
   Means: I exercised and as a result lost a lot of weight.

2. 운동해서 살을 뺐어요. (I got rid of my fat)
   Means: I execised and made myself lose a lot of weight.

Look at the next two sentences and see how another similar sentence is different based on context.

Context: We ran out of milk and soft drinks in the house.
1. 물만 마셔서 살이 빠졌어요.
   I lost weight because I only drank water.

Context: I chose not to drink water.
2. 물만 마셔서 살을 뺐어요.
   I lost weight by drinking only water.

15 | Test Yourself Activities 연습 문제

● **A15-1. Fix the mistake**
Correct the Korean sentence, then finish the translation on the line below.

1. 저는 배고프지만 아침부터 아무데나 안 먹었어요.

   Korean _____

   English I am hungry but_____

2. 친구가 만화책을 그리고 싶는다고 했어요.

   Korean _____

   English My friend said_____

3. 학교 후배가 내 이름을 벌써 잊어버린다고 했어!

   Korean _____

   English _____already forgot my name!

● **A15-2. Listening skills**
Go to **http://fromzero.com/korean/kfz3/A2** OR scan the QR code. Enter the code. Write the Korean then the English.

1. 15A Korean _____

   English _____

2. 15B Korean _____

   English _____

3. 15C Korean _____

   English _____

● A15-3. Fill in the blanks

Fill in the missing word or particle based on the English sentence.

1. 언니가 강남역에서 내릴 ＿＿＿＿＿＿ 했어요.
   My older sister said she will get off at Gangnam station.

2. 카메라를 잃어버려서 여행할 때 사진을 못 ＿＿＿＿＿ 했어요.
   They said they couldn't take any pictures when they travelled since they lost their camera.

3. 제 여자친구가 백화점 앞에서 저를 ＿＿＿＿＿＿ 했어요.
   My girlfriend said she is waiting for me in front of the department store.

4. 매일 피자를 안 먹으면 ＿＿＿＿＿＿요.
   If you don't eat pizza everyday it's easy to lose weight. (get rid of your weight)

5. 눈이 오면 ＿＿＿＿＿＿ 못 가요.
   If it rains I can't go anywhere.

● A15-4. Mark and Translate

Mark the Korean sentence without mistakes then translate it.

1. ○ 선배가 괜찮다고 해지만 아직 화가 난 것 같아요.
   ○ 선배가 괜찮다고 했지만 아직 화가 난 것 같아요.
   ○ 선배가 괜찮다고 했지만 아직 화가 난 걸 같아요.

   Translation:＿＿＿＿＿＿＿＿＿＿＿＿＿＿＿＿＿＿＿＿＿

2. ○ 여차친구랑 싸운 다음 날에 항상 화해한다고 했어요.
   ○ 여차친구랑 싸운 다음 날에 한장 화해한다고 했어요.
   ○ 여차친구랑 싸운 다음 날에 항상 화해할 가라고 했어요.

   Translation:＿＿＿＿＿＿＿＿＿＿＿＿＿＿＿＿＿＿＿＿＿

3. ○ 지윤 씨가 아무거나 가서 먹을 수 있다고 했어요.
   ○ 지윤 씨가 아무 데나 가서 먹을 수 있다고 했어요.
   ○ 지윤 씨가 아무나 가서 먹을 수 있다고 했어요.

   Translation:＿＿＿＿＿＿＿＿＿＿＿＿＿＿＿＿＿＿＿＿＿

15 | Self Test Answers 연습 문제 정답

● A15-1. Fix the mistake (answers)

1. 저는 배고프지만 아침부터 아무것도 안 먹었어요.
   I am hungry but I didn't eat anything since morning.

2. 친구가 만화책을 그리고 싶다고 했어요.
   My friend said he wants to draw a comic book.

3. 학교 후배가 내 이름을 벌써 잊어버렸다고 했어!
   My school under classman already forgot my name!

● A15-2. Listening skills (answers)

1. 새벽에 강남역 앞에 이상한 남자가 있었어요!
   In the early morning there was a strange man in front of Gangnam station.

2. 제가 만든 커피는 어때요? 괜찮아요?
   How is the coffee I made? Is it okay?

3. 아무 데나 앉으세요.
   Sit anywhere.

● A15-3. Fill in the blanks (answers)

1. 언니가 강남역에서 내릴 거라고 했어요.

2. 카메라를 잃어버려서 여행할 때 사진을 못 찍었다고 했어요.

3. 제 여자친구가 백화점 앞에서 저를 기다린다고 했어요.

4. 매일 피자를 안 먹으면 살을 빼기 쉬워요.

5. 눈이 오면 아무 데도 못 가요.

● A15-4. Best Sentence Search (answers)

1. ○ 선배가 괜찮다고 해지만 아직 화가 난 것 같아요.
   ✓ 선배가 괜찮다고 했지만 아직 화가 난 것 같아요.
   ○ 선배가 괜찮다고 했지만 아직 화가 난 걸 같아요.
   Translation: My upper classmate said it's okay, but I think he is still mad.

2. ✓ 여자친구랑 싸운 다음 날에 항상 화해한다고 했어요.
   ○ 여자친구랑 싸운 다음 날에 한장 화해한다고 했어요.
   ○ 여자친구랑 싸운 다음 날에 항상 화해할 가라고 했어요.
   Translation: He said they always make up the day after they fight.

3. ○ 지윤 씨가 아무거나 가서 먹을 수 있다고 했어요.
   ✓ 지윤 씨가 아무 데나 가서 먹을 수 있다고 했어요.
   ○ 지윤 씨가 아무나 가서 먹을 수 있다고 했어요.
   Translation: Jiyoon said she can go and eat anywhere.

15 | Vocabulary Builder 단어 구축

There are so many things in the house!

■ Group J: In the house 집안

다리미	iron
압력밥솥	pressure rice cooker
토스터	toaster
세탁기	washing machine
건조기	clothes dryer
가습기	humidifier
제습기	dehumidifier
정수기	water purifier
식기 세척기	dishwasher
김치 냉장고	kimchi fridge (most Korean houses have this)

■ Vocabulary Sentences

The following sentences will use grammar / verbs / adjectives that may or may not have been covered in any prior lesson. Sometimes you might learn something new.

1. 지금 남편의 셔츠를 다리미로 다리는 중이예요.
   I am in the middle of ironing my husband's shirt with an iron right now.

2. 압력 밥솥으로 한 밥은 맛있어요.
   Rice that was cooked with a pressure cooker is delicious.

3. 아침마다 토스터에 빵을 구워 먹어요.
   Every morning I toast bread in the toaster and eat it.

4. 빨래는 세탁기와 건조기가 해요.
   Do the laundry in the washer and dryer.

5. 날씨가 너무 건조해서 가습기가 필요해요.
   The weather is so dry that I need a humidifier.

6. 여름에는 날씨가 매우 습하게 느껴지기 때문에 제습기를 사용해요.
   Because it feels very humid in summer, I use a dehumidifier.

7. 정수기의 필터는 매 달 갈아주는 것이 좋아요.
It's good to change out the water purifier filter every month.

8. 한국에서는 김치를 김치 냉장고에 보관해요.
In Korea kimchi is stored in the kimchi fridge.

16 Lesson 16: Like this, Like that

16 | New Words 새로운 단어

New Nouns etc.

백설공주	princess Snow White
야식	late night snack

New Adjectives

하얗다	white
까맣다	black
파랗다	blue
빨갛다	red
노랗다	yellow
어떻다	how?, in what way?, what kind of?
이렇다	to be like this, this way, this kind of
그렇다	to be like that, that way, that kind of
저렇다	to be like that over there, that way, that kind of
뚱뚱하다	to be fat
통통하다	to be chubby
날씬하다	to be skinny
어지럽다	to be dizzy

16 | Grammar and Usage 문법과 사용법

● 16-1. Conjugating 'ㅎ' irregulars

There aren't that many ㅎ irregulars. We have already presented the rules for conjugating ㅎ irregulars in the beginning of this book in Lesson 2. Here is a portion of that chart.

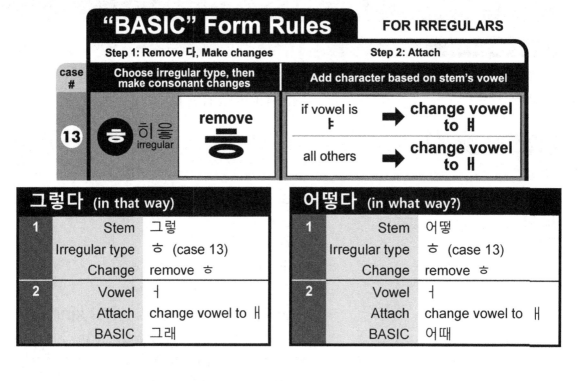

● 16-2. This way, that way etc. 이렇다, 그렇다

이렇다, 그렇다, 저렇다 and 어떻다 are all ㅎ irregulars so they conjugate as described above. They are used to state a fact or action is a certain way.

Similarly to 이것, 그것, and 저것 you choose which one to use based on the distance from the speaker or listener. However, instead of a physical object location, you choose which word to use based on the perceived distance of the ACTION or IDEA to the situation.

Example sentences (simple)
1. 어때요?   Which way is it? How?
2. 그래요.   It's that way. / It's true.
3. 이래요.   It's this way. / This is the case.
4. 저래요.   In that way (far away). (not common)

Let's look at each word one by one since they're SO heavily used in Korean.

어떻다 (how?, in what way?)

어떻다 was introduced in book 1 as just 어때요? (How is it?) and 어땠어요? (How was it?) because we needed these important questions to make relevant conversation. The usage is very straightforward.

> **Example Q&A**
> **1. Q: 어때요?**   **How is it?**
>   A: 재미있어요.   It's interesting.
>   A: 맛있어요.   It's delicious.
> **2. Q: 어땠어요?**   **How was it?**
>   A: 괜찮았어요.   It was fine.
>   A: 비쌌어요.   It was expensive.

이렇다 (in this way)

We can use combine 이렇다 with existing grammar taught so far in the Korean From Zero! series.

> **Example sentences**
> 1. 이렇다고 생각해요.   I think it's this way.
> 2. 이런 것 같아요.   I think it's like this.
> 3. 이런 줄 알았어요.   I thought it was this way.
> 4. 왜 이래요?   Why is it this way?

그렇다 (in that way)

It's not an exaggeration to say that 그렇다 is one of the MOST used words in the Korean language. It can simply mean "yes" or "I agree" or "that's right" when used as 그래. But it's real power comes in the multitudes of grammar patterns that it's used in. From this point forward and in book 4 we will introduce many of these patterns.

> **Example Q&A**
> **1. Q: 한국어는 어려워!**   **Korean is difficult.**
>   A: 그래요!   That's right!
>   A: 안 그래요!   It's not true. / That's not the case.
>   A: 그렇지 않아요!   It's not true. / That's not the case.
>   A: 그럴 것 같아요.   I think so.
>   A: 그래요?   Is that so?

Some familiar expressions you already know are made with 그렇다:

1. 그런데...   but, however
2. 그럼...   Well then / if that's the case
3. 그래서...   so / therefore / that's why

The following expressions are easily made using grammar you already know.

4. 그러면...   if that is so...
5. 왜 그래?   Why are you that way?
                                   Why is it that way?

저렇다 (in this way)

저렇다 is probably the least used of the ~렇다 words. It's used when talking about an ACTION or IDEA that isn't close to both the speaker or the listener.

Two men talking about noisy cats heard in the distance.

1. A: 왜 이렇게 시끄러워요?
   B: 저 공원에는 고양이가 많아서 시끄러워요.
   A: 매일 저래요?
   B: 네 항상 저래요.
   _____

   A: Why is it so loud like this?
   B: It's loud because there are a lot of cats in that park over there.
   A: Is it like that every day?
   B: Yes it's always that way.

● **16-3. Doing something in a certain way ~게**

If you are asked 어떻게 했어요? (How did you do it?) you can answer with 이렇게 (this way) etc while demonstrating how you did it.

Examples

1. 이렇게 먹어요.   You eat it like this.
2. 그렇게 하세요.   Do it like that.
3. 저렇게 춤을 춰봐요.   Try dancing like that (over there).

Friends looking at a drawing.

1. A: 와! 이 그림이 너무 예뻐요. 어떻게 그렸어요?
   B: 간단해요! 이렇게 그렸어요.
   _____

   A: Wow! This drawing is really pretty. How did you draw it?
   B: It's easy! I drew it this way.

Wife watching husband do housework.
2. A: 왜 그렇게 해?
   B: 몰라! 어떻게 해?
   A: 이렇게 해야 해!

   A: Why are you doing it that way?
   B: I don't know! How do you do it?
   A: You have to do it like this! (demonstrating)

Two girls walking in 신사역 which is close to many surgery clinics.
3. A: 성형수술을 할까요?
   B: 네. 하지만 저렇게 하지 마세요. (pointing at a large surgery ad)
   A: 이렇게 할 거예요. (pointing at another ad)
   B: 좋아요! 그렇게 하세요.

   A: Should I get plastic surgery?
   B: Yes. But don't do it that way.
   A: I am going to do it this way.
   B: Good! Do it that way.

16-4. Making adverbs out of any adjective using ~게

By adding 게 after any adjective stem you can turn the adjective into an adverb. Adverbs are used to modify how something is done.

Example sentences
1. 맵게 만드세요.   Make it spicy.
2. 달게 만드세요.   Make it sweet.
3. 짜게 만드세요.   Make it salty.

4. 섹시하게 춤을 추세요.   Dance sexily.
5. 귀엽게 춤을 추세요.   Dance cute(ly).
6. 멋있게 춤을 추세요.   Dance cool(ly).

7. 더 크게 말하세요.   Speak more loudly (bigger).
8. 더 착하게 말하세요.   Speak more kindly.
9. 더 부드럽게 말하세요.   Speak more softly.

10. 따뜻하게 입으세요.   Dress warm(ly).
11. 가볍게 입으세요.   Dress lightly.
12. 섹시하게 입으세요.   Dress sexily.

● 16-5. 뚱뚱하다 (to be fat), 통통하다 (to be chubby), 날씬하다 (to be thin)

뚱뚱하다	TYPE	하다 adjective	BASIC FORM	뚱뚱해
통통하다	TYPE	하다 adjective	BASIC FORM	통통해
날씬하다	TYPE	하다 adjective	BASIC FORM	날씬해

Instead of 뚱뚱하다 (to be fat) you could just call someone 통통하다 (to be chubby). Try not to be rude!

Example sentences

1. 야식을 매일 먹어서 뚱뚱해졌어요.
   I got fat because I eat late night snacks everyday.

2. 저렇게 뚱뚱한 사람은 처음 봤어요.
   It's the first time I saw such a fat person (like that).

3. 엄마는 제 동생이 좀 통통하다고 생각했어요.
   My mother thought my brother/sister was a bit chubby.

4. 우리 가족은 다 날씬해요.
   My (our) family is all thin.

Dialogue between two people starring in a KDRAMA.

1. A: 지윤 씨는 왜 남자친구가 없어요?
   B: 뚱뚱해서 남자친구가 없는 것 같아요.
   A: 안타까워요.

   A: Why doesn't Jiyoon have a boyfriend?
   B: I think she doesn't have a boyfriend because she is fat.
   A: That's unfortunate.

● 16-6. 어지럽다 (to get dizzy)

어지럽다	TYPE	ㅂ irregular adjective	BASIC FORM	어지러워

Example sentences

1. 오랫동안 달려서 머리가 아프고 어지러웠어요.
   Because I ran for a long time my head hurt and I was dizzy.

2. 감기에 걸려서 너무 어지러워요.
   I'm so dizzy because I caught a cold.

● **16-7. Becoming pretty, loud etc. (~게 되다 vs ~지다)**
With our new ~게 grammar pattern we can combine ADJECTIVE 게 + 되다 (to become) to show how something has changed.

> **Example sentences**
> 1. 우리 한국어 수업은 갑자기 어렵게 됐어요.
>   Our Korean class suddenly became difficult.
>
> 2. 우리 엄마가 전보다 착하게 됐어요.
>   My mother became kinder than before.

● **16-8. How are ~게 되다 and ~지다 different?**
Previously we learned how to say something changes using ~지다. So we can say: 추워졌어요 (It got cold.) ~지다 and 게 되다 are often used in exactly the same way by Koreans, however there are official differences.

~지다 shows change over time. The change is slow and gradual, or natural change. The exact point of change is not easily known.

> **Improved as she aged...**
> 여자친구가 예뻐졌어요.
> Girlfriend became pretty.

~게 되다 is used when the point of change is known. For example, perhaps the prices of fruit didn't raise overtime, but instead rose due to a big storm and loss of crops. In this case, 비싸게 됐어요 is better than 비싸졌어요 even though they both translate to "became expensive" in English.

> **Put on makeup and clothes...**
> 여자친구가 예쁘게 됐어요.
> Girlfriend became pretty.

◆◆◆ IMPORTANT NOTE ◆◆◆

Most Koreans don't differentiate between ~지다 and ~게 되다. As with many things, context + word usage can make both versions work in most situations despite the "official" differences. So use what makes sense to you without worrying about the academics.

● **16-9. The color verbs**

Review the section on colors in book 1 lesson 17 prior to this section.

하얗다 (white)	**TYPE**	ㅎ irregular	**BASIC FORM**	하얘

까맣다 (black)	**TYPE**	ㅎ irregular	**BASIC FORM**	까매

파랗다 (blue)	**TYPE**	ㅎ irregular	**BASIC FORM**	파래

빨갛다 (red)	**TYPE**	ㅎ irregular	**BASIC FORM**	빨개

노랗다 (yellow)	**TYPE**	ㅎ irregular	**BASIC FORM**	노래

Example sentences

> 빨다 (to wash, clean) is used for washing clothes.

1. 백설공주는 눈보다 하얀 것 같아요.
   I think Snow White is whiter than snow.

2. 운동화를 일 년 동안 빨지 않아서 까맣게 됐어요.
   Since I didn't wash my tennis shoes for a year they turned black.

3. 바다가 너무 파랗게 보여요.
   The ocean looks really blue.

4. 저렇게 빨간 사과는 처음 봐요!
   It's my first time seeing such a red apple!

5. 삼 일 동안 아파서 얼굴이 노랗게 됐어요.
   I was sick for 3 days so my face got yellow.

If you want to say something is a certain color, the most efficient way is using the noun versions of the colors. (color + 이다)

빨간색	red	파란색	blue
노란색	yellow	초록색	green
검은색	black	주황색	orange
흰색	white	보라색	purple
갈색	brown	하늘색	light blue
분홍색	pink	무슨 색깔?	which color?

● 16-10. How can I~? How do I~? 어떻게 하면~

어떻게 하면 is used to ask advice from someone.

Example sentences

1. **어떻게 하면** 돼요?	How do I do this?
2. **어떻게 하면** 갈 수 있어요?	How can I go?
3. **어떻게 하면** 좋을까요?	What can / should I do?

You can sometimes change the verb after 어떻게 to say how can I 'verb'.
However 어떻게 하면 is the most commonly used expression.

Both of the sentences below make the same point.

4. 강남역에 어떻게 가면 돼요?
   어떻게 하면 강남역에 갈 수 있어요?
   How do I go to Gangnam station?

Here are a few more examples to show you how 어떻게 하면 can be used.

Example sentences

1. **어떻게 하면** 살을 뺄 수 있어요?
   What can I do to lose weight?

2. **어떻게 하면** 한글을 잘 쓸까요?
   How can I write Hangul well.

3. **어떻게 하면** 명동까지 제일 빨리 갈 수 있어요?
   How can I get to Myeongdong in the fastest way?

4. 컴퓨터가 고장이 났을 때 어떻게 하면 돼요?
   When the computer breaks what should / can I do?

5. **어떻게 하면** 의사가 될 수 있어요?
   What can I do to be able to become a doctor?
   (How can I become a doctor?)

6. **어떻게 하면** 아이폰으로 예쁜 사진을 찍을 수 있어요?
   How can I take pretty photos on the iPhone?

---

16 | Test Yourself Activities 연습 문제

● A16-1. Fix the mistake
Correct the Korean sentence, then finish the translation on the line below.

1. 그렇게 계속 많이 먹으면 뚱뚱하기 것 같아요.

    Korean _____

    English I think you will get fat if _____

2. 어지럽다 때는 약을 먹으면 괜찮아져요.

    Korean _____

    English If you take medicine when_____

3. 제일 크게 말하지 않으면 못 들어요.

    Korean _____

    English If you don't speak louder_____

● A16-2. Listening skills
Go to **http://fromzero.com/korean/kfz3/A2** OR scan the QR code. Enter the code. Write the Korean then the English.

1. 16A Korean _____

    English _____

2. 16B Korean _____

    English _____

3. 16C Korean _____

    English _____

● **A16-3. Fill in the blanks**
Fill in the missing word or particle based on the English sentence.

1. 왜 그렇게 _____ 옷을 입었어요?
   Why are you wearing such strange clothes?

2. _____ 더 빨리 끝날 수 있어요._____
   If you do it this way you can finish it faster.

3. 저는 _____ 색깔의 모자를 쓰기 싫어요.
   I don't like wearing this kind of color hat.

4. 남동이 부끄러워서 얼굴이 _____ 됐어요.
   My little brother's face got red because he was embarrassed.

5. 우리 할아버지랑 말할 때 _____ 말해야 돼요.
   When you talk with our grandfather you have to speak loudly.

● **A16-4. Mark and Translate**
Mark the Korean sentence without mistakes then translate it.

1. ○ 저는 귀우게 말했지만 남편이 귀엽지 않다고 했어요.
   ○ 저는 귀엽게 말했지만 남편이 귀엽지 않다고 했어요.
   ○ 저는 귀엽개 말했지만 남편이 귀엽지 않다고 했어요.

   Translation:_____

2. ○ 저는 어릴 때부터 통통한 여자들을 정말 좋아해요.
   ○ 저는 이럴 때부터 통통한 여자들을 정말 좋아해요.
   ○ 저는 어릴 때부터 통통하는 여자들을 정말 좋아해요.

   Translation:_____

3. ○ 우리 아들은 좋아하는 여자를 보면 얼굴이 빨갛게 돼요.
   ○ 우리 아들은 좋아하는 여자를 보면 얼굴이 빨개게 돼요.
   ○ 우리 아들은 좋아하는 여자를 보면 올걸이 빨갛게 돼요.

   Translation:_____

16 | Self Test Answers 연습 문제 정답

● A16-1. Fix the mistake

1. 그렇게 계속 많이 먹으면 뚱뚱해질 것 같아요.
   I think you will get fat if you continuously eat so much.

2. 어지러울 때는 약을 먹으면 괜찮아져요.
   If you take medicine when you are dizzy you will get better (okay).

3. 더 크게 말하지 않으면 못 들어요.
   If you don't speak louder I can't hear you.

● A16-2. Listening skills

1. 와! 이 그림이 너무 예뻐요! 어떻게 그렸어요?
   Wow! This drawing is really pretty. How did you draw it?

2. 뚱뚱한 고양이보다 날씬한 고양이가 빨리 달릴 수 있어요.
   Thin cats can run faster than fat cats.

3. 어떻게 하면 화장을 더 예쁘게 할 수 있어요?
   What can I do to make my makeup prettier?

● A16-3. Fill in the blanks

1. 왜 그렇게 이상한 옷을 입었어요?
2. 이렇게 하면 더 빨리 끝날 수 있어요.
3. 저는 이런 색깔의 모자를 쓰기 싫어요.
4. 남동이 부끄러워서 얼굴이 빨강게 됐어요.
5. 우리 할아버지랑 말 할 때 크게 말해야 돼요.

● A16-4. Best Sentence Search

1. ○ 저는 귀우게 말했지만 남편이 귀엽지 않다고 했어요.
   ✓ 저는 귀엽게 말했지만 남편이 귀엽지 않다고 했어요.
   ○ 저는 귀엽개 말했지만 남편이 귀엽지 않다고 했어요.
   Translation: I spoke cute, but my husband said it wasn't cute.

2. ✓ 저는 어릴 때부터 통통한 여자들을 정말 좋아해요.
   ○ 저는 이럴 때부터 톰톰한 여자들을 정말 좋아해요.
   ○ 저는 어릴 때부터 통통하는 여자들을 정말 좋아해요.
   Translation: Since I was young I have really liked chubby girls.

3. ✓ 우리 아들은 좋아하는 여자를 보면 얼굴이 빨강게 돼요.
   ○ 우리 아들은 좋아하는 여자를 보면 얼굴이 빨개게 돼요.
   ○ 우리 아들은 좋아하는 여자를 보면 올걸이 빨강게 돼요.
   Translation: When our son sees the girl he likes his face gets red.

16 | **Vocabulary Builder** 단어 구축

There are so many things in just our solar system. Get off Uranus and learn them!

■ Group K: The solar system 태양계

태양계	solar system
행성	planet
왜소행성	dwarf planet
별	star
태양	The Sun
달	The Moon
수성	Mercury
금성	Venus
지구	Earth
화성	Mars
목성	Jupiter
토성	Saturn
천왕성	Uranus
해왕성	Neptune
명왕성	Pluto

■ Vocabulary Sentences

The following sentences will use grammar and words that may or may not have been covered in any prior lesson. Sometimes you might learn something new.

1. 태양계에는 여덟 개의 행성이 있어요.
   There are eight planets in the solar system.

2. 목성은 태양계에서 가장 큰 행성이예요.
   Jupiter is the largest planet in the solar system.

3. 태양은 태양계에서 유일한 별이예요.
   The sun is the only star in our solar system.

4. 해왕성은 고리들로 둘러싸여 있어요.
   Neptune is surrounded by rings.

5. 지구에는 인간이 살지만 달에는 인간이 살지 않아요.
   Humans live on Earth, however humans don't live on the moon.

6. 수성은 태양에서 제일 가까워요.
   Mercury is the closest to the sun.

7. 명왕성은 행성이 아니라 왜소행성이에요.
   Pluto isn't a planet, but it's a dwarf planet.

8. 목성은 토성보다 더 커요.
   Jupiter is bigger than Saturn.

9. 화성에는 외계인이 살고 있는 것 같아요.
   I think aliens live on Mars.

10. 토성은 아름다운 고리들로 유명해요.
    Saturn is famous for it's beautiful rings.

17 Lesson 17: Asking Permission

17 | New Words 새로운 단어

New Nouns etc.

미술관	art gallery
쓰레기	trash
담배	cigarette
하나님	God (the "one")
산타클로스	Santa Claus
일기	diary, journal
거짓말쟁이	liar
도시락	lunchbox
졸업식	graduation ceremony
외계인	alien (from another planet)

New Adverbs

조용히	quietly
아까	just now, a minute ago

New Verbs

고장이 나다	to be broken
열이 나다	to have a fever
가져가다	to take (a thing)
데려가다	to take (a person)
가져오다	to bring (a thing)
데려오다	to bring (a person)
떠들다	to make noise
믿다	to believe, to trust
담배를 피우다	to smoke
바람을 피우다	to have an affair, to cheat

17 | Grammar and Usage 문법과 사용법

● **17-1. Should, would be good if, (으)면 되다**
Before we learn the main goal of this lesson, which is "asking permission" we need to learn (으)면 되다 to prevent confusion between two similar sounding patterns.

(으)면 되다 is used to say, if a certain state is met, or if a certain action is done, there will be no problems. It's also used to say that those actions are the least that you should do to accomplish the result.

Example sentences
1. 살을 빼고 싶으면 건강한 음식을 먹으면 돼요.
    If you want to lose weight, you should eat healthy food.

2. 지윤 씨랑 죽을 때까지 같이 있고 싶으면 결혼하면 돼요.
    If you want to be with Jiyoon until you die, you should marry her.

3. 일본에 가기전에 일본어를 공부하면 돼요.
    Before you go to Japan you should study Japanese.

4. 우울할 때는 운동을 하면 돼요.
    When you are depressed, you should exercise.

> The implied goal is "not being depressed".

Example conversations
1. Q: 시험 공부를 많이 해야 돼요?
    A: 네. 하지만 수학만 공부하면 돼요.
    A: 아니요. 저는 성적이 좋아서 괜찮아요.
    A: 조금만 더 하면 돼요.

    Q: Do you have to do a lot of test study?
    A: Yes. But I only have to study math.
    A: No. Since my grades are good I'm fine.
    A: I just have to do only a bit more. (It's good if I do just a bit more)

> We are bending the English to sound natural. It translates to "It's good if I only~"

2. Q: 강남역까지 어떻게 가면 돼요?
    A: 버스를 타고 가면 돼요.
    A: 그 쪽으로 걸어가면 돼요.

    Q: How can (should) I go to Gangnam station?
    A: You should ride a bus and go.
    A: You should walk that way.

● **17-2. Asking for permission in Korean**
BASIC + 도 되다 is the pattern for asking permission to do something.
This form can translate to "May I~", "Can I~" and "Is it okay if I~".

Example sentences

1. 먹어도 돼요?	May I eat? / Can I eat?
2. 봐도 돼요?	May I see? / Can I see?
3. 앉아도 돼요?	May I sit? / Can I sit?
4. 말해도 돼요?	May I speak? / Can I speak?
5. 가도 돼요?	May I go? / Can I go?

If someone asks you permission and you are answering YES then the
following pattern is used.

Example sentences

1. 네 먹어도 돼요.	Yes, you may eat. / You can eat.
2. 네 봐도 돼요.	Yes, you may see. / You can see.
3. 네 앉아도 돼요.	Yes, you may sit. / You can sit.
4. 네 말해도 돼요.	Yes, you may speak. / You can speak.
5. 네 가도 돼요.	Yes, you may go. / You can go.

To tell someone that they do NOT have permission, the pattern changes to:
~(으)면 안 되다. You can also simply tell someone to not do something using
this pattern. It's another way to say "Don't do~".

Example sentences

1. 아니요 먹으면 안 돼요.	No, you may not eat. / You can't eat.
2. 아니요 보면 안 돼요.	No, you may not see. / You can't see.
3. 아니요 앉으면 안 돼요.	No, you may not sit. / You can't sit.
4. 아니요 말하면 안 돼요.	No, you may not speak. / You can't speak.
5. 아니요 가면 안 돼요.	You may not go. / You can't go.

If you are answering a "Can I" question, then you can drop 네 (yes) and
아니요 (no) since it's understood.

● 17-3. 믿다 (to trust, to believe)

믿다	TYPE	regular verb	BASIC FORM	믿어

Example sentences

1. 하나님을 믿어요?
   Do you believe in God?

2. 그를 다시 믿으면 후회할 것 같아요.
   If I trust him again I think I will regret it.

3. 널 못 믿어!
   I don't believe you!

> You can put the IDEA that someone believes as indirect speech and combine it with 믿다.

> With ㄹ irregular verbs, ㄹ is dropped then ㄴ added.

4. 정말로 외계인이 지구에 산다고 믿어요?
   Do you really believe that aliens are living on Earth?

5. 우리 아이들은 어릴 때 산타클로스를 믿었지만 지금은 안 그래요.
   Our children believed in Santa Claus when they were young but now that isn't the case.

● 17-4. 담배를 피우다 (to smoke cigarettes), 바람을 피우다 (to have an affair, to cheat)

담배를 피우다	TYPE	regular verb	BASIC FORM	담배를 피워
바람을 피우다	TYPE	regular verb	BASIC FORM	바람을 피워

피우다 by itself has other meanings and usages for example you can "make a fire" with 불을 피우다 or "stir up dust" with 먼지를 피우다.

The 바람 from 바람을 피우다 does not mean "wind". 바람 actually means "relationship" in this case. So in a sense you are "fostering" or "stirring up" your "relationship" when you have an affair.

It's common that over time words that started out as slang or popular expressions become an official part of the language.

From the 표준국어대사전 (Standard Language Encyclopedia) operated by the 국립국어원 (The National Institute of Korean Language) they list 바람을 피우다 as just 바람피우다. So while it's interesting to know the history of how a common verb was made, you could spend a lot of time like we did researching each verb.

In the end it's more important that you know what something means and not the history of it! Now on to some example sentences!

Example sentences

1. 담배를 피우면 건강에 나빠요.
   It's not good for your health if you smoke.

2. 병원에서는 절대 담배를 피우지 마세요.
   Never smoke at the hospital.

3. 남자친구가 제 친구와 바람을 피운 것 같아요.
   I think my boyfriend cheated with my friend.

Example Q&A
1. **Q: 왜 담배를 피워요?**
   A: 담배를 피우면 기분이 좋아져요.
   A: 그냥 멋있어 보여서 담배를 피워요.
   A: 여자친구가 피워서 저도 담배를 피워요.

   Q: Why do you smoke?
   A: I feel better when I smoke.
   A: I smoke just because it looks cool.
   A: Because my girlfriend smokes, I also smoke.

> **A note from us.**
> 1. Smoking only feels good if you are addicted.
> 2. Smoking isn't cool.
> 3. Smoking won't get you a girlfriend.
> 4. None of us at Korean From Zero smoke!

Conversation: A woman confronts her boyfriend.
1. A: 어젯밤에 뭐했어?
   B: 도서관에서 공부 했어.
   A: 거짓말쟁이! 너랑 다른 여자가 담배 피우는 걸 봤어!
   B: 미안해. 하지만 바람을 피우지는 않았어.
   A: 믿어도 돼?

   A: What did you do last night?
   B: I studied at the library.
   A: Liar! I saw you smoking with a different girl!
   B: I'm sorry. But I didn't cheat.
   A: Can I trust you?

> Adding 는 after 지 makes it stronger emphasis.

● **17-5. ~(으)니까 Because (reason)**
We have been using 그래서 (because) and BASIC + 서 to say "because", "since", and "so". The usage of 그래서 is limited because it can never be followed with a command or suggestion. Instead you can only say the result.

(으)니까 can do everything that BASIC + 서 does and can be followed with commands and suggestions. It's the stronger version of "because".

Example sentences

1. 건강에 나쁘니까 담배를 피우지 마세요.
   Don't smoke because it's bad for your health.

2. 너무 더우니까 시원한 것을 먹을 거예요.
   I am going to eat something cool since it's so hot.

3. 택시가 비싸니까 버스를 타면 돼요.
   You should take the bus because taxis are expensive.

4. 숙제를 다 했으니까 콘서트에 가도 돼요.
   You can go to the concert, because you did all of your homework.

5. 밥이 없으니까 빵을 먹을게.
   I am going to eat bread since we don't have any rice.

6. 담배를 피우니까 기분이 좋아졌어요.
   I feel better since I smoked.

7. 중국어가 어려우니까 한국어를 배우면 돼요.
   Because Chinese is difficult you should learn Korean.

● 17-6. 고장이 나다 (to be broken)

TYPE	regular verb	BASIC FORM	고장이 나

Example sentences

1. 제 차가 고장이 났어요.
   My car broke.

2. 어젯밤 에어컨이 고장이 나서 오늘 집이 너무 더웠어요.
   Last night our air conditioner broke so our house was really hot today.

3. 컴퓨터가 고장이 나서 숙제를 못 했어요.
   I couldn't do my homework since our computer is broken.

4. 고장이 난 컴퓨터는 필요 없으니까 버리면 돼요.
   We don't need the broken computer so you should throw it away.

5. 히터가 고장이 났지만 오늘 안 추우니까 괜찮아요.
   The heater is broken but since today isn't cold it will be okay.

Example conversation
1. A: 왜 화가 났어요?
   B: 아까 카메라가 고장이 났어요.
   A: 제 카메라를 빌려 줄까요?
   B: 괜찮아요. 아이폰으로 사진을 찍을 거예요.

   A: Why did you get mad?
   B: Just now my camera broke.
   A: Shall I lend you my camera?
   B: It's okay. I will take pictures with my iPhone.

● **17-7. 가져가다 (to take a thing), 가져오다 (to bring a thing)**

가져가다	TYPE	regular verb	BASIC FORM	가져가

가져오다	TYPE	regular verb	BASIC FORM	가져와

Example sentences
1. 저는 오늘 도시락을 가져왔어요.
   Today I brought lunch.

2. 이번 학기의 학비는 현금으로 가져오세요.
   Please bring your tuition for this semester as cash.

3. 고모의 생일날에 케이크를 가져갈 거예요.
   I am taking a cake on my aunt's birthday.

4. 오늘 저녁에 비가 올 것 같아서 우산을 가져왔어요.
   I brought an umbrella because I think it's going to rain this evening.

5. 사장님께 선물로 받은 와인을 가져가고 싶어요.
   I want to take the wine that I got as a present from the president.

Example Q&A (question asked on the phone)
1. Q: 책을 다음 주까지 가져가도 돼요?
   A: 아니요. 다음 주에 가져오면 안돼요. 내일 가져오세요.
   A: 물론이에요. 내일 가져와도 돼요.
   A: 그럼요. 다음주도 괜찮아요.

   Q: Is it okay if I bring back the book by next week?
   (note: In English "take back" sounds wrong so we used "bring back".)
   A: No. You can't bring it back next week. Bring it tomorrow.
   A: Of course. You can bring it back tomorrow.
   A: Sure. Next week is also okay.

● **17-8. 데려가다 (to take a person), 데려오다 (to bring a person)**

데려가다	TYPE	regular verb	BASIC FORM	데려가

데려오다	TYPE	regular verb	BASIC FORM	데려와

데려가다 and 데려오다 usage is exactly the same as 가져가다 and 가져오다 except that 데려~ is used for people and animals only and 가져~ can only be used for non-living things.

Example sentences
1. 미술관에 동물이나 아이들을 데려오지 마세요.
   Don't bring animals or children to the art gallery.

2. 생일 파티에 새로 생긴 남자친구를 데려갈 것 같아요.
   I think I will take my new boyfriend to the birthday party.

3. 졸업식에 부모님을 데려갈 거예요.
   I am taking my parents to my graduation ceremony.

> 시끄럽다 can also mean "bothersome"

4. 시끄러우니까 교회에 강아지를 데려오면 안 돼요.
   You shouldn't bring your puppy to church because it will be bothersome.

● **17-9. 열이 나다 (to have a fever)**

TYPE	regular verb	BASIC FORM	열이 나

Example sentences
1. 오늘 학교에서 시험을 볼 때 어지럽고 열이 났어요.
   Today when I was taking the test at school I got dizzy and got a fever.

2. 열이 나면 이 약을 먹으면 돼요.
   If you get a fever you should take this medicine.

3. 얼굴이 빨개서 열이 나는 줄 알았어요.
   I thought you had a fever because your face was red.

● **17-10. 조용히 하다 (to be quiet)**

TYPE	하다 adjective	BASIC FORM	조용히 해

조용히 하다 is really just 조용히 (quietly) in front of 하다. We only have it here to represent the opposite of 떠들다 (to make a noise).

Example sentences
1. 미술관 안에서는 조용히 하세요.
   Be quiet inside the art gallery.

2. 아기들이 잠을 자서 조용히 해야 돼요.
   Because the children are sleeping we have to be quiet.

● **17-11. 떠들다 (to make noise, to clamour)**

TYPE	ㄹ irregular verb	BASIC FORM	떠들어

Example sentences
1. 아버지께서 주무시니까 떠들면 안 돼요.
   Because father is sleeping you shouldn't make any noise.

2. 아이들은 공원에서 시끄럽게 떠들었어요.
   The children clamoured loudly in the park.

Special Information 특별 정보

When telling someone that they can't do something, you can completely remove the verb and just say 안 돼요. 안 돼요, and the informal 안 돼 are strong ways to say "no" in Korean.

Example Q&A
1. Q: 네 일기를 읽어도 돼?   Can I read your diary?
   A: 안 돼!   No!

2. Q: 이거 먹어도 돼요?   Can I eat this?
   A: 안 돼요.   No.

3. Q: 술을 마셔도 됩니까?   Can I drink alcohol?
   A: 안 됩니다.   No.

17 | Test Yourself Activities 연습 문제

● **A17-1. Fix the mistake**
Correct the Korean sentence, then finish the translation on the line below.

1. 오늘 머리가 아파서 학교에 좀 늦게 가야도 돼요?

   | Korean | _____

   | English | Since my head hurts_____

2. 매일 일하기 힘드니까 이번 주말에 쉬워야 돼요.

   | Korean | _____

   | English | Because working everyday is exhausting_____

3. 돈이 없으시면 은행에 가시면 됩니다.

   | Korean | _____

   | English | If you don't have any money_____

● **A17-2. Listening skills**
Go to **http://fromzero.com/korean/kfz3/A2** OR scan the QR code. Enter the code. Write the Korean then the English.

1. 17A | Korean | _____

   | English | _____

2. 17B | Korean | _____

   | English | _____

3. 17C | Korean | _____

   | English | _____

● A17-3. Fill in the blanks
Fill in the missing word or particle based on the English sentence.

1. 선생님에게 숙제를 내면 밖에서 _____요.
   If you turn in your homework to the teacher you can play outside.

2. 고속도로에서 차가 _____서 집까지 걸어갔어요.
   I walked all the way to my house because my car brokedown on the highway.

3. 선생님이 지금 _____ 조용히 하세요.
   Be quiet since the teacher is talking now.

4. 병원 앞에 담배를 _____요.
   You cannot smoke cigarettes in front of the hospital.

5. 정말로 일본어보다 중국어가 더 _____ 믿어요?
   Do you really believe that Chinese is more difficult than Japanese?

● A17-4. Mark and Translate
Mark the Korean sentence without mistakes then translate it.

1. ○ 우리 고양이가 개를 싫어하니까 강아지를 가져오면 안 돼요.
   ○ 우리 고양이가 개를 싫어하니까 강아지를 데려오면 안 돼요.
   ○ 우리 고양이가 개 이니까 강아지를 가져오면 안 돼요.

   Translation:_____
   _____

2. ○ 교회 안에 시끄럽게 떠들면 엄마가 화나요.
   ○ 교회 속에 시끄럽게 떠들면 엄마가 화나요.
   ○ 교회 안에 시끄롭게 떠들면 엄마가 화나요.

   Translation:_____
   _____

3. ○ 손이 제대로 씻지 않았으니까 열이 났어요.
   ○ 손을 제대로 씨지 않았으니까 열이 났어요.
   ○ 손을 제대로 씻지 않았으니까 열이 났어요.

   Translation:_____
   _____

17 | Self Test Answers 연습 문제 정답

● A17-1. Fix the mistake
1. 오늘 머리가 아파서 학교에 좀 늦게 가도 돼요?
   Since my head hurts may I go to school a little late today?
2. 매일 일하기 힘드니까 이번 주말에 쉬어야 돼요.
   Because working everyday is exhausting, I must rest this weekend.
3. 돈이 없으시면 은행에 가시면 됩니다.
   If you don't have any money you should go to the bank.

● A17-2. Listening skills
1. 위험하니까 수영장에 아기를 데려가지 마세요.
   Don't take your baby to the pool because it's dangerous.
2. 좀 어려운 질문을 물어봐도 돼요?
   Is it okay if I ask a bit of a hard question?
3. 강남역까지 어떻게 가면 돼요?
   How can (should) I go to Gangnam station?

● A17-3. Fill in the blanks
1. 선생님에게 숙제를 내면 밖에서 놀면 돼요.
2. 고속도로에서 차가 고장이 나서 집까지 걸어갔어요.
3. 선생님이 지금 말하니까 조용히 하세요.
4. 병원 앞에 담배를 피우면 안 돼요.
5. 정말로 일본어보다 중국어가 더 어렵다고 믿어요?

● A17-4. Best Sentence Search
1. ○ 우리 고양이가 개를 싫어하니까 강아지를 가져오면 안 돼요.
   ✓ 우리 고양이가 개를 싫어하니까 강아지를 데려오면 안 돼요.
   ○ 우리 고양이가 개 이니까 강아지를 가져오면 안 돼요.
   You shouldn't bring your puppy because our cat doesn't like dogs.

2. ✓ 교회 안에 시끄럽게 떠들면 엄마가 화나요.
   ○ 교회 속에 시끄럽게 떠들면 엄마가 화나요.
   ○ 교회 안에 시끄롭게 떠들면 엄마가 화나요.
   Translation: If you loudly make noise in the church Mom will get mad.

3. ○ 손이 제대로 씻지 않았으니까 열이 났어요.
   ○ 손을 제대로 씨지 않았으니까 열이 났어요.
   ✓ 손을 제대로 씻지 않았으니까 열이 났어요.
   Translation: You got a fever because you didn't properly wash your hands.

SR! Super Review and Quiz #4: Lessons 14-17

SR | Question and Answer 질문과 대답

Hide the English and try to translate the Korean. Take notes on words or grammar patterns that confuse you then review them if necessary.

1. **Q: 수학 시험 공부를 많이 했어요?**
   A: 네, 언니가 도와줘서 공부하기 쉬웠어요.
   A: 아니요, 머리가 아프고 어지러워서 공부하기 어려웠어요.
   A: 아니요. 시험 보기 30분 전에 공부하면 돼요.

   Q: Did you do a lot of math test study?
   A: Yes, my older sister helped me so it was easy to study.
   A: No, my head hurt and I was dizzy so it was hard to study.
   A: No, it's okay if I study 30 minutes before taking the test.

2. **Q: 어제 본 영화는 어땠어요?**
   A: 영화가 슬플 거라고 생각했지만 별로 안 슬펐어요.
   A: 이상했어요. 재미있을 거라고 기대하지 마세요.
   A: 괜찮았어요. 많은 사람들이 지루하다고 했지만 재미있었어요.

   Q: How was the movie you saw yesterday?
   A: I thought the movie would be sad, but it wasn't that sad.
   A: It was weird. Don't expect it to be interesting.
   A: It was okay. Maybe people said it was boring, but it was interesting.

3. **Q: 어떻게 살을 뺐어요?**
   A: 기숙사의 밥이 맛없어서 살을 빼기 쉬웠어요.
   A: 몰라요. 매일 야식을 먹어서 살이 찔 거라고 생각 했지만 살이 빠졌어요.
   A: 저녁 7시부터는 아무것도 먹지 않고 물만 마셨어요.

   Q: How did you lose weight?
   A: It was easy to lose weight since the dorm food is not good (tasteless)
   A: I don't know. I ate late night snacks everyday so I thought I would gain weight but I lost weight.
   A: I didn't eat anything from 7 at night and only drank water.

4. **Q: 이 컴퓨터를 써도 돼요?**
   A: 네, 그 컴퓨터를 써도 돼요.
   A: 아니요, 그 컴퓨터는 쓰면 안 돼요.
   A: 아니요, 그 컴퓨터는 고장이 났으니까 이 컴퓨터를 쓰세요.

   Q: Can I use this computer?
   A: Yes, you can use that computer.
   A: No, you can't use that computer.
   A: No, that computer is broken so use this computer.

5. **Q: 여기서 담배를 피워도 돼요?**
   A: 네, 피워도 돼요.
   A: 아니요, 여기는 미술관이니까 담배를 피우면 안돼요.
   A: 네, 피워도 되지만 담배는 건강에 나빠요.

   Q: Can I smoke here?
   A: Yes, you can smoke.
   A: No, since this is an art museum you can't smoke.
   A: Yes, you can smoke but cigarettes are bad for your health.

6. **Q: 이 색은 어떻게 생각해요?**
   A: 파래서 예뻐요.
   A: 노란색 보다 빨간색이 더 좋아요.
   A: 너무 하얘서 뚱뚱해 보여요.

   Q: How do you think about this color?
   A: It's pretty because it's red.
   A: The blue is better than the yellow.
   A: It's too white so you look fat.

SR | Conversation 대화 K-E

Hide the English and try to translate the Korean. Take notes on words or grammar patterns that confuse you then review them if necessary.

1. **A mixed conversation between an English speaker and a Korean.**
   존: 무슨 색의 눈을 좋아해?
   민지: 파란 눈이 좋아요. 존은요?
   존: 난 까만 눈이 좋아.
   민지: 그래요? 한국 사람들의 눈은 거의 다 까매요.

John: What color eyes do you like?

Minzy: Blue eyes are good. What about you John?

John: I like black eyes.

Minzy: Is that so? Almost all Korean people's eyes are black.

2. A polite conversation between an an English speaker and a Korean.

폴: 오늘 저녁 때 요리를 할 거예요?

다라: 네. 아까 여기저기서 신선한 재료를 샀어요.

폴: 한국 요리는 만들기 쉽나요?

다라: 미국 요리보다 만들기 어렵지만 요리책을 보면서 만들면 돼요.

Paul: Are you going to cook dinner today?

Dara: Yes. I just went here and there and bought fresh ingredients.

Paul: Is Korean cooking easy to make?

Dara: It's harder than American cooking but it's okay if I cook while looking at a cookbook.

3. A polite conversation between international friends.

조지: 왜 안 먹어요?

현아: 친구들이 요즘 제가 뚱뚱해졌다고 해서요.

조지: 정말로 살이 빠지고 싶으면 매일 운동을 하면 돼요.

현아: 매일 운동하는 게 어렵지만, 그렇게 해 볼게요.

George: Why aren't you eating?

Hyuna: Because my friends said recently I got fat.

George: If you really want to lose weight you should exercise everyday.

Hyuna: Exercising everyday is hard, but I will try to do so.

4. A polite conversation between friends.

미나: 왜 우산을 가지고 있어요?

초아: 오후에 비가 올 것 같아요.

미나: 그래요? 근데 구름이 없어요.

초아: 저를 믿으세요. 비가 올 거예요.

미나: 알겠어요. 비를 기대할게요.

Mina: Why do you have an umbrella?

Choa: I think it's going to rain in the afternoon.

Mina: Is that so? But there aren't any clouds.

Choa: Trust me. It's going to rain.

Mina: Got it. I will expect rain.

SR | Quiz Yourself 퀴즈

● 1. Sentence maker
Complete the sentences using the **Indirect Speech (Verbs)** patterns below.

> - stem ~겠다고 VERB FUTURE
> - stem ~(으)ㄹ 거라고 VERB FUTURE
> - stem ~ㄴ/는다고 VERB PRESENT
> - past tense stem ~다고 VERB PAST

> **Sample**
> 지윤: 어제 차를 샀어요.
> 한국어: 지윤씨가 어제 차를 샀다고 했어요.
> English: Jiyoon said she bought a car yesterday.

1. 현빈: 아침에 백화점에서 빨간색 바지를 샀어요.

   한국어: _____

   English:_____

2. 조지: 지금 배가 고프니까 밥을 먹을거예요.

   한국어: _____

   English:_____

3. 원준: 월말에 회사 근처로 이사할거예요.

   한국어: _____

   English:_____

4. 소현: 아영의 생일때 예쁜 구두를 선물 했어.

   한국어: _____

   English:_____

5. 상민: 저는 매일 아기의 사진을 찍어요.

   한국어: _____

   English:_____

6. 효정: 지난 주에 감기에 걸렸어요.

   한국어: _____

   English:_____

● **2. Fill in the blanks**
Fill in the missing part of the sentence with the Korean that best matches the provided English. The on the following line write the English translation.

> **Sample**
> **Ex.** Because it's raining~
> _____우산을 쓰세요. (because it's raining)
> Translation: <u>Use an umbrella since it's raining.</u>

1. Because I'm busy today~

    _____ 내일 만나자.

    Translation: _____.

2. Since you have a fever~

    _____ 약을 먹으세요.

    Translation: _____.

3. Since it's this place (here) is a library~

_____ 조용히 하세요.

Translation: _____.

4. Since I am not carrying my wallet right now~

_____ 돈을 빌려 주세요.

Translation: _____.

5. Because the baby is sleeping~

_____ 떠들면 안 돼요.

Translation: _____.

● 3. Question VS answer blanks
Look at the following Q&A and fill in the missing parts.

1. Q: 여기서 담배를 피워도 돼요?

   A: 네, _____.

   A: 아니요, _____.

2. Q: 파티에_____?

   A: 네, 친구를 3 명까지 데려가도 돼요.

   A: 아니요, 사람이 많으니까 데려가면 안 돼요.

3. Q: 이것을_____?

   A: 네, 하지만 읽은 후에 웃지 마세요.

   A: 아니요, 이건 제 일기예요.

● **4. Reading comprehension**
Read the following selection then answer the questions.

몸이 아파서 오늘 병원에 갔어요. 의사 선생님이 요즘 유행하는 감기라고 했어요. 이 감기에 걸리면 열이 나면서 어지러울 거라고 들었어요. 저도 그렇게 됐어요. 의사 선생님이 준 약을 먹으면 이틀 후에 괜찮아질 거예요. 이 약을 먹기 전에 커피를 마시면 안 된다고 했어요. 의사 선생님을 믿고 오늘 저녁부터 약을 먹을 거예요.

1. 이 사람은 오늘 공원에 갔어요? 아니면 어디에 갔어요?

   _____

2. 이 사람은 어디가 아파요?

   _____

3. 이 감기에 걸리면 무슨 증상이 있어요?

   _____

4. 어떻게 하면 괜찮아질 수 있어요?

   _____

5. 오늘이 월요일이라면 목요일에는 이 사람은 어떨까요?

   _____

● **5. Korean to English Translation**
Translate the following sentences into Korean.

1. 한국에 갈 거라고 기대했지만 가족이 가면 안 된다고 했어요.

   _____

2. 저는 매일 점심 밥을 먹은 후에 초콜릿을 먹어서 뚱뚱해졌어요.

   _____

3. 그렇게 하면 고장이 날 거예요.

_____

4. 제 손을 잡았을 때 부끄러워서 얼굴이 빨갛게 됐어요.

_____

SR | Super Review Answers 연습 문제 정답

● 1. Sentence maker (answers)

1. 현빈씨가 백화점에서 바지를 샀다고 했어요.
   Hyeonbin said he bought pants at the department store

2. 조지가 지금 배고프니까 밥을 먹을거라고/먹겠다고 했어요.
   George said he's going to eat because he's hungry now.

3. 원준이 월말에 회사 근처로 이사할거라고/이사하겠다고 했어요.
   Wonjun said he was moving nearby the company on Monday.

4. 소현이 아영의 생일 때 예쁜 구두를 선물했다고 했어요.
   Sohyeon said on Ayeong's birthday he gave him brown shoes.

5. 상민은 매일 아기의 사진을 찍는다고 했어요.
   Sangmin said he takes pictures of his baby everyday.

6. 효정은 지난 주에 감기에 걸렸다고 했어요.
   Hyojeong said she caught a cold last week.

● 2. Fill in the blanks (answers)

1. 오늘 바쁘니까 내일 만나자.
   Since I am busy today let's meet tomorrow.

2. 열이 나니까 약을 먹으세요.
   Since you have a fever take this medicine.

3. 여기는 도서관이니까 조용히 하세요.
   Since this place (here) is a library be quiet.

4. 지금 지갑을 안 가지니까 돈을 빌려 주세요.
   Since I am not carrying my wallet right now please loan me money.

5. 아기가 잠을 자니까 떠들면 안 돼요.
   Because the baby is sleeping you shouldn't make any sound.

● 3. Question VS answer blanks (answers)

1. Q: 여기서 담배를 피워도 돼요?
   A: 네, (담배를) 피워도 돼요.
   A: 아니요, 담배를 피우면 안 돼요.

   Q: Is it okay if I smoke here?
   A: Yes, you can smoke.
   A: No you can't smoke.

2. Q: 파티에 친구를 데려가도 돼요?
   A: 네, 친구를 3 명까지 데려와도 돼요.
   A: 아니요, 사람이 많으니까 데려가면 안 돼요.

   Q: Can I take a friend to the party?
   A: Yes, you can up bring up to 3 friends.
   A: No, you can't bring anyone because there are a lot of people.

3. Q: 이것을 읽어도 돼요?
   A: 네, 하지만 읽은 후에 웃지 마세요.
   A: 아니요, 이건 제 일기예요.

   Q: Can I read this?
   A: Yes, but after you read it don't laugh.
   A: No, that's my diary.

● 4. Reading comprehension (answers)

Because I'm sick (my body hurts) I went to the hospital today. The doctor said that recently there is a cold going around. I heard that if you catch this cold you get dizzy while having a fever. I also got this way. If I take the medicine that the doctor gave me I will get better after two days. He said that I can't drink coffee after taking this medicine. I will trust the doctor and take the medicine from this evening.

1. Translation: Did this person go the park today? If not, where did he go?
   Answer: 아니요. 병원에 갔어요.

2. Translation: Why is this person sick?
   Answer: 감기에 걸렸어요.

3. Translation: If you catch this cold what symptons are there?
   Answer: 열이 나면서 어지러워요.

4. Translation: How can he get better?
   Answer: 약을 먹으면 돼요.

5. Translation: If today is Monday, on Thursday how will this person be?
   Answer: 괜찮을 거예요.

● 5. Korean to English Translation (answers)

1. I was expecting to go to Korea, but my family said I couldn't go.
2. I got fat because I eat chocolate everyday after I eat lunch.
3. If you do it that way it will break.
4. When you grabbed my hand, I was so embarrassed that my face got red.

Verb Conjugation Reference

You should already know how to conjugate the verbs without using charts, but every now and then it's nice to confirm what you already know.

NOTE: We have not included any of the 하다 verbs / adjectives since they are so common.

가르치다
to teach

regular verb

STEM	BASIC	으 FORM
가르치	가르쳐	가르치
PAST	PRESENT	FUTURE
가르쳤	가르치는	가르칠

PRESENT	가르쳐요.
FUTURE	가르칠 거예요.
PAST	가르쳤어요.
IF	가르치면~
WHEN	가르칠 때~
BECAUSE	가르치니까~, 가르쳐서~

가다
to go

regular verb

STEM	BASIC	으 FORM
가	가	가
PAST	PRESENT	FUTURE
갔	가는	갈

PRESENT	가요.
FUTURE	갈 거예요.
PAST	갔어요.
IF	가면~
WHEN	갈 때~
BECAUSE	가니까~, 가서~

가져오다
to bring (a thing)

regular verb

STEM	BASIC	으 FORM
가져오	가져와	가져오
PAST	PRESENT	FUTURE
가져왔	가져오는	가져올

PRESENT	가져와요.
FUTURE	가져올 거예요.
PAST	가져왔어요.
IF	가져오면~
WHEN	가져올 때~
BECAUSE	가져오니까~, 가져와서~

가져가다
to take (a thing)

regular verb

STEM	BASIC	으 FORM
가져가	가져가	가져가
PAST	PRESENT	FUTURE
가져갔	가져가는	가져갈

PRESENT	가져가요.
FUTURE	가져갈 거예요.
PAST	가져갔어요.
IF	가져가면~
WHEN	가져갈 때~
BECAUSE	가져가니까~, 가져가서~

감기에 걸리다
to catch a cold

regular verb

STEM	BASIC	으 FORM
감기에 걸리	감기에 걸려	감기에 걸리
PAST	PRESENT	FUTURE
감기에 걸렸	감기에 걸리	감기에 걸릴

PRESENT	감기에 걸려요.
FUTURE	감기에 걸릴 거예요.
PAST	감기에 걸렸어요.
IF	감기에 걸리면~
WHEN	감기에 걸릴 때~
BECAUSE	감기에 걸리니까~, 감기에

갈아타다
to transfer, to change

regular verb

STEM	BASIC	으 FORM
갈아타	갈아타	갈아타
PAST	PRESENT	FUTURE
갈아탔	갈아타는	갈아탈

PRESENT	갈아타요.
FUTURE	갈아탈 거예요.
PAST	갈아탔어요.
IF	갈아타면~
WHEN	갈아탈 때~
BECAUSE	갈아타니까~, 갈아타서~

고르다
to choose

르 irregular verb

STEM	BASIC	으 FORM
고르	골라	고르
PAST	PRESENT	FUTURE
골랐	고르는	고를

PRESENT	골라요.
FUTURE	고를 거예요.
PAST	골랐어요.
IF	고르면~
WHEN	고를 때~
BECAUSE	고르니까~, 골라서~

강하다
to be strong (non-physical)

regular adjective

STEM	BASIC	으 FORM
강하	강해	강하
PAST	PRESENT	FUTURE
강했	강한	강할

PRESENT	강해요.
FUTURE	강할 거예요.
PAST	강했어요.
IF	강하면~
WHEN	강할 때~
BECAUSE	강하니까~, 강해서~

그렇다
to be like that

ㅎ irregular adjective

STEM	BASIC	으 FORM
그렇	그래	그러
PAST	PRESENT	FUTURE
그랬	그러는	그럴

PRESENT	그래요.
FUTURE	그럴 거예요.
PAST	그랬어요.
IF	그러면~
WHEN	그럴 때~
BECAUSE	그러니까~, 그래서~

괜찮다
to be okay, to be fine

regular adjective

STEM	BASIC	으 FORM
괜찮	괜찮아	괜찮으
PAST	PRESENT	FUTURE
괜찮았	괜찮은	괜찮을

PRESENT	괜찮아요.
FUTURE	괜찮을 거예요.
PAST	괜찮았어요.
IF	괜찮으면~
WHEN	괜찮을 때~
BECAUSE	괜찮으니까~, 괜찮아서~

금지하다
to be forbidden, to be prohibited

하다 verb

STEM	BASIC	으 FORM
금지하	금지해	금지하
PAST	PRESENT	FUTURE
금지했	금지하는	금지할

PRESENT	금지해요.
FUTURE	금지할 거예요.
PAST	금지했어요.
IF	금지하면~
WHEN	금지할 때~
BECAUSE	금지하니까~, 금지해서~

그리다
to draw, to paint

regular verb

STEM	BASIC	으 FORM
그리	그려	그리
PAST	PRESENT	FUTURE
그렸	그리는	그릴

PRESENT	그려요.
FUTURE	그릴 거예요.
PAST	그렸어요.
IF	그리면~
WHEN	그릴 때~
BECAUSE	그리니까~, 그려서~

기억하다
to remember

하다 verb

STEM	BASIC	으 FORM
기억하	기억해	기억하
PAST	**PRESENT**	**FUTURE**
기억했	기억하는	기억할

PRESENT	기억해요.
FUTURE	기억할 거예요.
PAST	기억했어요.
IF	기억하면~
WHEN	기억할 때~
BECAUSE	기억하니까~, 기억해서~

기대하다
to expect

하다 verb

STEM	BASIC	으 FORM
기대하	기대해	기대하
PAST	**PRESENT**	**FUTURE**
기대했	기대하는	기대할

PRESENT	기대해요.
FUTURE	기대할 거예요.
PAST	기대했어요.
IF	기대하면~
WHEN	기대할 때~
BECAUSE	기대하니까~, 기대해서~

날씬하다
to be skinny

하다 adjective

STEM	BASIC	으 FORM
날씬하	날씬해	날씬하
PAST	**PRESENT**	**FUTURE**
날씬했	날씬한	날씬할

PRESENT	날씬해요.
FUTURE	날씬할 거예요.
PAST	날씬했어요.
IF	날씬하면~
WHEN	날씬할 때~
BECAUSE	날씬하니까~, 날씬해서~

끼다
to put on gloves, glasses etc.

regular verb

STEM	BASIC	으 FORM
끼	껴	끼
PAST	**PRESENT**	**FUTURE**
꼈	끼는	낄

PRESENT	껴요.
FUTURE	낄 거예요.
PAST	꼈어요.
IF	끼면~
WHEN	낄 때~
BECAUSE	끼니까~, 껴서~

놀라다
to be surprised

regular verb

STEM	BASIC	으 FORM
놀라	놀라	놀라
PAST	**PRESENT**	**FUTURE**
놀랐	놀라는	놀랄

PRESENT	놀라요.
FUTURE	놀랄 거예요.
PAST	놀랐어요.
IF	놀라면~
WHEN	놀랄 때~
BECAUSE	놀라니까~, 놀라서~

낮다
to be low

regular adjective

STEM	BASIC	으 FORM
낮	낮아	낮으
PAST	**PRESENT**	**FUTURE**
낮았	낮은	낮을

PRESENT	낮아요.
FUTURE	낮을 거예요.
PAST	낮았어요.
IF	낮으면~
WHEN	낮을 때~
BECAUSE	낮으니까~, 낮아서~

눕다
to lay down

ㅂ irregular verb		
STEM	BASIC	으 FORM
눕	누워	누우
PAST	PRESENT	FUTURE
누웠	눕는	누울
PRESENT	누워요.	
FUTURE	누울 거예요.	
PAST	누웠어요.	
IF	누우면~	
WHEN	누울 때~	
BECAUSE	누우니까~, 누워서~	

높다
to be high

regular adjective		
STEM	BASIC	으 FORM
높	높아	높으
PAST	PRESENT	FUTURE
높았	높은	높을
PRESENT	높아요.	
FUTURE	높을 거예요.	
PAST	높았어요.	
IF	높으면~	
WHEN	높을 때~	
BECAUSE	높으니까~, 높아서~	

다니다
to attend, to frequent

regular verb		
STEM	BASIC	으 FORM
다니	다녀	다니
PAST	PRESENT	FUTURE
다녔	다니는	다닐
PRESENT	다녀요.	
FUTURE	다닐 거예요.	
PAST	다녔어요.	
IF	다니면~	
WHEN	다닐 때~	
BECAUSE	다니니까~, 다녀서~	

느끼다
to feel

regular verb		
STEM	BASIC	으 FORM
느끼	느껴	느끼
PAST	PRESENT	FUTURE
느꼈	느끼는	느낄
PRESENT	느껴요.	
FUTURE	느낄 거예요.	
PAST	느꼈어요.	
IF	느끼면~	
WHEN	느낄 때~	
BECAUSE	느끼니까~, 느껴서~	

답답하다
to be cramped, stifled, frustrated

regular adjective		
STEM	BASIC	으 FORM
답답하	답답해	답답하
PAST	PRESENT	FUTURE
답답했	답답한	답답할
PRESENT	답답해요.	
FUTURE	답답할 거예요.	
PAST	답답했어요.	
IF	답답하면~	
WHEN	답답할 때~	
BECAUSE	답답하니까~, 답답해서~	

담배를 피우다
to smoke

regular verb		
STEM	BASIC	으 FORM
담배를 피우	담배를 피워	담배를 피우
PAST	PRESENT	FUTURE
담배를 피웠	담배를 피우	담배를 피울
PRESENT	담배를 피워요.	
FUTURE	담배를 피울 거예요.	
PAST	담배를 피웠어요.	
IF	담배를 피우면~	
WHEN	담배를 피울 때~	
BECAUSE	담배를 피우니까~, 담배를	

데려오다
to bring (a person)

regular verb		
STEM	BASIC	으 FORM
데려오	데려와	데려오
PAST	PRESENT	FUTURE
데려왔	데려오는	데려올
PRESENT	데려와요.	
FUTURE	데려올 거예요.	
PAST	데려왔어요.	
IF	데려오면~	
WHEN	데려올 때~	
BECAUSE	데려오니까~, 데려와서~	

데려가다
to take (a person)

regular verb		
STEM	BASIC	으 FORM
데려가	데려가	데려가
PAST	PRESENT	FUTURE
데려갔	데려가는	데려갈
PRESENT	데려가요.	
FUTURE	데려갈 거예요.	
PAST	데려갔어요.	
IF	데려가면~	
WHEN	데려갈 때~	
BECAUSE	데려가니까~, 데려가서~	

듣다
to hear

ㄷ irregular verb		
STEM	BASIC	으 FORM
듣	들어	들으
PAST	PRESENT	FUTURE
들었	듣는	들을
PRESENT	들어요.	
FUTURE	들을 거예요.	
PAST	들었어요.	
IF	들으면~	
WHEN	들을 때~	
BECAUSE	들으니까~, 들어서~	

돈이 생기다
to make money

regular verb		
STEM	BASIC	으 FORM
돈이 생기	돈이 생겨	돈이 생기
PAST	PRESENT	FUTURE
돈이 생겼	돈이 생기는	돈이 생길
PRESENT	돈이 생겨요.	
FUTURE	돈이 생길 거예요.	
PAST	돈이 생겼어요.	
IF	돈이 생기면~	
WHEN	돈이 생길 때~	
BECAUSE	돈이 생기니까~, 돈이 생겨	

떠나다
to leave

regular verb		
STEM	BASIC	으 FORM
떠나	떠나	떠나
PAST	PRESENT	FUTURE
떠났	떠나는	떠날
PRESENT	떠나요.	
FUTURE	떠날 거예요.	
PAST	떠났어요.	
IF	떠나면~	
WHEN	떠날 때~	
BECAUSE	떠나니까~, 떠나서~	

딱딱하다
to be hard

regular adjective		
STEM	BASIC	으 FORM
딱딱하	딱딱해	딱딱하
PAST	PRESENT	FUTURE
딱딱했	딱딱한	딱딱할
PRESENT	딱딱해요.	
FUTURE	딱딱할 거예요.	
PAST	딱딱했어요.	
IF	딱딱하면~	
WHEN	딱딱할 때~	
BECAUSE	딱딱하니까~, 딱딱해서~	

똑똑하다
to be smart

regular adjective

STEM	BASIC	으 FORM
똑똑하	똑똑해	똑똑하
PAST	**PRESENT**	**FUTURE**
똑똑했	똑똑한	똑똑할

PRESENT	똑똑해요.
FUTURE	똑똑할 거예요.
PAST	똑똑했어요.
IF	똑똑하면~
WHEN	똑똑할 때~
BECAUSE	똑똑하니까~, 똑똑해서~

떠들다
to make noise

ㄹ irregular verb

STEM	BASIC	으 FORM
떠들	떠들어	떠들
PAST	**PRESENT**	**FUTURE**
떠들었	떠드는	떠들

PRESENT	떠들어요.
FUTURE	떠들 거예요.
PAST	떠들었어요.
IF	떠들면~
WHEN	떠들 때~
BECAUSE	떠드니까~, 떠들어서~

마시다
to drink

regular verb

STEM	BASIC	으 FORM
마시	마셔	마시
PAST	**PRESENT**	**FUTURE**
마셨	마시는	마실

PRESENT	마셔요.
FUTURE	마실 거예요.
PAST	마셨어요.
IF	마시면~
WHEN	마실 때~
BECAUSE	마시니까~, 마셔서~

뚱뚱하다
to be fat

하다 adjective

STEM	BASIC	으 FORM
뚱뚱하	뚱뚱해	뚱뚱하
PAST	**PRESENT**	**FUTURE**
뚱뚱했	뚱뚱한	뚱뚱할

PRESENT	뚱뚱해요.
FUTURE	뚱뚱할 거예요.
PAST	뚱뚱했어요.
IF	뚱뚱하면~
WHEN	뚱뚱할 때~
BECAUSE	뚱뚱하니까~, 뚱뚱해서~

말하다
to speak, tell, talk

하다 verb

STEM	BASIC	으 FORM
말하	말해	말하
PAST	**PRESENT**	**FUTURE**
말했	말하는	말할

PRESENT	말해요.
FUTURE	말할 거예요.
PAST	말했어요.
IF	말하면~
WHEN	말할 때~
BECAUSE	말하니까~, 말해서~

만나다
to meet

regular verb

STEM	BASIC	으 FORM
만나	만나	만나
PAST	**PRESENT**	**FUTURE**
만났	만나는	만날

PRESENT	만나요.
FUTURE	만날 거예요.
PAST	만났어요.
IF	만나면~
WHEN	만날 때~
BECAUSE	만나니까~, 만나서~

먹다
to eat

regular verb		
STEM	BASIC	으 FORM
먹	먹어	먹으
PAST	PRESENT	FUTURE
먹었	먹는	먹을
PRESENT	먹어요.	
FUTURE	먹을 거예요.	
PAST	먹었어요.	
IF	먹으면~	
WHEN	먹을 때~	
BECAUSE	먹으니까~, 먹어서~	

매다
to wear, put on, tie (neckties etc.)

regular verb		
STEM	BASIC	으 FORM
매	매	매
PAST	PRESENT	FUTURE
맸	매는	맬
PRESENT	매요.	
FUTURE	맬 거예요.	
PAST	맸어요.	
IF	매면~	
WHEN	맬 때~	
BECAUSE	매니까~, 매서~	

못생기다
to be unattractive, ugly (not formed well)

regular verb		
STEM	BASIC	으 FORM
못생기	못생겨	못생기
PAST	PRESENT	FUTURE
못생겼	못생기는	못생길
PRESENT	못생겨요.	
FUTURE	못생길 거예요.	
PAST	못생겼어요.	
IF	못생기면~	
WHEN	못생길 때~	
BECAUSE	못생기니까~, 못생겨서~	

멍청하다
to be dumb

regular adjective		
STEM	BASIC	으 FORM
멍청하	멍청해	멍청하
PAST	PRESENT	FUTURE
멍청했	멍청한	멍청할
PRESENT	멍청해요.	
FUTURE	멍청할 거예요.	
PAST	멍청했어요.	
IF	멍청하면~	
WHEN	멍청할 때~	
BECAUSE	멍청하니까~, 멍청해서~	

미치다
to go crazy

regular verb		
STEM	BASIC	으 FORM
미치	미쳐	미치
PAST	PRESENT	FUTURE
미쳤	미치는	미칠
PRESENT	미쳐요.	
FUTURE	미칠 거예요.	
PAST	미쳤어요.	
IF	미치면~	
WHEN	미칠 때~	
BECAUSE	미치니까~, 미쳐서~	

문제가 생기다
to have a problem happen

regular verb		
STEM	BASIC	으 FORM
문제가 생기	문제가 생겨	문제가 생기
PAST	PRESENT	FUTURE
문제가 생겼	문제가 생기	문제가 생길
PRESENT	문제가 생겨요.	
FUTURE	문제가 생길 거예요.	
PAST	문제가 생겼어요.	
IF	문제가 생기면~	
WHEN	문제가 생길 때~	
BECAUSE	문제가 생기니까~, 문제가	

바람을 피우다
to have an affair, to cheat

regular verb

STEM	BASIC	으 FORM
바람을 피우	바람을 피워	바람을 피우
PAST	**PRESENT**	**FUTURE**
바람을 피웠	바람을 피우	바람을 피울
PRESENT	바람을 피워요.	
FUTURE	바람을 피울 거예요.	
PAST	바람을 피웠어요.	
IF	바람을 피우면~	
WHEN	바람을 피울 때~	
BECAUSE	바람을 피우니까~, 바람을	

믿다
to believe, to trust

regular verb

STEM	BASIC	으 FORM
믿	믿어	믿으
PAST	**PRESENT**	**FUTURE**
믿었	믿는	믿을
PRESENT	믿어요.	
FUTURE	믿을 거예요.	
PAST	믿었어요.	
IF	믿으면~	
WHEN	믿을 때~	
BECAUSE	믿으니까~, 믿어서~	

벌다
to earn (money)

ㄹ irregular verb

STEM	BASIC	으 FORM
벌	벌어	벌
PAST	**PRESENT**	**FUTURE**
벌었	버는	벌
PRESENT	벌어요.	
FUTURE	벌 거예요.	
PAST	벌었어요.	
IF	벌면~	
WHEN	벌 때~	
BECAUSE	버니까~, 벌어서~	

발표하다
to give a speech, make a presentation

noun

STEM	BASIC	으 FORM
발표하	발표해	발표하
PAST	**PRESENT**	**FUTURE**
발표했	발표하는	발표할
PRESENT	발표해요.	
FUTURE	발표할 거예요.	
PAST	발표했어요.	
IF	발표하면~	
WHEN	발표할 때~	
BECAUSE	발표하니까~, 발표해서~	

부드럽다
to be soft

ㅂ irregular adjective

STEM	BASIC	으 FORM
부드럽	부드러워	부드러우
PAST	**PRESENT**	**FUTURE**
부드러웠	부드러운	부드러울
PRESENT	부드러워요.	
FUTURE	부드러울 거예요.	
PAST	부드러웠어요.	
IF	부드러우면~	
WHEN	부드러울 때~	
BECAUSE	부드러우니까~, 부드러워서	

벗다
to take off clothes etc

regular verb

STEM	BASIC	으 FORM
벗	벗어	벗으
PAST	**PRESENT**	**FUTURE**
벗었	벗는	벗을
PRESENT	벗어요.	
FUTURE	벗을 거예요.	
PAST	벗었어요.	
IF	벗으면~	
WHEN	벗을 때~	
BECAUSE	벗으니까~, 벗어서~	

부탁하다
to request, to ask

하다 verb

STEM	BASIC	으 FORM
부탁하	부탁해	부탁하
PAST	PRESENT	FUTURE
부탁했	부탁하는	부탁할
PRESENT	부탁해요.	
FUTURE	부탁할 거예요.	
PAST	부탁했어요.	
IF	부탁하면~	
WHEN	부탁할 때~	
BECAUSE	부탁하니까~, 부탁해서~	

부럽다
to be envious

ㅂ irregular adjective

STEM	BASIC	으 FORM
부럽	부러워	부러우
PAST	PRESENT	FUTURE
부러웠	부러운	부러울
PRESENT	부러워요.	
FUTURE	부러울 거예요.	
PAST	부러웠어요.	
IF	부러우면~	
WHEN	부러울 때~	
BECAUSE	부러우니까~, 부러워서~	

빼다
to take off rings, gloves etc.

regular verb

STEM	BASIC	으 FORM
빼	빼	빼
PAST	PRESENT	FUTURE
뺐	빼는	뺄
PRESENT	빼요.	
FUTURE	뺄 거예요.	
PAST	뺐어요.	
IF	빼면~	
WHEN	뺄 때~	
BECAUSE	빼니까~, 빼서~	

불다
to play a wind instrument

ㄹ irregular verb

STEM	BASIC	으 FORM
불	불어	불
PAST	PRESENT	FUTURE
불었	부는	불
PRESENT	불어요.	
FUTURE	불 거예요.	
PAST	불었어요.	
IF	불면~	
WHEN	불 때~	
BECAUSE	부니까~, 불어서~	

사업하다
to do a business

noun

STEM	BASIC	으 FORM
사업하	사업해	사업하
PAST	PRESENT	FUTURE
사업했	사업하는	사업할
PRESENT	사업해요.	
FUTURE	사업할 거예요.	
PAST	사업했어요.	
IF	사업하면~	
WHEN	사업할 때~	
BECAUSE	사업하니까~, 사업해서~	

뿌리다
to put on perfume etc.

regular verb

STEM	BASIC	으 FORM
뿌리	뿌려	뿌리
PAST	PRESENT	FUTURE
뿌렸	뿌리는	뿌릴
PRESENT	뿌려요.	
FUTURE	뿌릴 거예요.	
PAST	뿌렸어요.	
IF	뿌리면~	
WHEN	뿌릴 때~	
BECAUSE	뿌리니까~, 뿌려서~	

살을 빼다
to lose weight (make effort to lose)

regular verb

STEM	BASIC	으 FORM
살을 빼	살을 빼	살을 빼
PAST	PRESENT	FUTURE
살을 뺐	살을 빼는	살을 뺄
PRESENT	살을 빼요.	
FUTURE	살을 뺄 거예요.	
PAST	살을 뺐어요.	
IF	살을 빼면~	
WHEN	살을 뺄 때~	
BECAUSE	살을 빼니까~, 살을 빼서~	

사용하다
to use

하다 verb

STEM	BASIC	으 FORM
사용하	사용해	사용하
PAST	PRESENT	FUTURE
사용했	사용하는	사용할
PRESENT	사용해요.	
FUTURE	사용할 거예요.	
PAST	사용했어요.	
IF	사용하면~	
WHEN	사용할 때~	
BECAUSE	사용하니까~, 사용해서~	

살이 찌다
to gain weight

regular verb

STEM	BASIC	으 FORM
살이 찌	살이 쪄	살이 찌
PAST	PRESENT	FUTURE
살이 쪘	살이 찌는	살이 찔
PRESENT	살이 쪄요.	
FUTURE	살이 찔 거예요.	
PAST	살이 쪘어요.	
IF	살이 찌면~	
WHEN	살이 찔 때~	
BECAUSE	살이 찌니까~, 살이 쪄서~	

살이 빠지다
to lose weight (become less fat)

regular verb

STEM	BASIC	으 FORM
살이 빠지	살이 빠져	살이 빠지
PAST	PRESENT	FUTURE
살이 빠졌	살이 빠지는	살이 빠질
PRESENT	살이 빠져요.	
FUTURE	살이 빠질 거예요.	
PAST	살이 빠졌어요.	
IF	살이 빠지면~	
WHEN	살이 빠질 때~	
BECAUSE	살이 빠지니까~, 살이 빠져	

생기다
to happen, to occur, to make, to form

regular verb

STEM	BASIC	으 FORM
생기	생겨	생기
PAST	PRESENT	FUTURE
생겼	생기는	생길
PRESENT	생겨요.	
FUTURE	생길 거예요.	
PAST	생겼어요.	
IF	생기면~	
WHEN	생길 때~	
BECAUSE	생기니까~, 생겨서~	

생각하다
to consider, to think of

하다 verb

STEM	BASIC	으 FORM
생각하	생각해	생각하
PAST	PRESENT	FUTURE
생각했	생각하는	생각할
PRESENT	생각해요.	
FUTURE	생각할 거예요.	
PAST	생각했어요.	
IF	생각하면~	
WHEN	생각할 때~	
BECAUSE	생각하니까~, 생각해서~	

성공하다
to succeed

noun		
STEM	BASIC	으 FORM
성공하	성공해	성공하
PAST	PRESENT	FUTURE
성공했	성공하는	성공할
PRESENT	성공해요.	
FUTURE	성공할 거예요.	
PAST	성공했어요.	
IF	성공하면~	
WHEN	성공할 때~	
BECAUSE	성공하니까~, 성공해서~	

서다
to stand

regular verb		
STEM	BASIC	으 FORM
서	서	서
PAST	PRESENT	FUTURE
섰	서는	설
PRESENT	서요.	
FUTURE	설 거예요.	
PAST	섰어요.	
IF	서면~	
WHEN	설 때~	
BECAUSE	서니까~, 서서~	

숨을 쉬다
to breathe

regular verb		
STEM	BASIC	으 FORM
숨을 쉬	숨을 쉬어	숨을 쉬
PAST	PRESENT	FUTURE
숨을 쉬었	숨을 쉬는	숨을 쉴
PRESENT	숨을 쉬어요.	
FUTURE	숨을 쉴 거예요.	
PAST	숨을 쉬었어요.	
IF	숨을 쉬면~	
WHEN	숨을 쉴 때~	
BECAUSE	숨을 쉬니까~, 숨을 쉬어서	

세다
to be strong (physical)

regular adjective		
STEM	BASIC	으 FORM
세	세	세
PAST	PRESENT	FUTURE
셌	센	셀
PRESENT	세요.	
FUTURE	셀 거예요.	
PAST	셌어요.	
IF	세면~	
WHEN	셀 때~	
BECAUSE	세니까~, 세서~	

시간이 생기다
to get time (time opened up)

regular verb		
STEM	BASIC	으 FORM
시간이 생기	시간이 생겨	시간이 생기
PAST	PRESENT	FUTURE
시간이 생겼	시간이 생기	시간이 생길
PRESENT	시간이 생겨요.	
FUTURE	시간이 생길 거예요.	
PAST	시간이 생겼어요.	
IF	시간이 생기면~	
WHEN	시간이 생길 때~	
BECAUSE	시간이 생기니까~, 시간이	

스키를 타다
to ski

regular verb		
STEM	BASIC	으 FORM
스키를 타	스키를 타	스키를 타
PAST	PRESENT	FUTURE
스키를 탔	스키를 타는	스키를 탈
PRESENT	스키를 타요.	
FUTURE	스키를 탈 거예요.	
PAST	스키를 탔어요.	
IF	스키를 타면~	
WHEN	스키를 탈 때~	
BECAUSE	스키를 타니까~, 스키를 타	

시험을 보다
to take a test

regular verb		
STEM	BASIC	ㅇ FORM
시험을 보	시험을 봐	시험을 보
PAST	PRESENT	FUTURE
시험을 봤	시험을 보는	시험을 볼
PRESENT	시험을 봐요.	
FUTURE	시험을 볼 거예요.	
PAST	시험을 봤어요.	
IF	시험을 보면~	
WHEN	시험을 볼 때~	
BECAUSE	시험을 보니까~, 시험을 봐	

시원하다
to be cool

regular adjective		
STEM	BASIC	ㅇ FORM
시원하	시원해	시원하
PAST	PRESENT	FUTURE
시원했	시원한	시원할
PRESENT	시원해요.	
FUTURE	시원할 거예요.	
PAST	시원했어요.	
IF	시원하면~	
WHEN	시원할 때~	
BECAUSE	시원하니까~, 시원해서~	

신선하다
to be fresh

regular adjective		
STEM	BASIC	ㅇ FORM
신선하	신선해	신선하
PAST	PRESENT	FUTURE
신선했	신선한	신선할
PRESENT	신선해요.	
FUTURE	신선할 거예요.	
PAST	신선했어요.	
IF	신선하면~	
WHEN	신선할 때~	
BECAUSE	신선하니까~, 신선해서~	

신다
to wear on feet

regular verb		
STEM	BASIC	ㅇ FORM
신	신어	신으
PAST	PRESENT	FUTURE
신었	신는	신을
PRESENT	신어요.	
FUTURE	신을 거예요.	
PAST	신었어요.	
IF	신으면~	
WHEN	신을 때~	
BECAUSE	신으니까~, 신어서~	

실패하다
to fail

noun		
STEM	BASIC	ㅇ FORM
실패하	실패해	실패하
PAST	PRESENT	FUTURE
실패했	실패하는	실패할
PRESENT	실패해요.	
FUTURE	실패할 거예요.	
PAST	실패했어요.	
IF	실패하면~	
WHEN	실패할 때~	
BECAUSE	실패하니까~, 실패해서~	

실수하다
to make a mistake

noun		
STEM	BASIC	ㅇ FORM
실수하	실수해	실수하
PAST	PRESENT	FUTURE
실수했	실수하는	실수할
PRESENT	실수해요.	
FUTURE	실수할 거예요.	
PAST	실수했어요.	
IF	실수하면~	
WHEN	실수할 때~	
BECAUSE	실수하니까~, 실수해서~	

쓰다
to spend (money)

regular verb

STEM	BASIC	으 FORM
쓰	써	쓰
PAST	**PRESENT**	**FUTURE**
썼	쓰는	쓸

PRESENT	써요.
FUTURE	쓸 거예요.
PAST	썼어요.
IF	쓰면~
WHEN	쓸 때~
BECAUSE	쓰니까~, 써서~

심심하다
to be bored

regular adjective

STEM	BASIC	으 FORM
심심하	심심해	심심하
PAST	**PRESENT**	**FUTURE**
심심했	심심한	심심할

PRESENT	심심해요.
FUTURE	심심할 거예요.
PAST	심심했어요.
IF	심심하면~
WHEN	심심할 때~
BECAUSE	심심하니까~, 심심해서~

아기가 생기다
to form a baby (to get pregnant)

regular verb

STEM	BASIC	으 FORM
아기가 생기	아기가 생겨	아기가 생기
PAST	**PRESENT**	**FUTURE**
아기가 생겼	아기가 생기	아기가 생길

PRESENT	아기가 생겨요.
FUTURE	아기가 생길 거예요.
PAST	아기가 생겼어요.
IF	아기가 생기면~
WHEN	아기가 생길 때~
BECAUSE	아기가 생기니까~, 아기가

씻다
to wash

regular verb

STEM	BASIC	으 FORM
씻	씻어	씻으
PAST	**PRESENT**	**FUTURE**
씻었	씻는	씻을

PRESENT	씻어요.
FUTURE	씻을 거예요.
PAST	씻었어요.
IF	씻으면~
WHEN	씻을 때~
BECAUSE	씻으니까~, 씻어서~

안전하다
to be safe

regular adjective

STEM	BASIC	으 FORM
안전하	안전해	안전하
PAST	**PRESENT**	**FUTURE**
안전했	안전한	안전할

PRESENT	안전해요.
FUTURE	안전할 거예요.
PAST	안전했어요.
IF	안전하면~
WHEN	안전할 때~
BECAUSE	안전하니까~, 안전해서~

아프다
to be sick, to hurt

regular adjective

STEM	BASIC	으 FORM
아프	아파	아프
PAST	**PRESENT**	**FUTURE**
아팠	아픈	아플

PRESENT	아파요.
FUTURE	아플 거예요.
PAST	아팠어요.
IF	아프면~
WHEN	아플 때~
BECAUSE	아프니까~, 아파서~

앉다
to sit

regular verb		
STEM	BASIC	으 FORM
앉	앉아	앉으
PAST	PRESENT	FUTURE
앉았	앉는	앉을
PRESENT	앉아요.	
FUTURE	앉을 거예요.	
PAST	앉았어요.	
IF	앉으면~	
WHEN	앉을 때~	
BECAUSE	앉으니까~, 앉아서~	

안타깝다
to be unfortunate, regrettable

ㅂ irregular adjective		
STEM	BASIC	으 FORM
안타깝	안타까워	안타까우
PAST	PRESENT	FUTURE
안타까웠	안타까운	안타까울
PRESENT	안타까워요.	
FUTURE	안타까울 거예요.	
PAST	안타까웠어요.	
IF	안타까우면~	
WHEN	안타까울 때~	
BECAUSE	안타까우니까~, 안타까워서	

약혼하다
to get engaged to be married

noun		
STEM	BASIC	으 FORM
약혼하	약혼해	약혼하
PAST	PRESENT	FUTURE
약혼했	약혼하는	약혼할
PRESENT	약혼해요.	
FUTURE	약혼할 거예요.	
PAST	약혼했어요.	
IF	약혼하면~	
WHEN	약혼할 때~	
BECAUSE	약혼하니까~, 약혼해서~	

약하다
to be weak (physical and non)

regular adjective		
STEM	BASIC	으 FORM
약하	약해	약하
PAST	PRESENT	FUTURE
약했	약한	약할
PRESENT	약해요.	
FUTURE	약할 거예요.	
PAST	약했어요.	
IF	약하면~	
WHEN	약할 때~	
BECAUSE	약하니까~, 약해서~	

어지럽다
to be dizzy

ㅂ irregular adjective		
STEM	BASIC	으 FORM
어지럽	어지러워	어지러우
PAST	PRESENT	FUTURE
어지러웠	어지러운	어지러울
PRESENT	어지러워요.	
FUTURE	어지러울 거예요.	
PAST	어지러웠어요.	
IF	어지러우면~	
WHEN	어지러울 때~	
BECAUSE	어지러우니까~, 어지러워서	

어리다
to be young

regular adjective		
STEM	BASIC	으 FORM
어리	어려	어리
PAST	PRESENT	FUTURE
어렸	어린	어릴
PRESENT	어려요.	
FUTURE	어릴 거예요.	
PAST	어렸어요.	
IF	어리면~	
WHEN	어릴 때~	
BECAUSE	어리니까~, 어려서~	

연주하다
to play an instrument (any)

하다 verb		
STEM	BASIC	○ FORM
연주하	연주해	연주하
PAST	PRESENT	FUTURE
연주했	연주하는	연주할
PRESENT	연주해요.	
FUTURE	연주할 거예요.	
PAST	연주했어요.	
IF	연주하면~	
WHEN	연주할 때~	
BECAUSE	연주하니까~, 연주해서~	

엄격하다
to be strict

regular adjective		
STEM	BASIC	○ FORM
엄격하	엄격해	엄격하
PAST	PRESENT	FUTURE
엄격했	엄격한	엄격할
PRESENT	엄격해요.	
FUTURE	엄격할 거예요.	
PAST	엄격했어요.	
IF	엄격하면~	
WHEN	엄격할 때~	
BECAUSE	엄격하니까~, 엄격해서~	

오다
to come

regular verb		
STEM	BASIC	○ FORM
오	와	오
PAST	PRESENT	FUTURE
왔	오는	올
PRESENT	와요.	
FUTURE	올 거예요.	
PAST	왔어요.	
IF	오면~	
WHEN	올 때~	
BECAUSE	오니까~, 와서~	

열이 나다
to have a fever

regular verb		
STEM	BASIC	○ FORM
열이 나	열이 나	열이 나
PAST	PRESENT	FUTURE
열이 났	열이 나는	열이 날
PRESENT	열이 나요.	
FUTURE	열이 날 거예요.	
PAST	열이 났어요.	
IF	열이 나면~	
WHEN	열이 날 때~	
BECAUSE	열이 나니까~, 열이 나서~	

위험하다
to be dangerous

regular adjective		
STEM	BASIC	○ FORM
위험하	위험해	위험하
PAST	PRESENT	FUTURE
위험했	위험한	위험할
PRESENT	위험해요.	
FUTURE	위험할 거예요.	
PAST	위험했어요.	
IF	위험하면~	
WHEN	위험할 때~	
BECAUSE	위험하니까~, 위험해서~	

외우다
to memorize

regular verb		
STEM	BASIC	○ FORM
외우	외워	외우
PAST	PRESENT	FUTURE
외웠	외우는	외울
PRESENT	외워요.	
FUTURE	외울 거예요.	
PAST	외웠어요.	
IF	외우면~	
WHEN	외울 때~	
BECAUSE	외우니까~, 외워서~	

이렇다
to be like this

ㅎ irregular adjective		
STEM	BASIC	으 FORM
이렇	이래	이러
PAST	PRESENT	FUTURE
이랬	이러는	이럴
PRESENT	이래요.	
FUTURE	이럴 거예요.	
PAST	이랬어요.	
IF	이러면~	
WHEN	이럴 때~	
BECAUSE	이러니까~, 이래서~	

이기다
to win, to beat

regular verb		
STEM	BASIC	으 FORM
이기	이겨	이기
PAST	PRESENT	FUTURE
이겼	이기는	이길
PRESENT	이겨요.	
FUTURE	이길 거예요.	
PAST	이겼어요.	
IF	이기면~	
WHEN	이길 때~	
BECAUSE	이기니까~, 이겨서~	

이상하다
to be strange, weird

regular adjective		
STEM	BASIC	으 FORM
이상하	이상해	이상하
PAST	PRESENT	FUTURE
이상했	이상한	이상할
PRESENT	이상해요.	
FUTURE	이상할 거예요.	
PAST	이상했어요.	
IF	이상하면~	
WHEN	이상할 때~	
BECAUSE	이상하니까~, 이상해서~	

이사하다
to move (to a new place)

하다 verb		
STEM	BASIC	으 FORM
이사하	이사해	이사하
PAST	PRESENT	FUTURE
이사했	이사하는	이사할
PRESENT	이사해요.	
FUTURE	이사할 거예요.	
PAST	이사했어요.	
IF	이사하면~	
WHEN	이사할 때~	
BECAUSE	이사하니까~, 이사해서~	

인쇄하다
to print

하다 verb		
STEM	BASIC	으 FORM
인쇄하	인쇄해	인쇄하
PAST	PRESENT	FUTURE
인쇄했	인쇄하는	인쇄할
PRESENT	인쇄해요.	
FUTURE	인쇄할 거예요.	
PAST	인쇄했어요.	
IF	인쇄하면~	
WHEN	인쇄할 때~	
BECAUSE	인쇄하니까~, 인쇄해서~	

이혼하다
to get a divorce

noun		
STEM	BASIC	으 FORM
이혼하	이혼해	이혼하
PAST	PRESENT	FUTURE
이혼했	이혼하는	이혼할
PRESENT	이혼해요.	
FUTURE	이혼할 거예요.	
PAST	이혼했어요.	
IF	이혼하면~	
WHEN	이혼할 때~	
BECAUSE	이혼하니까~, 이혼해서~	

입다
to wear clothes

regular verb		
STEM	BASIC	으 FORM
입	입어	입으
PAST	PRESENT	FUTURE
입었	입는	입을
PRESENT	입어요.	
FUTURE	입을 거예요.	
PAST	입었어요.	
IF	입으면~	
WHEN	입을 때~	
BECAUSE	입으니까~, 입어서~	

읽다
to read

regular verb		
STEM	BASIC	으 FORM
읽	읽어	읽으
PAST	PRESENT	FUTURE
읽었	읽는	읽을
PRESENT	읽어요.	
FUTURE	읽을 거예요.	
PAST	읽었어요.	
IF	읽으면~	
WHEN	읽을 때~	
BECAUSE	읽으니까~, 읽어서~	

있다
to exist, to have

regular verb		
STEM	BASIC	으 FORM
있	있어	있으
PAST	PRESENT	FUTURE
있었	있는	있을
PRESENT	있어요.	
FUTURE	있을 거예요.	
PAST	있었어요.	
IF	있으면~	
WHEN	있을 때~	
BECAUSE	있으니까~, 있어서~	

입학하다
to enter school

하다 verb		
STEM	BASIC	으 FORM
입학하	입학해	입학하
PAST	PRESENT	FUTURE
입학했	입학하는	입학할
PRESENT	입학해요.	
FUTURE	입학할 거예요.	
PAST	입학했어요.	
IF	입학하면~	
WHEN	입학할 때~	
BECAUSE	입학하니까~, 입학해서~	

잘생기다
to be handsome, pretty (formed well)

noun		
STEM	BASIC	으 FORM
잘생기	잘생겨	잘생기
PAST	PRESENT	FUTURE
잘생겼	잘생기는	잘생길
PRESENT	잘생겨요.	
FUTURE	잘생길 거예요.	
PAST	잘생겼어요.	
IF	잘생기면~	
WHEN	잘생길 때~	
BECAUSE	잘생기니까~, 잘생겨서~	

자다
to sleep

regular verb		
STEM	BASIC	으 FORM
자	자	자
PAST	PRESENT	FUTURE
잤	자는	잘
PRESENT	자요.	
FUTURE	잘 거예요.	
PAST	잤어요.	
IF	자면~	
WHEN	잘 때~	
BECAUSE	자니까~, 자서~	

졸업하다
to graduate

하다 verb

STEM	BASIC	으 FORM
졸업하	졸업해	졸업하
PAST	PRESENT	FUTURE
졸업했	졸업하는	졸업할
PRESENT	졸업해요.	
FUTURE	졸업할 거예요.	
PAST	졸업했어요.	
IF	졸업하면~	
WHEN	졸업할 때~	
BECAUSE	졸업하니까~, 졸업해서~	

저렇다
to be like that over there

ㅎ irregular adjective

STEM	BASIC	으 FORM
저렇	저래	저러
PAST	PRESENT	FUTURE
저랬	저러는	저럴
PRESENT	저래요.	
FUTURE	저럴 거예요.	
PAST	저랬어요.	
IF	저러면~	
WHEN	저럴 때~	
BECAUSE	저러니까~, 저래서~	

즐겁다
to be joyful

ㅂ irregular adjective

STEM	BASIC	으 FORM
즐겁	즐거워	즐거우
PAST	PRESENT	FUTURE
즐거웠	즐거운	즐거울
PRESENT	즐거워요.	
FUTURE	즐거울 거예요.	
PAST	즐거웠어요.	
IF	즐거우면~	
WHEN	즐거울 때~	
BECAUSE	즐거우니까~, 즐거워서~	

주다
to give

regular verb

STEM	BASIC	으 FORM
주	줘	주
PAST	PRESENT	FUTURE
줬	주는	줄
PRESENT	줘요.	
FUTURE	줄 거예요.	
PAST	줬어요.	
IF	주면~	
WHEN	줄 때~	
BECAUSE	주니까~, 줘서~	

지루하다
to be boring

regular adjective

STEM	BASIC	으 FORM
지루하	지루해	지루하
PAST	PRESENT	FUTURE
지루했	지루한	지루할
PRESENT	지루해요.	
FUTURE	지루할 거예요.	
PAST	지루했어요.	
IF	지루하면~	
WHEN	지루할 때~	
BECAUSE	지루하니까~, 지루해서~	

지다
to lose

regular verb

STEM	BASIC	으 FORM
지	져	지
PAST	PRESENT	FUTURE
졌	지는	질
PRESENT	져요.	
FUTURE	질 거예요.	
PAST	졌어요.	
IF	지면~	
WHEN	질 때~	
BECAUSE	지니까~, 져서~	

차다
to put on a watch

regular verb		
STEM	BASIC	으 FORM
차	차	차
PAST	PRESENT	FUTURE
찼	차는	찰
PRESENT	차요.	
FUTURE	찰 거예요.	
PAST	찼어요.	
IF	차면~	
WHEN	찰 때~	
BECAUSE	차니까~, 차서~	

지우다
to take off makeup

regular verb		
STEM	BASIC	으 FORM
지우	지워	지우
PAST	PRESENT	FUTURE
지웠	지우는	지울
PRESENT	지워요.	
FUTURE	지울 거예요.	
PAST	지웠어요.	
IF	지우면~	
WHEN	지울 때~	
BECAUSE	지우니까~, 지워서~	

축하하다
to celebrate

하다 verb		
STEM	BASIC	으 FORM
축하하	축하해	축하하
PAST	PRESENT	FUTURE
축하했	축하하는	축하할
PRESENT	축하해요.	
FUTURE	축하할 거예요.	
PAST	축하했어요.	
IF	축하하면~	
WHEN	축하할 때~	
BECAUSE	축하하니까~, 축하해서~	

청소를 하다
to clean

하다 verb		
STEM	BASIC	으 FORM
청소를 하	청소를 해	청소를 하
PAST	PRESENT	FUTURE
청소를 했	청소를 하는	청소를 할
PRESENT	청소를 해요.	
FUTURE	청소를 할 거예요.	
PAST	청소를 했어요.	
IF	청소를 하면~	
WHEN	청소를 할 때~	
BECAUSE	청소를 하니까~, 청소를 해	

출장가다
to go on a business trip

regular verb		
STEM	BASIC	으 FORM
출장가	출장가	출장가
PAST	PRESENT	FUTURE
출장갔	출장가는	출장갈
PRESENT	출장가요.	
FUTURE	출장갈 거예요.	
PAST	출장갔어요.	
IF	출장가면~	
WHEN	출장갈 때~	
BECAUSE	출장가니까~, 출장가서~	

출근하다
to go to work

하다 verb		
STEM	BASIC	으 FORM
출근하	출근해	출근하
PAST	PRESENT	FUTURE
출근했	출근하는	출근할
PRESENT	출근해요.	
FUTURE	출근할 거예요.	
PAST	출근했어요.	
IF	출근하면~	
WHEN	출근할 때~	
BECAUSE	출근하니까~, 출근해서~	

취업하다
to get a job

noun		
STEM	BASIC	으 FORM
취업하	취업해	취업하
PAST	PRESENT	FUTURE
취업했	취업하는	취업할
PRESENT	취업해요.	
FUTURE	취업할 거예요.	
PAST	취업했어요.	
IF	취업하면~	
WHEN	취업할 때~	
BECAUSE	취업하니까~, 취업해서~	

출퇴근하다
to commute (to work)

하다 verb		
STEM	BASIC	으 FORM
출퇴근하	출퇴근해	출퇴근하
PAST	PRESENT	FUTURE
출퇴근했	출퇴근하는	출퇴근할
PRESENT	출퇴근해요.	
FUTURE	출퇴근할 거예요.	
PAST	출퇴근했어요.	
IF	출퇴근하면~	
WHEN	출퇴근할 때~	
BECAUSE	출퇴근하니까~, 출퇴근해서	

친구가 생기다
to make a girlfriend

regular verb		
STEM	BASIC	으 FORM
친구가 생기	친구가 생겨	친구가 생기
PAST	PRESENT	FUTURE
친구가 생겼	친구가 생기	친구가 생길
PRESENT	친구가 생겨요.	
FUTURE	친구가 생길 거예요.	
PAST	친구가 생겼어요.	
IF	친구가 생기면~	
WHEN	친구가 생길 때~	
BECAUSE	친구가 생기니까~, 친구가	

치다
to play a stringed instrument

regular verb		
STEM	BASIC	으 FORM
치	쳐	치
PAST	PRESENT	FUTURE
쳤	치는	칠
PRESENT	쳐요.	
FUTURE	칠 거예요.	
PAST	쳤어요.	
IF	치면~	
WHEN	칠 때~	
BECAUSE	치니까~, 쳐서~	

태어나다
to be born

regular verb		
STEM	BASIC	으 FORM
태어나	태어나	태어나
PAST	PRESENT	FUTURE
태어났	태어나는	태어날
PRESENT	태어나요.	
FUTURE	태어날 거예요.	
PAST	태어났어요.	
IF	태어나면~	
WHEN	태어날 때~	
BECAUSE	태어나니까~, 태어나서~	

키가 크다
to be tall

regular adjective		
STEM	BASIC	으 FORM
키가 크	키가 커	키가 크
PAST	PRESENT	FUTURE
키가 컸	키가 큰	키가 클
PRESENT	키가 커요.	
FUTURE	키가 클 거예요.	
PAST	키가 컸어요.	
IF	키가 크면~	
WHEN	키가 클 때~	
BECAUSE	키가 크니까~, 키가 커서~	

퇴근하다
to get off work

하다 verb

STEM	BASIC	으 FORM
퇴근하	퇴근해	퇴근하
PAST	**PRESENT**	**FUTURE**
퇴근했	퇴근하는	퇴근할

PRESENT	퇴근해요.
FUTURE	퇴근할 거예요.
PAST	퇴근했어요.
IF	퇴근하면~
WHEN	퇴근할 때~
BECAUSE	퇴근하니까~, 퇴근해서~

통통하다
to be chubby

regular adjective

STEM	BASIC	으 FORM
통통하	통통해	통통하
PAST	**PRESENT**	**FUTURE**
통통했	통통한	통통할

PRESENT	통통해요.
FUTURE	통통할 거예요.
PAST	통통했어요.
IF	통통하면~
WHEN	통통할 때~
BECAUSE	통통하니까~, 통통해서~

팔리다
to be sold

regular verb

STEM	BASIC	으 FORM
팔리	팔려	팔리
PAST	**PRESENT**	**FUTURE**
팔렸	팔리는	팔릴

PRESENT	팔려요.
FUTURE	팔릴 거예요.
PAST	팔렸어요.
IF	팔리면~
WHEN	팔릴 때~
BECAUSE	팔리니까~, 팔려서~

퇴직하다
to retire

noun

STEM	BASIC	으 FORM
퇴직하	퇴직해	퇴직하
PAST	**PRESENT**	**FUTURE**
퇴직했	퇴직하는	퇴직할

PRESENT	퇴직해요.
FUTURE	퇴직할 거예요.
PAST	퇴직했어요.
IF	퇴직하면~
WHEN	퇴직할 때~
BECAUSE	퇴직하니까~, 퇴직해서~

하다
to put on accessories

하다 verb

STEM	BASIC	으 FORM
하	해	하
PAST	**PRESENT**	**FUTURE**
했	하는	할

PRESENT	해요.
FUTURE	할 거예요.
PAST	했어요.
IF	하면~
WHEN	할 때~
BECAUSE	하니까~, 해서~

풀다
to take off ties, hair ribbons

regular verb

STEM	BASIC	으 FORM
풀	풀어	풀으
PAST	**PRESENT**	**FUTURE**
풀었	풀는	풀을

PRESENT	풀어요.
FUTURE	풀을 거예요.
PAST	풀었어요.
IF	풀으면~
WHEN	풀을 때~
BECAUSE	풀으니까~, 풀어서~

허가하다
to permit, to grant

하다 verb

STEM	BASIC	ㅇ FORM
허가하	허가해	허가하
PAST	PRESENT	FUTURE
허가했	허가하는	허가할
PRESENT	허가해요.	
FUTURE	허가할 거예요.	
PAST	허가했어요.	
IF	허가하면~	
WHEN	허가할 때~	
BECAUSE	허가하니까~, 허가해서~	

합격하다
to pass (a test)

하다 verb

STEM	BASIC	ㅇ FORM
합격하	합격해	합격하
PAST	PRESENT	FUTURE
합격했	합격하는	합격할
PRESENT	합격해요.	
FUTURE	합격할 거예요.	
PAST	합격했어요.	
IF	합격하면~	
WHEN	합격할 때~	
BECAUSE	합격하니까~, 합격해서~	

후회하다
to regret

noun

STEM	BASIC	ㅇ FORM
후회하	후회해	후회하
PAST	PRESENT	FUTURE
후회했	후회하는	후회할
PRESENT	후회해요.	
FUTURE	후회할 거예요.	
PAST	후회했어요.	
IF	후회하면~	
WHEN	후회할 때~	
BECAUSE	후회하니까~, 후회해서~	

회의하다
to have a meeting

noun

STEM	BASIC	ㅇ FORM
회의하	회의해	회의하
PAST	PRESENT	FUTURE
회의했	회의하는	회의할
PRESENT	회의해요.	
FUTURE	회의할 거예요.	
PAST	회의했어요.	
IF	회의하면~	
WHEN	회의할 때~	
BECAUSE	회의하니까~, 회의해서~	

Glossary
E-K

1

1 billion - 십 억

1 book - 한 권

1 million - 백 만

1 piece - 한 장

1 piece - 한 조각

1 quadrillion - 천 조

1 trillion - 조

1 units - 한 대

10 billion - 백 억

10 million - 천 만

10 thousand - 만

10 trillion - 십 조

10,000 books - 만 권

10,000 pieces - 만 장

10,000 pieces - 만 조각

10,000 units - 만 대

100 billion - 천 억

100 books - 백 권

100 million - 억

100 pieces - 백 장

100 pieces - 백 조각

100 thousand - 십 만

100 trillion - 백 조

100 units - 백 대

1st, 2nd, 3rd etc. (order counter) - ~번째

2

2 books - 두 권

2 pieces - 두 장

2 pieces - 두 조각

2 units - 두 대

3

3 books - 세 권

3 pieces - 세 장

3 pieces - 세 조각

3 units - 세 대

4

4 books - 네 권

4 pieces - 네 장

4 pieces - 네 조각

4 units - 네 대

5

5 books - 다섯 권

5 pieces - 다섯 장

5 pieces - 다섯 조각

5 units - 다섯 대

A

account - 계좌

account number - 계좌번호

age - 나이

air - 공기

album (photo, record, cd) - 앨범

alien (from another planet) - 외계인

Alzheimer's - 치매

anemia - 빈혈

any body / anyone - 아무나

any place / anywhere - 아무 데나

anything - 아무거나

Apple © - 애플

approximately, roughly - 약

art gallery - 미술관

B

bamboo - 대나무

bank book - 통장

bar - 술집

battery - 건전지

belt - 벨트

Bill Gates - 빌 게이츠

birthday - 생일

birthday - 생일날

black - 검은색

black - 까맣다

blender - 믹서기

blind date - 소개팅

blue - 파란색

blue - 파랗다

body aches - 몸살

books, magazine - ~권

bracelet - 팔찌

brown - 갈색

bruise - 타박상

business meeting - 회의

business trip - 출장

business, enterprise - 사업

C

cactus - 선인장

camera - 카메라

cancer - 암

canola flower - 유채꽃

cash - 현금

casual speech - 반말

charger - 충전기

check - 수표

cherry blossoms - 벚꽃

cherry tree - 벚나무

Chinese - 중국말

chrysanthemum - 국화

cigarette - 담배

classmate - 급우

clock, watch - 시계

clothes dryer - 건조기

coat - 코트

cold - 감기

colleague, co-worker - 동료

competition - 경기

contact lens - 렌즈

convertible car - 오픈카

cook, chef - 요리사

cough - 기침

D

dandelion - 민들레

dehumidifier - 제습기

deposit - 입금

diabetes - 당뇨병

diarrhea - 설사

dishwasher - 식기 세척기

diversity - 다양성

divorce - 이혼

dormitory - 기숙사

drawing, painting - 그림

dress - 드레스

dress shows - 구두

drums - 드럼

during a conference - 회의 때

during party - 파티 때

during school - 학교 때

dwarf planet - 왜소행성

E

earrings - 귀걸이

Earth - 지구

eighth - 여덟 번째

electric fan - 선풍기

electric toothbrush - 전기 칫솔

electronic dictionary - 전자 사전

elementary school - 초등학교

employment, get a job - 취업

end of month - 월말

end of year - 연말

engagement - 약혼

exit; way out - 출구

F

failure - 실패

fat - 살

fee - 수수료

fever - 열

fifth - 다섯 번째

finally - 드디어

fir - 전나무

first - 첫 번째

first of all, before anything else - 먼저

flat objects, paper - ~장

flute - 플루트

fool, idiot, dummy - 바보

formal speech - 존댓말

forth - 네 번째

French - 프랑스말

G

gaze, glare of eye - 눈빛

gender - 성별

get off work - 퇴근

glass - 유리

glasses - 안경

gloves - 장갑

go to work - 출근

God (the "one") - 하나님

graduation ceremony - 졸업식

green - 초록색

guitar - 기타

gym - 헬스장

H

happening, event - 일

hard, diligently, enthusiastically - 열심히

harmonica - 하모니카

hat - 모자

headache - 두통

headband - 머리 띠

health - 건강

heart disease - 심장병

here and there - 여기저기

high school - 고등학교

highway - 고속도로

hobby - 취미

honorific speech - 높임말

house - 집

housework - 집안일

how - 어떻다

How many books? - 몇 권?

How many pieces? - 몇 장?

How many pieces? - 몇 조각?

How many units? - 몇 대?

how?, in what way?, what kind of? - 어떻다

humidifier - 가습기

I

idea, thought - 생각

importance - 중요성

infection - 전염병

ingredients - 재료

insomnia - 불면증

iron - 다리미

J

Japanese - 일본말

Jupiter - 목성

just now, a minute ago - 아까

K

kilograms - ~킬로그램

kilometers - ~킬로미터

kimchi fridge (most Korean houses have this) - 김치 냉장고

Korean - 한국말

L

language - 언어

late night snack - 야식

laughter - 웃음

liar - 거짓말쟁이

light blue - 하늘색

lily - 백합

line # (only for subways subways) - 호선

linguistics, the study of language - 어학

long, a long time - 오래

lunchbox - 도시락

M

machinery, equipment, cars etc. - ~대

malnutrition - 영양실조

married couple, husband and wife - 부부

Mars - 화성

mask - 마스크

meal / cooked rice - 밥

meeting room - 회의실

Mercury - 수성

middle aged man - 삼촌

middle aged woman - 이모

middle school - 중학교

mind, spirit - 정신

mistake - 실수

mobile phone - 핸드폰

morning glory - 나팔꽃

most (similar to 제일) - 가장

Mr., Mrs. etc - 씨

much, far, a lot, considerably, way - 훨씬

musical instrument - 악기

N

name - 이름

nature - 자연

nausea - 메스꺼움

nearby, in the area - 근처

necessity - 필요성

necktie - 넥타이

Neptune - 해왕성

news (tv news cast) - 뉴스

ninth - 아홉 번째

no one / nobody / anyone - 아무도

no place / anywhere - 아무 데도

nothing / not any / anything - 아무것도

novel (book) - 소설

O

oak wood - 참나무

odor, smell - 냄새

office - 사무실

older man - 아저씨

older woman - 아줌마

on my birthday - 생일 때

one piece dress - 원피스

orange - 주황색

other person - 남

outside - 밖

P

pancakes - 팬케이크

pants - 바지

paper - 종이

password (secret number) - 비밀번호

patient - 환자

pay day - 지급일

perfume, cologne - 향수

person - 사람

phrase - 어구

piano - 피아노

pieces, slices - ~조각

pine - 소나무

pink - 분홍색

planet - 행성

plans - 계획

plastic surgery - 성형수술

Pluto - 명왕성

pneumonia - 폐렴

pork belly - 삼겹살

possibility, likelyhood - 가능성

power, energy - 힘

presentation, speech - 발표

pressure rice cooker - 압력밥솥

price - 가격

princess Snow White - 백설공주

properly - 제대로

property, asset, wealth - 재산

purple - 보라색

puzzle - 퍼즐

Q

quietly - 조용히

R

recorder - 녹음기

recorder - 리코더

red - 빨간색

red - 빨갛다

regret - 후회

relatives - 친척

request - 부탁

retire - 퇴직

ring - 반지

riskiness, jeopardy - 위험성

rose - 장미

rose of sharon - 무궁화

running nose (mucus) - 콧물

S

salary, monthly pay - 월급

salesperson, store clerk - 점원

Samsung © - 삼성

Santa Claus - 산타클로스

Saturn - 토성

saxophone - 색소폰

scarf - 목도리

second - 두 번째

seconds - ~초

selfie - 셀카

selflish - 이기적

send money - 송금

service - 서비스

seventh - 일곱 번째

shirt - 셔츠

shoelaces – 신발 끈

short break - 휴식

sickness - 병

sixth - 여섯 번째

slang - 속어

solar system - 태양계

Spanish - 스페인말

star - 별

still (not), even now - 아직도

story, talk - 얘기

strawberry - 딸기

style - 스타일

subject marker - 이/가

success - 성공

sunflower - 해바라기

sunlight - 햇빛

T

tambourine - 탬버린

tenth - 열 번째

terminology - 용어

Thai - 태국말

the end of the year - 연말

The Moon - 달

The Sun - 태양

the week after next - 다다음주

the whole world - 전 세계

third - 세 번째

to / from - 에게/한테

to attend, to frequent - 다니다

to be bored - 심심하다

to be boring - 지루하다

to be born - 태어나다

to be broken - 고장이 나다

to be chubby - 통통하다

to be cool - 시원하다

to be cramped, stifled, frustrated - 답답하다

to be dangerous - 위험하다

to be dizzy - 어지럽다

to be dumb - 멍청하다

to be easy - 간단해요

to be envious - 부럽다

to be fat - 뚱뚱하다

to be forbidden, to be prohibited - 금지하다

to be fresh - 신선하다

to be handsome, pretty (formed well) - 잘생기다

to be hard - 딱딱하다

to be high - 높다

to be joyful - 즐겁다

to be like that - 그렇다

to be like that over there - 저렇다

to be like that over there, - 저렇다

to be like that, that way, that kind of - 그렇다

to be like this - 이렇다

to be like this, this way, this kind of - 이렇다

to be low - 낮다

to be okay, to be fine - 괜찮다

to be safe - 안전하다

to be sick, to hurt - 아프다

to be skinny - 날씬하다

to be smart - 똑똑하다

to be soft - 부드럽다

to be sold - 팔리다

to be strange, weird - 이상하다

to be strict - 엄격하다

to be strong (non-physical) - 강하다

to be strong (physical) - 세다

to be surprised - 놀라다

to be tall - 키가 크다

to be unattractive, ugly (not formed well) - 못생기다

to be unfortunate, regrettable - 안타깝다

to be weak (physical and non) - 약하다

to be young - 어리다

to believe, to trust - 믿다

to breathe - 숨을 쉬다

to bring (a person) - 데려오다

to bring (a thing) - 가져오다

to catch a cold - 감기에 걸리다

to celebrate - 축하하다

to change/to transfer - 갈아타다

to choose - 고르다

to clean - 청소를 하다

to come - 오다

to commute (to work) - 출퇴근하다

to consider, to think of - 생각하다

to do - 하다

to do a business - 사업하다

to draw, to paint - 그리다

to drink - 마시다

to earn (money) - 벌다

to eat - 먹다

to enter school - 입학하다

to exist, to have - 있다

to expect - 기대하다

to fail - 실패하다

to feel - 느끼다

to form a baby (to get pregnant) - 아기가 생기다

to gain weight - 살이 찌다

to get a divorce - 이혼하다

to get a job - 취업하다

to get engaged to be married - 약혼하다

to get off work - 퇴근하다

to get time (time opened up) - 시간이 생기다

to give - 주다

to give a speech, make a presentation - 발표하다

to go - 가다

to go crazy - 미치다

to go on a business trip - 출장가다

to go to work - 출근하다

to graduate - 졸업하다

to happen, to occur, to make, to form - 생기다

to have a fever - 열이 나다

to have a meeting - 회의하다

to have a problem happen - 문제가 생기다

to have an affair, to cheat - 바람을 피우다

to hear - 듣다

to lay down - 눕다

to leave - 떠나다

to lose - 지다

to lose weight (become less fat) - 살이 빠지다

to lose weight (make effort to lose) - 살을 빼다

to make a mistake - 실수하다

to make money - 돈이 생기다

to make noise - 떠들다

to make/get a girlfriend - 친구가 생기다

to meet - 만나다

to memorize - 외우다

to move (to a new place) - 이사하다

to pass (a test) - 합격하다

to permit, to grant - 허가하다

to play a stringed instrument - 치다

to play a wind instrument - 불다

to play an instrument (any) - 연주하다

to print - 인쇄하다

to put on a watch - 차다

to put on accessories - 하다

to put on accessories, bracelets, earrings, hair bows - 하다

to put on contact lenses, rings - 끼다

to put on glasses, gloves, watches, bracelets - 끼다

to put on gloves, glasses etc. - 끼다

to put on hats, beanies, glasses, masks, wigs - 쓰다

to put on makeup - 하다

to put on perfume etc. - 뿌리다

to put on perfume, aftershave, cologne - 뿌리다

to put on shirts, pants, underwear, jackets, suits, robes - 입다

to put on socks, shoes, boots, nylons - 신다

to put on ties, neckties, bow tie, belts, shoelaces, scarf - 매다

to put on watches, bracelets - 차다

to read - 읽다

to regret - 후회하다

to remember - 기억하다

to request, to ask - 부탁하다

to retire - 퇴직하다

to sit - 앉다

to ski - 스키를 타다

to sleep - 자다

to smoke - 담배를 피우다

to speak, tell, talk - 말하다

to spend (money) - 쓰다

to stand - 서다

to succeed - 성공하다

to take (a person) - 데려가다

to take (a thing) - 가져가다

to take a test - 시험을 보다

to take off accessories, bracelets, earrings, hair bows - 벗다

to take off clothes etc - 벗다

to take off contact lenses, rings - 빼다

to take off glasses, gloves, watches, bracelets - 벗다

to take off hats, beanies, glasses, masks, wigs - 벗다

to take off makeup - 지우다

to take off rings, gloves etc. - 빼다

to take off shirts, pants, underwear, jackets, suits, robes - 벗다

to take off socks, shoes, boots, nylons - 벗다

to take off ties, hair ribbons - 풀다

to take off ties, neckties, bow tie, belts, shoelaces, scarf - 풀다

to take off watches, bracelets - 벗다

to teach - 가르치다

to use - 사용하다

to wash - 씻다

to wear clothes - 입다

to wear on feet - 신다

to wear on head - 쓰다

to wear ties, neck etc. - 매다

to win, to beat - 이기다

toaster - 토스터

topic marker - 은/는

traffic accident - 교통사고

transfer - 이체

trash - 쓰레기

treadmill - 런닝머신

trumpet - 트럼펫

tuba - 튜바

tulip - 튤립

U

ukulele - 우쿨렐레

umbrella - 우산

under classman - 후배

underwear - 속옷

upper classman - 선배

Uranus - 천왕성

us, our, we - 우리

usage - 사용

V

vacation (only from school) - 방학

vacation, day off - 휴가

vacuum cleaner - 청소기

value, worth - 값

Venus - 금성

W

washing machine - 세탁기

water purifier - 정수기

wedding rings - 결혼반지

weekday - 평일

when in elementary school - 중학교 때

when was 18 years old - 열 여섯 살 때

when was 2 years old - 두 살 때

when was 30 years old - 서른 살 때

when was 40 years old - 마흔 살 때

when was college - 대학교 때

when was in high school - 고등학교 때

which color? - 무슨 색깔?

which? - 몇 번째

while on a trip - 여행 때

white - 하얗다

white - 흰색

withdrawal - 예금인출

word, vocabulary - 단어

words - 말

X

xylophone - 실로폰

Y

yellow - 노란색

yellow - 노랗다

yoga - 요가

young man - 오빠 (girls only)

young man - 형 (men say)

young single man - 총각

young woman - 누나 (men say)

young woman - 아가씨

young woman - 언니 (girls only)

young woman - 처녀

youngest (child) – 막내

Glossary K-E

ㄱ

~권 - books, magazine

~대 - machinery, equipment, cars etc.

~번째 - 1st, 2nd, 3rd etc. (order counter)

~장 - flat objects, paper

~조각 - pieces, slices

~초 - seconds

~킬로그램 - kilograms

~킬로미터 - kilometers

ㄱ

가격 - price

가능성 - possibility, likelyhood

가다 - to go

가르치다 - to teach

가습기 - humidifier

가장 - most (similar to 제일)

가져가다 - to take (a thing)

가져오다 - to bring (a thing)

간단해요 - to be easy

갈색 - brown

갈아타다 - to change/to transfer

감기 - cold

감기에 걸리다 - to catch a cold

값 - value, worth

강하다 - to be strong (non-physical)

거짓말쟁이 - liar

건강 - health

건전지 - battery

건조기 - clothes dryer

검은색 - black

결혼반지 - wedding rings

경기 - competition

계좌 - account

계좌번호 - account number

계획 - plans

고등학교 - high school

고등학교 때 - when was in high school

고르다 - to choose

고속도로 - highway

고장이 나다 - to be broken

공기 - air

괜찮다 - to be okay, to be fine

교통사고 - traffic accident

구두 - dress shows

국화 - chrysanthemum

귀걸이 - earrings

그렇다 - to be like that

그렇다 - to be like that, that way, that kind of

그리다 - to draw, to paint

그림 - drawing, painting

근처 - nearby, in the area

금성 - Venus

금지하다 - to be forbidden, to be prohibited

급우 - classmate

기대하다 - to expect

기숙사 - dormitory

기억하다 - to remember

기침 - cough

기타 - guitar

김치 냉장고 - kimchi fridge (most Korean houses have this)

ㄲ

까맣다 - black

끼다 - to put on contact lenses, rings

끼다 - to put on glasses, gloves, watches, bracelets
끼다 - to put on gloves, glasses etc.

ㄴ

나이 - age
나팔꽃 - morning glory
날씬하다 - to be skinny
남 - other person
낮다 - to be low
냄새 - odor, smell
네 권 - 4 books
네 대 - 4 units
네 번째 - forth
네 장 - 4 pieces
네 조각 - 4 pieces
넥타이 - necktie
노란색 - yellow
노랗다 - yellow
녹음기 - recorder
놀라다 - to be surprised
높다 - to be high
높임말 - honorific speech
누나 (men say) - young woman
눈빛 - gaze, glare of eye
눕다 - to lay down
뉴스 - news (tv news cast)
느끼다 - to feel

ㄷ

다니다 - to attend, to frequent
다다음주 - the week after next
다리미 - iron

다섯 권 - 5 books
다섯 대 - 5 units
다섯 번째 - fifth
다섯 장 - 5 pieces
다섯 조각 - 5 pieces
다양성 - diversity
단어 - word, vocabulary
달 - The Moon
담배 - cigarette
담배를 피우다 - to smoke
답답하다 - to be cramped, stifled, frustrated
당뇨병 - diabetes
대나무 - bamboo
대학교 때 - when was college
데려가다 - to take (a person)
데려오다 - to bring (a person)
도시락 - lunchbox
돈이 생기다 - to make money
동료 - colleague, co-worker
두 권 - 2 books
두 대 - 2 units
두 번째 - second
두 살 때 - when was 2 years old
두 장 - 2 pieces
두 조각 - 2 pieces
두통 - headache
드디어 - finally
드럼 - drums
드레스 - dress
듣다 - to hear

ㄸ

딱딱하다 - to be hard
딸기 - strawberry

떠나다 - to leave
떠들다 - to make noise
똑똑하다 - to be smart
뚱뚱하다 - to be fat

ㄹ

런닝머신 - treadmill
렌즈 - contact lens
리코더 - recorder

ㅁ

마스크 - mask
마시다 - to drink
마흔 살 때 - when was 40 years old
막내 - youngest (child)
만 - 10 thousand
만 권 - 10,000 books
만 대 - 10,000 units
만 장 - 10,000 pieces
만 조각 - 10,000 pieces
만나다 - to meet
말 - words
말하다 - to speak, tell, talk
매다 - to put on ties, neckties, bow tie, belts, shoelaces, scarf
매다 - to wear ties, neck etc.
머리 띠 - headband
먹다 - to eat
먼저 - first of all, before anything else
멍청하다 - to be dumb
메스꺼움 - nausea
명왕성 - Pluto
몇 권? - How many books?

몇 대? - How many units?
몇 번째 - which?
몇 장? - How many pieces?
몇 조각? - How many pieces?
모자 - hat
목도리 - scarf
목성 - Jupiter
몸살 - body aches
못생기다 - to be unattractive, ugly (not formed well)
무궁화 - rose of sharon
무슨 색깔? - which color?
문제가 생기다 - to have a problem happen
미술관 - art gallery
미치다 - to go crazy
믹서기 - blender
민들레 - dandelion
믿다 - to believe, to trust

ㅂ

바람을 피우다 - to have an affair, to cheat
바보 - fool, idiot, dummy
바지 - pants
밖 - outside
반말 - casual speech
반지 - ring
발표 - presentation, speech
발표하다 - to give a speech, make a presentation
밥 - meal / cooked rice
방학 - vacation (only from school)
백 권 - 100 books
백 대 - 100 units
백 만 - 1 million
백 억 - 10 billion

백 장 - 100 pieces

백 조 - 100 trillion

백 조각 - 100 pieces

백설공주 - princess Snow White

백합 - lily

벌다 - to earn (money)

벗다 - to take off accessories, bracelets, earrings, hair bows

벗다 - to take off clothes etc

벗다 - to take off glasses, gloves, watches, bracelets

벗다 - to take off hats, beanies, glasses, masks, wigs

벗다 - to take off shirts, pants, underwear, jackets, suits, robes

벗다 - to take off socks, shoes, boots, nylons

벗다 - to take off watches, bracelets

벚꽃 - cherry blossoms

벚나무 - cherry tree

벨트 - belt

별 - star

병 - sickness

보라색 - purple

부드럽다 - to be soft

부럽다 - to be envious

부부 - married couple, husband and wife

부탁 - request

부탁하다 - to request, to ask

분홍색 - pink

불다 - to play a wind instrument

불면증 - insomnia

비밀번호 - password (secret number)

빈혈 - anemia

빌 게이츠 - Bill Gates

ㅃ

빨간색 - red

빨갛다 - red

빼다 - to take off contact lenses, rings

빼다 - to take off rings, gloves etc.

뿌리다 - to put on perfume etc.

뿌리다 - to put on perfume, aftershave, cologne

ㅅ

사람 - person

사무실 - office

사업 - business, enterprise

사업하다 - to do a business

사용 - usage

사용하다 - to use

산타클로스 - Santa Claus

살 - fat

살을 빼다 - to lose weight (make effort to lose)

살이 빠지다 - to lose weight (become less fat)

살이 찌다 - to gain weight

삼겹살 - pork belly

삼성 - Samsung ©

삼촌 - middle aged man

색소폰 - saxophone

생각 - idea, thought

생각하다 - to consider, to think of

생기다 - to happen, to occur, to make, to form

생일 - birthday

생일 때 - on my birthday

생일날 - birthday

서다 - to stand

서른 살 때 - when was 30 years old

서비스 - service

선배 - upper classman

선인장 - cactus

선풍기 - electric fan

설사 - diarrhea

성공 - success

성공하다 - to succeed

성별 - gender

성형수술 - plastic surgery

세 권 - 3 books

세 대 - 3 units

세 번째 - third

세 장 - 3 pieces

세 조각 - 3 pieces

세다 - to be strong (physical)

세탁기 - washing machine

셀카 - selfie

셔츠 - shirt

소개팅 - blind date

소나무 - pine

소설 - novel (book)

속어 - slang

속옷 - underwear

송금 - send money

수성 - Mercury

수수료 - fee

수표 - check

술집 - bar

숨을 쉬다 - to breathe

스키를 타다 - to ski

스타일 - style

스페인말 - Spanish

시간이 생기다 - to get time (time opened up)

시계 - clock, watch

시원하다 - to be cool

시험을 보다 - to take a test

식기 세척기 - dishwasher

신다 - to put on socks, shoes, boots, nylons

신다 - to wear on feet

신발 끈 - shoelaces

신선하다 - to be fresh

실로폰 - xylophone

실수 - mistake

실수하다 - to make a mistake

실패 - failure

실패하다 - to fail

심심하다 - to be bored

심장병 - heart disease

십 만 - 100 thousand

십 억 - 1 billion

십 조 - 10 trillion

ㅆ

쓰다 - to put on hats, beanies, glasses, masks, wigs

쓰다 - to spend (money)

쓰다 - to wear on head

쓰레기 - trash

씨 - Mr., Mrs. etc

씻다 - to wash

#

아가씨 - young woman

아기가 생기다 - to form a baby (to get pregnant)

아까 - just now, a minute ago

아무 데나 - any place / anywhere

아무 데도 - no place / anywhere

아무거나 - anything

아무것도 - nothing / not any / anything

아무나 - any body / anyone

아무도 - no one / nobody / anyone

아저씨 - older man

아줌마 - older woman

아직도 - still (not), even now

아프다 - to be sick, to hurt

아홉 번째 - ninth

악기 - musical instrument

안경 - glasses

안전하다 - to be safe

안타깝다 - to be unfortunate, regrettable

앉다 - to sit

암 - cancer

압력밥솥 - pressure rice cooker

애플 - Apple ©

앨범 - album (photo, record, cd)

야식 - late night snack

약 - approximately, roughly

약하다 - to be weak (physical and non)

약혼 - engagement

약혼하다 - to get engaged to be married

얘기 - story, talk

어구 - phrase

어떻다 - how

어떻다 - how?, in what way?, what kind of?

어리다 - to be young

어지럽다 - to be dizzy

어학 - linguistics, the study of language

억 - 100 million

언니 (girls only) - young woman

언어 - language

엄격하다 - to be strict

에게/한테 - to / from

여기저기 - here and there

여덟 번째 - eighth

여섯 번째 - sixth

여행 때 - while on a trip

연말 - end of year

연말 - the end of the year

연주하다 - to play an instrument (any)

열 - fever

열 번째 - tenth

열 여섯 살 때 - when was 18 years old

열심히 - hard, diligently, enthusiastically

열이 나다 - to have a fever

영양실조 - malnutrition

예금인출 - withdrawal

오다 - to come

오래 - long, a long time

오빠 (girls only) - young man

오픈카 - convertible car

왜소행성 - dwarf planet

외계인 - alien (from another planet)

외우다 - to memorize

요가 - yoga

요리사 - cook, chef

용어 - terminology

우리 - us, our, we

우산 - umbrella

우쿨렐레 - ukulele

웃음 - laughter

원피스 - one piece dress

월급 - salary, monthly pay

월말 - end of month

위험성 - riskiness, jeopardy

위험하다 - to be dangerous

유리 - glass

유채꽃 - canola flower

은/는 - topic marker

이/가 - subject marker

이기다 - to win, to beat

이기적 - selfish

이렇다 - to be like this

이렇다 - to be like this, this way, this kind of

이름 - name

이모 - middle aged woman

이사하다 - to move (to a new place)

이상하다 - to be strange, weird

이체 - transfer

이혼 - divorce

이혼하다 - to get a divorce

인쇄하다 - to print

일 - happening, event

일곱 번째 - seventh

일본말 - Japanese

읽다 - to read

입금 - deposit

입다 - to put on shirts, pants, underwear, jackets, suits, robes

입다 - to wear clothes

입학하다 - to enter school

있다 - to exist, to have

ㅈ

자다 - to sleep

자연 - nature

잘생기다 - to be handsome, pretty (formed well)

장갑 - gloves

장미 - rose

재료 - ingredients

재산 - property, asset, wealth

저렇다 - to be like that over there

저렇다 - to be like that over there,

전 세계 - the whole world

전기 칫솔 - electric toothbrush

전나무 - fir

전염병 - infection

전자 사전 - electronic dictionary

점원 - salesperson, store clerk

정수기 - water purifier

정신 - mind, spirit

제대로 - properly

제습기 - dehumidifier

조 - 1 trillion

조용히 - quietly

존댓말 - formal speech

졸업식 - graduation ceremony

졸업하다 - to graduate

종이 - paper

주다 - to give

주황색 - orange

중국말 - Chinese

중요성 - importance

중학교 - middle school

중학교 때 - when in elementary school

즐겁다 - to be joyful

지구 - Earth

지급일 - pay day

지다 - to lose

지루하다 - to be boring

지우다 - to take off makeup

집 - house

집안일 - housework

ㅊ

차다 - to put on a watch

차다 - to put on watches, bracelets

참나무 - oak wood

처녀 - young woman

천 만 - 10 million

천 억 - 100 billion

천 조 - 1 quadrillion

천왕성 - Uranus

첫 번째 - first

청소기 - vacuum cleaner

청소를 하다 - to clean

초등학교 - elementary school

초록색 - green

총각 - young single man

축하하다 - to celebrate

출구 - exit; way out

출근 - go to work

출근하다 - to go to work

출장 - business trip

출장가다 - to go on a business trip

출퇴근하다 - to commute (to work)

충전기 - charger

취미 - hobby

취업 - employment, get a job

취업하다 - to get a job

치다 - to play a stringed instrument

치매 - Alzheimer's

친구가 생기다 - to make/get a girlfriend

친척 - relatives

카메라 - camera

코트 - coat

콧물 - running nose (mucus)

키가 크다 - to be tall

타박상 - bruise

태국말 - Thai

태양 - The Sun

태양계 - solar system

태어나다 - to be born

탬버린 - tambourine

토성 - Saturn

토스터 - toaster

통장 - bank book

통통하다 - to be chubby

퇴근 - get off work

퇴근하다 - to get off work

퇴직 - retire

퇴직하다 - to retire

튜바 - tuba

튤립 - tulip

트럼펫 - trumpet

ㅍ

파란색 - blue

파랗다 - blue

파티 때 - during party

팔리다 - to be sold

팔찌 - bracelet

팬케이크 - pancakes

퍼즐 - puzzle

평일 - weekday

폐렴 - pneumonia

풀다 - to take off ties, hair ribbons

풀다 - to take off ties, neckties, bow tie, belts,

shoelaces, scarf
프랑스말 - French
플루트 - flute
피아노 - piano
필요성 - necessity

ㅎ

하나님 - God (the "one")
하늘색 - light blue
하다 - to do
하다 - to put on accessories
하다 - to put on accessories, bracelets, earrings, hair bows
하다 - to put on makeup
하모니카 - harmonica
하얗다 - white
학교 때 - during school
한 권 - 1 book
한 대 - 1 units
한 장 - 1 piece
한 조각 - 1 piece
한국말 - Korean
합격하다 - to pass (a test)
해바라기 - sunflower
해왕성 - Neptune
핸드폰 - mobile phone
햇빛 - sunlight
행성 - planet
향수 - perfume, cologne
허가하다 - to permit, to grant
헬스장 - gym
현금 - cash
형 (men say) - young man
호선 - line # (only for subways subways)
화성 - Mars
환자 - patient
회의 - business meeting
회의 때 - during a conference
회의실 - meeting room
회의하다 - to have a meeting

후배 - under classman
후회 - regret
후회하다 - to regret
훨씬 - much, far, a lot, considerably, way
휴가 - vacation, day off
휴식 - short break
흰색 - white
힘 - power, energy

SOUTH KOREA 대한민국
Provinces & Major Cities Map

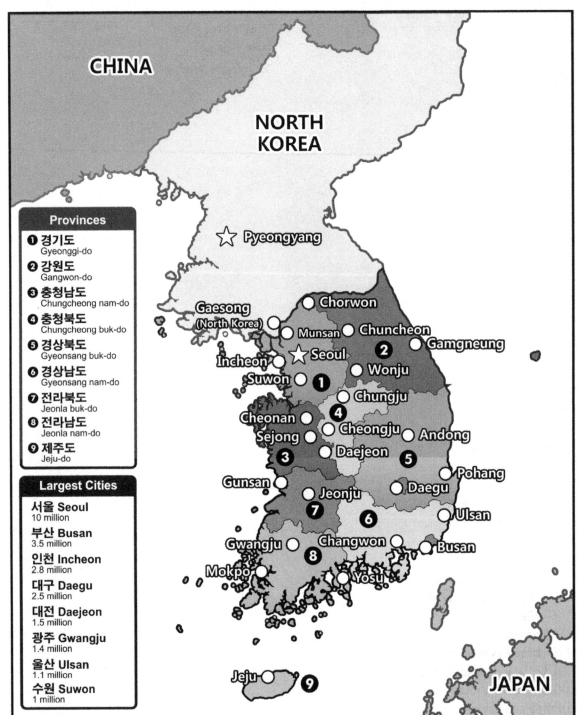

Provinces

❶ 경기도
Gyeonggi-do

❷ 강원도
Gangwon-do

❸ 충청남도
Chungcheong nam-do

❹ 충청북도
Chungcheong buk-do

❺ 경상북도
Gyeonsang buk-do

❻ 경상남도
Gyeonsang nam-do

❼ 전라북도
Jeonla buk-do

❽ 전라남도
Jeonla nam-do

❾ 제주도
Jeju-do

Largest Cities

서울 Seoul
10 million

부산 Busan
3.5 million

인천 Incheon
2.8 million

대구 Daegu
2.5 million

대전 Daejeon
1.5 million

광주 Gwangju
1.4 million

울산 Ulsan
1.1 million

수원 Suwon
1 million

CHINA

NORTH KOREA

☆ Pyeongyang

Gaesong (North Korea)

Chorwon

Munsan

Chuncheon

Gamgneung

Incheon

☆ Seoul

Wonju

❷

Suwon

❶

Chungju

Cheonan

❹

Cheongju

Andong

Sejong

❸

Daejeon

❺

Pohang

Gunsan

Daegu

Jeonju

❼

❻

Ulsan

Gwangju

Changwon

Busan

❽

Mokpo

Yosu

Jeju

❾

JAPAN

"BASIC" Form Rules — FOR REGULARS

case #	Step 1: Remove 다! Choose last vowel or character	Step 2: Make changes If there isn't a 받침 do this step ELSE go to Step 3	Step 3: Attach Only when there is a 받침
1	하	if the last character is 하 하 ➡ 해	add 아
2	ㅗ	ㅗ ➡ ㅘ	add 아
3	ㅏ	no changes	add 아
4	ㅓ ㅐ ㅔ	no changes	add 어
5	ㅣ	ㅣ ➡ ㅕ	add 어
6	ㅜ	ㅜ ➡ ㅝ	add 어
7	ㅡ	if prior vowel ㅏ or ㅗ ㅡ ➡ ㅏ all others ㅡ ➡ ㅓ	add 어
8	ㅟ ㅚ and others	with or without 받침 add 어	

"BASIC" Form Rules

FOR IRREGULARS

case #	Step 1: Remove 다, Make changes Choose irregular type, then make consonant changes		Step 2: Attach Add character based on stem's vowel	
9	ㄹ 리을 irregular	no changes	if vowel is ㅏ or ㅗ	➡ add 아
10	ㄷ 디귿 irregular	ㄷ ➡ ㄹ		
11	ㅅ 시옷 irregular	remove ㅅ	all others	➡ add 어
12	ㅂ 비읍 irregular	remove ㅂ	one character stems with ㅗ	➡ add 와
			all others	➡ add 워
13	ㅎ 히읗 irregular	remove ㅎ	if vowel is ㅑ	➡ change vowel to ㅒ
			all others	➡ change vowel to ㅐ
14	르 르 irregular	1. remove 르 2. attach ㄹ to bottom	if vowel is ㅏ or ㅗ	➡ add 라
			all others	➡ add 러

(으) Form Rules

ALL VERBS and ADJECTIVES

Remove 다. Choose verb type, make changes in B then do C.

A Verb Type?	**B** Make changes	**C** Add 으 / 우 or nothing
R regular	no change	if has 받침 add 으 if NO 받침 add nothing
ㄹ 리을 irregular	remove ㄹ	add nothing *
ㄷ 디귿 irregular	change ㄷ to ㄹ	add 으
ㅅ 시옷 irregular	remove ㅅ	add 으
ㅂ 비읍 irregular	remove ㅂ	add 우
ㅎ 히읗 irregular	remove ㅎ	add nothing
르 르 irregular	no change	add nothing

* ㄹ exception: In some grammar structures the ㄹ is not removed.

HANGUL CHARACTER NAME CHART

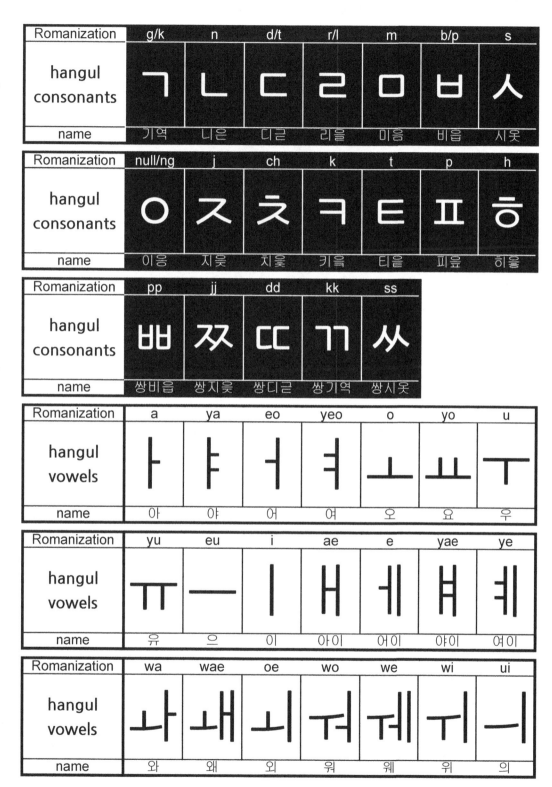

Romanization	g/k	n	d/t	r/l	m	b/p	s
hangul consonants	ㄱ	ㄴ	ㄷ	ㄹ	ㅁ	ㅂ	ㅅ
name	기역	니은	디귿	리을	미음	비읍	시옷

Romanization	null/ng	j	ch	k	t	p	h
hangul consonants	ㅇ	ㅈ	ㅊ	ㅋ	ㅌ	ㅍ	ㅎ
name	이응	지읒	치읓	키읔	티읕	피읖	히읗

Romanization	pp	jj	dd	kk	ss
hangul consonants	ㅃ	ㅉ	ㄸ	ㄲ	ㅆ
name	쌍비읍	쌍지읒	쌍디귿	쌍기역	쌍시옷

Romanization	a	ya	eo	yeo	o	yo	u
hangul vowels	ㅏ	ㅑ	ㅓ	ㅕ	ㅗ	ㅛ	ㅜ
name	아	야	어	여	오	요	우

Romanization	yu	eu	i	ae	e	yae	ye
hangul vowels	ㅠ	ㅡ	ㅣ	ㅐ	ㅔ	ㅒ	ㅖ
name	유	으	이	아이	어이	야이	여이

Romanization	wa	wae	oe	wo	we	wi	ui
hangul vowels	ㅘ	ㅙ	ㅚ	ㅝ	ㅞ	ㅟ	ㅢ
name	와	왜	외	워	웨	위	의

Cut out for reference.

Korean Keyboard Layout

© 2014 KoreanFromZero.com

Other From Zero! Books

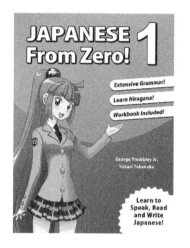

Chinese From Zero! Coming in 2016!

69957313R00186

Made in the USA
Middletown, DE
24 September 2019